Building
Sullivant's
Pyramid

Columbus Ohio
Dec'r 8th 1878

Prof. J R Smith
          Secreta'y of Faculty

Dear Sir

          I have the honor to acknowledge
the receipt of the Resolution of the Faculty
recognizing my interest and services
in behalf of the Ohio State University —
I need make no protestations of
_____ of the Faculty, that being
_____ action —
_____ my best wishes for
_____ ge of their respon-
_____ sincere hope that the
_____ have so long watched
_____ may continue to
_____ rish, proving indeed,
_____ igh place" to guide
_____ te into the paths of
_____ and useful
          very respectfully —
                    Sullivant

William A. Kinnison

BUILDING

SULLIVANT'S

PYRAMID

An Administrative History of the

Ohio State University, 1870–1907

Ohio State University Press

Ï●●

Published in observance of the 1970 Centennial
of the Ohio State University

Standard Book Number: 8142-0141-5
Library of Congress Catalogue Card Number: 77-105722
Printed in the United States of America

for AUDREY M.
and ERRETT LOWELL KINNISON

CONTENTS

Preface   *ix*

Prologue: The Morrill Act
in Perspective   3

Chapter One: The Cannon Act   21

Chapter Two: A Preliminary Consensus   35

Chapter Three: A Vanishing Enthusiasm   50

Chapter Four: Men and Ideas   68

Chapter Five: Freedom and Tenure   87

Chapter Six: Students and the Emergence
of the University   110

Chapter Seven: The Farmers' Victory   131

Chapter Eight: Peace with the Farmers:
A New Departure   144

Chapter Nine: Consensus through Structure
and Process   157

Chapter Ten: Unfinished Business   170

Epilogue: A Scattered Harvest   185

Bibliography   197

Index   215

Preface

Rutherford B. Hayes, as governor of Ohio, took an active interest in the creation of the Ohio State University and stamped it with his administrative style. He secured the university's establishment by the legislature, pressured discretely but successfully for its location at the state capital rather than in Springfield, Ohio, and appointed a board of trustees devoted to as broad a view of the university function as possible. "If anybody was its founder," he told his close political associate William Henry Smith, "in the words of Governor Corwin, 'A great part of it I am which.'"

Hayes reentered the life of the university some years later at the end of an eventful career which had carried him from the governor's chair to the White House. In 1887 he was appointed to the board of trustees of the Ohio State University and became its most influential member during a crucial period of policy determination. Like a great many others, however, Hayes worked on behalf of the university amid a host of conflicting and competing forces and interests. The interests of party politics in America's Civil War era, the hopes of agricultural reformers, the fears of rank and file farmers, the growing needs of expanding industries and fast rising cities, the hardships of worsening economic cycles, the maturation of an American educational profession, and the emergence of a new kind of student—these were among the factors that made the course of

institutional development difficult for contemporaries to chart but
interesting for the historian to study.

In the Morrill Land Grant Act of 1862, provision was made for
the education of the "industrial classes." In mid-nineteenth-century
America, many perceived two broad economic and social classes:
the professional and the industrial. The phrase "education for the
industrial classes" meant a new kind of education distinguishable
from that traditionally provided for the professional classes. The
term in its broadest sense referred to the new education designed
for the self-made men of industry and trade and of farm and factory
in place of the classical and traditional education designed for the
man of theology and the man of law. In its narrowest sense it meant
training for farmers and for mechanics. In either sense it denoted
a new perspective for higher education. But the interest in education for the industrial classes did not exist apart from broader concerns about reforming higher education which focused upon the
American college in the post–Civil War era. Rutherford B. Hayes
believed, however, that education for the industrial classes was the
dominant reason for passage of the Morrill Act and that its educational reform attacked one of the crucial issues emerging in industrial America. "Capital and Labor is the burning question," he said,
and he saw educational reform as a means of ameliorating class
struggle.

It is difficult to recapture the tenor of life in America in the
1860's, and particularly to delineate the perception of higher education as it existed then. Francis Wayland, president of Brown University, however, sensed the difference in his concern about the
impasse which seemed to exist between the traditional college and
the new emerging America. "Our colleges are not filled," Wayland
told his board of trustees, "because we do not furnish the education
desired by the people." He was convinced that the traditional
college produced an article for which the demand was diminishing,
and, he observed, "We sell it at less than cost, and the deficiency is
made up by charity. We give it away, and still the demand
diminishes."

With the passage of the Morrill Act, a specific and incisive
federal intervention into American higher education occurred

giving a decided assist to the development of education for the industrial classes. Without elaborate directives and detailed specifications, the federal government precipitated major changes in the structure and direction of American higher education. Through grants of land, the Congress secured state commitment to an undefined innovation and focused a decade of debate on the nature and function of higher education. The details of that decade of debate and the repercussions from it have not been sufficiently assessed in previous studies of the Land Grant movement. This study seeks to appraise this aspect of the Morrill Act as it related to the founding of the Ohio Agricultural and Mechanical College in Franklin County and to assess the implications of that development for higher education in the state.

The debate in Ohio focused on the attempt to found a state university offering the broadest possible curriculum as opposed to the agricultural and industrial college sought by the farming interests so influential in the legislature. In the face of such organized opposition, one of the earliest supporters of the total university concept was Trustee Joseph Sullivant, who designed the first university seal to symbolize the harmonious blending of the practical arts and liberal culture in the pyramid of knowledge. At the end of his term of service to the university in 1878, Joseph Sullivant wrote to the secretary of the faculty, Professor I. R. Smith, to express his continuing hope that the university would prove "'a light set on a high place' to guide the youth of the state into the paths of sound learning and useful citizenship." (See the Frontispiece for a reproduction of this letter, on deposit in the archives of the Ohio State University, and a later version of the university seal based on Joseph Sullivant's original design.) The fulfillment of this broader vision came closer to reality during the crucial term of Rutherford B. Hayes on the board of trustees, who ultimately succeeded in reconciling the rural forces of discontent and the advocates of a state university that would embrace all the arts of man.

The host of scholars to whom this writer is indebted are acknowledged in the notes to the text and in the bibliography. In addition thanks should be expressed specifically to Mr. Bruce

Harding, former archivist for Ohio State University, and his staff at the University Archives; to Watt P. Marchman, Ruth Ballenger, and the staff of the Rutherford B. Hayes Memorial Library in Fremont, Ohio; to the staff of the Ohio State University Library and the staff of the Ohio Historical Society Library in Columbus, Ohio. These professional persons were of immeasurable assistance in facilitating my research. John W. Gustad, Francis P. Weisenberger, Francis P. Robinson, Weldon A. Kefauver, the late John A. Ramseyer and the late William Best Hesseltine also come readily to mind as individual scholars to whom I am more than obligated for their contribution to my own development and to the development of this story.

I want to express special thanks, however, to William and Marie Flesher for the Flesher Fellowship at the Ohio State University which financially supported much of the research for this work. In addition a very helpful grant provided by Wittenberg University aided substantially in the preparation of the final manuscript. I am grateful also for the thorough and sympathetic editorial assistance of Jean Kuenn of the Ohio State University Press whose capacity for seeing the work whole as well as in its parts was extraordinary.

The greatest asset of any scholar, however, is a wife's good humor and candid editorial appraisal and children willing to share an adventure they do not really understand. The debt which I owe to Lenore, Bill, Linda and Amy, therefore, cannot be overstated.

WILLIAM A. KINNISON

Wittenberg University
Springfield, Ohio
October 22, 1969

Building
Sullivant's
Pyramid

The Morrill Act in Perspective

In 1862, Ohioans were at a loss to know what to do with the grant of lands bestowed upon them by the Morrill Land Grant College Act. Though some states acted immediately to claim and use the fund and others did so within a matter of a few years, it took Ohio's politicians until 1870 to resolve the conflicting issues sufficiently to found a college. Even then, they would probably have failed without the strong guiding hand of Governor Rutherford B. Hayes who compromised divergent views long enough to get the project underway. Although there were a multitude of reasons for this, three specific factors proved to be the determinants of the situation in Ohio. In the first place, the grant emerged from so much political in-fighting that its full importance was only slowly appreciated. Second, Ohio's agricultural reformers had developed some fairly definite preconceptions about what the bill should do, and these had very little relationship to what rank and file farmers had in mind. And third, the conflicting interests and educational needs of emerging urban and industrial centers put an emphasis upon mechanical and scientific education which was altogether unexpected by, and even unbelievable to, the agriculturists, who saw the Morrill Act primarily as a farm measure and not as an aid to scientific and industrial development and geological exploration.

Thus it was not so much the fact that Ohioans had no idea of what to do with so handsome a grant, but that there were too many divergent notions. Unity of purpose and agreement about objectives were impossible to obtain—at least for any great length of time. Moreover, the conflicting ideas of the few were hidden in massive statewide indifference and, at least originally, a preoccupation with the Civil War.

Many, to be sure, had originally supported political leaders who opposed the land grant idea altogether. The state's representatives in Congress, in fact, had been badly split over the issue for several years, and enactment of the measure found no more agreement than had existed previously. The Morrill Act was, in many respects, the child of agricultural reform and partisan politics, and neither was sufficient to carry the day in the Ohio legislature. Statesmen who sought a worthy purpose for which at least a part of the great public domain might be spent, found themselves leading a coalition of those who wanted agricultural reform and those who wanted to destroy the Democratic party. At least this was one of the reform impulses caught up in the great Republican crusade of the 1850's. When it was caught up in that crusade, however, in Ohio and elsewhere broader provisions for industrial education superseded narrower views about farm colleges.

Nevertheless, as a result, in the first session of the first Republican-controlled Congress in the history of the nation, despite the Civil War and its related problems, the Congress enacted the Morrill Land Grant College Act. The same Congress, incidentally, enacted a Homestead Act, giving free land to actual settlers, and separated the Department of Agriculture from the Patent Office and established it as an independent department.[1] The three enactments were closely related. They purported to give the West to the farmer; to dot it with colleges to foster his prosperity, while at the same time establishing similar institutions in the East; and to provide an independent bureau in Washington to look after his interests. Coupled with a policy of generous land grants for railroads,

1. Paul W. Gates, *Agriculture and the Civil War* (New York: Alfred A. Knopf, 1965), pp. 282–85.

the entire program was aimed at developing the West in keeping with the free-soil image.[2]

On all of these points—homesteads, colleges, railroads—North and South had differed prior to secession, and only the absence of southern congressmen made action possible in 1862. Even within the states of the North and the West, there had been great disagreement, but the absence of the southern legislators made the opposition very much a minority. These issues were of the warp and woof of the entire sectional controversy, which had grown increasingly bitter over the previous three decades. They were among the issues over which the Democratic party split in 1860, and they were of crucial importance in the destruction of the alliance of West and South which had dominated American politics since the day of Andrew Jackson.

In fact, the disposition of the nation's vast public domain became one of the most crucial domestic issues ever to face the nation. Whether the public domain, and especially the lands acquired in the war with Mexico, were to be slave or free was the fundamental question. Any plan for the judicious expenditure of land grants whether for railroads, homesteads, colleges, or whatever else had impact on that basic issue. Yet there were responsible men who forsaw the ultimate liquidation of the great public domain without any real achievement to demonstrate that such wealth had been handled with anything resembling statesmanlike stewardship. Though it might well be used to encourage the building of canals and railroads, to reward the nation's soldiers, and to compensate those men of vision who were to be found among real estate speculators, surely, this group felt, there was land enough to devote to some more lasting purpose.[3] It was this sentiment, then, which led many to look favorably upon the various ideas then current for agricultural and mechanical education. Jonathan B. Turner of Illinois was ahead of many in making his ideas about industrial

2. H. L. Trefousse, *Benjamin Franklin Wade: Radical Republican from Ohio*, (New York: Twayne Publishers, 1963), pp. 115, 188.

3. William Belmont Parker, *The Life and Public Service of Justin Smith Morrill*, (Boston and New York: Houghton Mifflin Co., 1924), pp. 262–63; Trefousse, op. cit., p. 100 ff.

education explicit. Norton S. Townshend of Ohio was busy at work in the field demonstrating the application of the professional school concept to the needs of the farmer. Justin Smith Morrill, congressman from Vermont, was aware of, and interested in, all such developments. Others responded to more mixed motives when they embraced the emerging land-grant college idea.

Benjamin Franklin Wade of Ohio, for instance—an early abolitionist and Republican leader—sought primarily a frontal assault on the institution of slavery and the Democratic party, which protected it. He was certain that the free-soil sentiment of the Northwest and the people who supported antislavery politicians like himself were strongly related to the agricultural community. Agricultural reform and abolition were therefore complementary issues for many Republicans, particularly in his district, and others could be motivated to support agricultural reform who might be less enthusiastic about abolition.[4]

Furthermore, the Democratic party was vulnerable on issues involving agricultural reform, as the Homestead bill and the Morrill bill revealed. Wade sought to embarrass them and to help destroy the western-southern alliance of Democrats by promoting these two bills. The Republicans could thereby reward their own farm supporters while they put Democrats in a vise between party regularity and home district sentiments. If northern Democrats voted for such issues in the face of southern opposition, the Democratic party would be further split; if they voted against them, they were in danger of losing the next election at home. Wade, fully cognizant of the situation, referred to President Buchanan's hold on the Democratic party by quipping, "I suppose if he takes snuff, every true Democrat ought to sneeze, or else be read out of the party." Whether the bills passed or not—and Wade felt that eventually they would—the Democratic party would be weakened if the Republicans pushed for them at once.[5]

In this political game the stakes were high and congressmen from Ohio and elsewhere were split almost evenly on the issue.

4. Ibid., p. 188.
5. *Congressional Globe,* 35th Cong., 1st sess., pp. 1120–24.

When the first Morrill Act passed in 1859, only to be vetoed by President Buchanan, eleven Ohioans in Congress opposed it and ten favored it. Senators Benjamin F. Wade, Republican, and George E. Pugh, Democrat, both of Ohio, argued on the floor of the Senate concerning the appropriateness of their respective actions and thereby dramatized the Ohio division and that of the nation. Senator Pugh insisted that Wade was under the instruction of the Ohio legislature to oppose the bill, but Wade insisted that the opposite was true. A change in party control of the legislature and vacillation in the home-state view of the issue accounted for the difference of opinion.[6]

Earlier in the session, Pugh had been instrumental in burying the proposal in committee, where most Democrats hoped it would stay. Wade, however, maneuvered to postpone all other business in order to bring the Morrill bill up for debate. His actions confounded Pugh and eventually sealed his doom in a bid for reelection. Opponents appealed to the crowded calendar of the Senate and other more urgent business to justify killing the troublesome bill in committee, but Wade threatened to throw the issue in the way of the appropriation bill every time it came up until he got a final vote.

Finally, Wade succeeded in getting the bill before the Senate, and Pugh led the opposition. He indicated that the Morrill bill had never received the support of the standing committees on agriculture in either house, and that it had come from the Senate Committee on the Public Lands without any recommendation for passage. "Those to whom Congress in each House has confided the special charge of the public domain," he lectured Wade, "have never given their assent to a proposition that proposes to alienate an empire, and for purposes wholly beyond the limits of the authority of this government."[7]

Pugh insisted that a sound federal land policy would prohibit the donation of the public lands to any person except the actual settler. He described the Morrill bill as a violation of the Constitution that would merely empower the state to sell land scrip to a host of

6. Ibid., part 2, pp. 713, 1742.
7. Ibid., pp. 713, 714, 784.

eastern land speculators, and within such a short period of time
that the price obtained would be too low to support any kind of
agricultural college at all. The bill authorized federal intervention
into the legitimate concerns of the states, he insisted, and he was
convinced that the results would not justify such a drastic rewriting
of the nation's organic law.

A colleague predicted that such profligate disbursement of the
public domain in such a short period would depress the price of
lands to between fifty and sixty cents per acre, a prediction close
to the average price eventually obtained. Earlier grants to the
nation's soldiers had forced the price of land from a dollar and a
quarter to ninety cents, he said, and, in view of the greater size of
this grant and the shorter period for its sale, the price would go
lower. The entire measure, the Senator conjectured, tripled the
opportunities for capitalists and speculators to tie up huge tracts of
land and scrip. As the price went down, he stated, the speculators'
money would cover increasingly larger tracts. The Morrill bill, he
insisted, would thus hasten the depletion of the federal land re-
serves, and in the long run place the great majority of Americans
at the mercy of speculators.

The people did not favor the bill, charged Senator Clay of Ala-
bama. They were beguiled into its advocacy without being told the
degree of direction from the federal government which it required
the states to accept. He characterized the bill as a scheme of
speculation and plunder, a bribe of the states suggested by Congress and pressed by greedy capitalists but not supported by the
honest tillers of the soil. "Agriculture is the mere name by whose
potential charms the people are to be defrauded of their rights," he
insisted. "The promotion of agriculture is but the incident, not the
great objective of this measure."[8]

Proponents of the measure had little to say, and Wade himself
spoke primarily to engineer the debate and to prevent the bill from
being sidetracked. He wanted action on this bill, as on the homestead bill, in order to draw the lines more clearly for the 1860

8. The prediction was that of Senator James S. Green of Missouri; ibid.,
pp. 723, 852.

election. It was not that he was playing mere politics. He wanted
these bills enacted, but he also hoped, he said, to preach the funeral
sermon of the Democratic party, and these measures would help.[9]

On February 7, 1859, the bill passed the Senate by a close vote of
25 to 22. Every vote cast against the measure was cast by a Democrat; but Democrats from Rhode Island, Wisconsin, California, and
New Jersey joined some former Democrats, Republicans, Old
Whigs, Unionists, Native Americans, and Free Soilers to pass the
measure.[10] Throughout the debate, the opposition was principally
southern and western in its origins, with negative votes from an
Ohioan, an Iowan, two senators from Indiana, two from Missouri,
and two from Minnesota joining with those of the South.[11]

With the narrow margin of victory, there was little hope that the
required majority to override a presidential veto could be obtained.
While Justin Smith Morrill, author of the bill, for a short while
entertained the hope that President Buchanan would sign his bill,
he vetoed it. As a result, many northern and western Democrats, as
Wade predicted, were faced with tough problems in their home
districts. The land-grant bill and the homestead bill were not the
only such issues emerging from this particular session of the Congress, but they added to the problems created for western Democrats by the national party's stance on rivers and harbors bills and
other legislation desired by the West. Western Democrats were
open to the criticism that while they went down the line for the
southern leadership of the party, they received nothing in return.[12]

At its 1860 convention, the Democratic party was unable to resolve the wide breaches within its ranks which issues like these had
helped to create. The convention broke up without nominating a
presidential candidate, and was unable to agree upon a national
platform. Later, two separate conventions, one northern and one
southern, nominated separate slates to run on different platforms,
and the way was cleared for Republican victory in the fall elections.

9. Parker, op. cit., p. 267; Trefousse, op. cit., p. 100.
10. *Congressional Globe,* 35th Cong., 2nd sess., 857; Parker, op. cit., p. 268.
11. *Congressional Globe,* 35th Cong., 2nd sess., pp. 712, 857.
12. Parker, op. cit., pp. 267–68; Trefousse, op. cit., p. 112; see also *New York Tribune,* February 2, 8, 28, 1859.

Senator Wade, with his characteristic bluntness, had drawn the issue very clearly during the recent session of Congress. It was, he said, simply a matter of "niggers for the niggerless", as advocated by the southern Democrats, or "land for the landless" as advocated by the Republicans, and he committed his party to a broad agricultural reform movement and called a halt to compromises with slavery.[13]

It was against this background that the Morrill bill was reintroduced in December of 1861. The representatives of the southern states were gone, and thus the most solid opposition to the bill was also gone. Since Morrill, as a tariff expert, was preoccupied with problems of war revenues—particularly, the internal revenue bill—and fearful that his agricultural colleges bill would fail of action as a result, he asked his friend "Old Ben Wade" of Ohio to introduce it in the Senate for him. With action there first, House action would require considerably less engineering and attention on his part. On June 10, 1862, the bill passed the Senate 32 to 7, and a week later it passed the House 90 to 25.

In the Senate, Wade allowed a popular western amendment that limited the amount of land which might be located in any one state to a million acres. This provision protected the western states but opened the territories to absorb the bulk of eastern claims. There was opposition to the original bill from westerners, who resented the fact that the largest grants would go to eastern states, and that their grants would monopolize a lot of western lands. Wade's maneuvers brought action reassuring them on these matters. Other opponents, however, advocated that lands be sold to finance the war in order to avoid an unpopular income tax rather than giving them away to finance peacetime luxuries like farmers' colleges. Morrill himself used this line of reasoning to oppose the Homestead bill and failed to recognize his own inconsistency. The two measures, how-

13. Trefousse, op. cit., pp. 111–12; 124–29; Murat Halstead, *Caucuses of 1860: A History of the National Conventions of the Current Presidential Campaign,* (Columbus, Ohio: Follett, 1860); for the role of Ohio Senator George E. Pugh in the split of the Democratic party in 1860, see Charles Robert Veeck, "The Senatorial Career of George E. Pugh, 1855–1861" (master's thesis, Ohio State University, 1949).

ever, were inseparable so far as the Republican party was concerned and it could never justify passing the one and not the other.[14]

On July 2, 1862, President Lincoln signed the Morrill Act without comment. The lack of fanfare reflected both the preoccupation with war which characterized the nation, and the thorough commitment of the Republican party to instigate the program at an early opportunity. Furthermore, the politically astute Lincoln, concerned about retaining the loyalty of the border states and generally unwilling to take issue needlessly with men whose support he might need on other issues, probably was not unaware of the large number of border state congressmen among the thirty-two who had opposed the bill. They represented, in large measure, the remnant of that once formidable southern and western coalition that had dominated the nation's politics for decades. They would take exception to any comment he might make. There was, however, widespread support and enthusiasm for the measure in areas where the Union cause was already strong. Nearly a score of states had instructed their representatives to support the measure, and, since 1857, large numbers of petitions from national and state agricultural societies and from private citizens had endorsed the bill. For these enthusiasts, the promulgation of the act was in itself sufficient reward.[15]

The newspapers in Ohio, however, took little or no notice of the passage of the act or of Lincoln's signing of the measure. Their pages were crowded with news of the war and the actions of Congress to raise and equip armies and to find ways of paying for them. A decade later, in Springfield, Ohio, newspapers took an avid interest in the disposal of the Ohio grant; but in 1862, in an outline of important legislation passed by Congress, they failed even to list the

14. *Congressional Globe*, 37th Cong., 2nd sess., pp. 1935, 2187, 2248 ff., 2630 ff., 2634; Parker, op. cit., p. 188; Gates, op. cit., p. 285.

15. Trefousse, op. cit.; pp. 100 ff.; for an appraisal of Lincoln's deferential treatment of border state sympathies, see Edward C. Smith, *The Borderland and the Civil War*, (New York: Macmillan Co., 1927); William Best Hesseltine, *Lincoln and the War Governors*, (New York: Alfred A. Knopf, 1955); and William Best Hesseltine, *Lincoln's Plan of Reconstruction* (Tuscaloosa, Ala.: Confederate Publishing Co., 1960), pp. 11–30.

Morrill Act. The *Ohio State Journal* listed it without comment or emphasis in a series giving the text of all laws passed in the second session of the Thirty-seventh Congress.[16]

Nevertheless, there were those who were interested. The Morrill Act attracted the immediate and enthusiastic attention of those committed to agricultural reform. The reform impulse in Ohio was rich and strong in the 1860's, and it had survived the expedients of politics. The reform of agriculture was moreover a major part of that reform zeal. The abolitionist movement, which highlighted the sectional crisis, was but one of many reform impulses to which Ohioians had given support in the years following the emergence of Jacksonian Democracy.[17]

To Ralph Waldo Emerson, it had seemed that no aspect of American life had escaped the reform energies of the American people. "Each person whom I address", he once said, "has felt his own call to cast aside all evil customs, timidities, and limitations, and to be in his place a free and helpful man, a reformer, a benefactor. . . ." The church, the state, literature, history, domestic custom, the marketing system, man's eating habits, the system of coinage—nothing escaped. "Christianity, the laws, commerce, schools, the farm, the laboratory . . ." all were subject to review and reform, said Emerson, and there was not a kingdom, town, statute, rite, calling, man, or woman who was not threatened by it.[18]

Certain reform movements, however, were just more popular and more effective than others. The movements for peace, temperance, and abolition were in the forefront of the concerns of men who made the history of the nineteenth century. Furthermore, the Civil

16. *Evening News* (Springfield, Ohio), July 23, 1862; *Ohio State Journal* (Columbus, Ohio), July 29, 1862.

17. For a full treatment of the reform impulse and the relationship between reform and religious fervor see Alice Felt Tyler, *Freedom's Ferment: Phases of American Social History to 1860*, (Minneapolis: University of Minnesota Press, 1944); the relationship to Jacksonian democracy is ably denoted in Arthur M. Schlesinger, Jr., *The Age of Jackson*, (Boston: Little, Brown and Co., 1945); also helpful is R. E. Riegel, *Young America: 1830–1840*, (Norman: University of Oklahoma Press, 1949).

18. Ralph Waldo Emerson, "Man the Reformer," a lecture read before the Mechanics Apprentices' Library Association, Boston, January 25, 1891, *Complete Works of Emerson*, Centenary Edition (Boston and New York: Houghton Mifflin Co., 1904), I, 225–56.

War focused the energies of the nation more specifically upon the issue of slavery, and at the same time eclipsed those less directly related to the one focal crisis which engulfed the nation.

Among these overshadowed reform movements, however, was the effort to change the face of agriculture. Emerson designated the movement as a reform of life and labor not altogether distinct from the abolition, temperance, and peace movements. While some focused primarily upon these, "others attacked the system of agriculture, the use of animal manures in farming, and the tyranny of man over brute nature," said Emerson.[19] Still others, however, attacked the tyranny of brute nature over man, the endless toil, and the cultural proverty of life on the farm.

There were two aspects to the movement for agricultural reform, and Caleb Atwater of Ohio indicated both of them in his *Essay on Education*, which he published in Cincinnati, in 1841.[20] Agriculture was an art, he insisted, and one that would be better pursued if a proper education were provided to its practitioners. The proper culture of the earth, how to prepare it, how to manure it and mix it with other earths, or cover it with compost or manures; what grain or plants the farm would best produce; what crop would be most profitable; what cattle, sheep, or hogs should be raised, how their breeds could be crossed—such practical matters of farming designed to raise production, end soil depletion, and make the farmers' lot more prosperous constituted an educational reform of the first magnitude.[21]

The movement, however, was a reform movement in the nineteenth century tradition of reform primarily because of its second aspect, which gave a high purpose to the mundane course of study Atwater had outlined. Atwater thought that the farmer was victimized by an envy of people living in towns, villages, and cities that corroded his heart. The farmer's own oppressive way of life, he said, had turned him against civilization, though secretly he envied it,

19. Ralph Waldo Emerson, "New England Reformers: A Lecture Read *before the Society in Amory Hall on Sunday, March 3, 1844," ibid.,* III, 249–86.

20. Caleb Atwater, *An Essay on Education,* (Cincinnati, Ohio: Kendall and Henry, 1841).

21. Ibid., pp. 54–55.

and had blinded him to the new way of life in which farmer, merchant, mechanic, lawyer, doctor, minister, and school teacher worked together for the common good and comfort. There was need for reform because the farmer was a slave to a bygone day and was missing out on the new, industrial society. "The farmer comes into town," observed Atwater, "and with envy sees the tailor . . . the shoemaker . . . the blacksmith . . . the cabinet maker," all of whom had more of this world's goods than he, though they neither planted nor harvested and, perhaps, owned no land at all. The difference, observed Atwater, was a difference in ways of life, a difference in systems of values, and the absence of a modern wisdom increasingly foreign to the farmer. None of these deficiencies, he felt, was likely to be repaired either for the farmer or for his children by the rudimentary and inadequate educational opportunities available to them.[22]

For some men, the changing of all this, the provision of a system to enlighten the farmer and to reform his way of life, to terminate soil-slavery, and to coordinate the life of the farm with the life of the city was much more important than the mere teaching of agriculture; it was a reform worthy of the greatest effort. Some who took up the cause were immigrants from the farm who had happy memories of their youthful drudgeries, but who, through the process of education, had become less and less inclined to return to the farm. They wanted, however, to do something to enlighten their less fortunate brethren. Others who took up the cause viewed their own farm origins quite differently and attacked with vigor the toil and drudgery, the provincialism, and the lack of educational opportunity which had smothered and stifled them until they had escaped.[23] The nature of the reforms sought differed somewhat for the representatives of these two orientations. The former sought to bring enlightenment to the farm; the latter, to bring the farmer to enlightenment. Both types, however, were inclined to view the theories of general reformers of education as somewhat irrelevant in their applicability to the problems of rural America.

22. Ibid., p. 56.
23. *Farm and Fireside*, August 1, 1887, X, no. 21, 343.

In the pursuit of agricultural reform, a group of persons emerged as leaders who were not divorced from the more general impulse for reform characteristic of the times. Like their compeers in the movements for abolition, temperance, peace, and similar reforms, they were interested in a host of good causes. Also, like their compeers in other vineyards, they advocated their reforms through the printed word. Two important Ohio journals devoted to agricultural reform, and characteristic of the several hundred published throughout the nation, were the *Ohio Cultivator*, published in Columbus, and the *Ohio Farmer*, established in Cleveland.[24] The first American college journal devoted to agriculture was the *Cincinnatus*, edited and published by the faculty of Farmers' College near Cincinnati.[25]

The *Ohio Cultivator*, through its editor and its writers, advocated women's rights, temperance, abolition, female education, and other good causes as well as agricultural reform. The editor of the *Ohio Farmer*, though less vociferous, endorsed women's rights as early as 1856 as the legitimate working out of the Declaration of Independence.[26] Hanna M. Tracy, a writer for the *Ohio Cultivator*, gave the magazine a modern flavor hardly equaled in any journal of the time whether devoted to farmers or city dwellers. A representative to the World Peace Congress in London in 1851 and a visitor to the World's Fair, she appeared in public in the new Bloomer costume and lectured on women's rights and the glories of Bloomerism. She was president of the Ohio Women's Rights Association; her co-worker, Mrs. M. B. Bateham, the wife of the journal's editor, served as president of the State Temperance Society.[27]

Writers for the agricultural press, however, wrote more specifically about reforming the land, restoring improverished soils, and ending the process of soil depletion followed by the westward migration. Their readers might easily have concluded that the great western movement in America's history was more the result of soil depletion in the East than the availability of plentiful land in

24. Albert Lowther Demaree, *The American Agricultural Press: 1819–1860*, (New York: Columbia University Press, 1941), p. 17.

25. Ibid., pp. 17, 55.

26. Ibid., pp. 162, 177n.

27. Ibid., pp. 164–67.

the West. Nevertheless, the editors carped at professors of chemistry who did not sufficiently understand the science they attempted to teach in its application to practical agriculture. They ridiculed the wise men of scientific agriculture who rushed to the farmer with half-baked revelations which in the end did nothing more than undermine the farmer's faith in education and scientific agriculture. Some of the "humbugs" of such scientific farmers, the editors lamented, would take a generation to undo and, in the meantime, another generation of farmers was shown the wisdom of their distrust of reform. The man who advised beekeepers to chloroform the bees to facilitate harvesting the honey crop had failed to discover in his research that the bees, unfortunately, did not recover. The editors of the farm journals observed that the farmer's faith in scientific agriculture failed to recover as well.[28]

The farm journals, however, supported and stimulated nation-wide agitation for federal land donations for agricultural institutions with an emphasis on the reform involved and not on the political impact of the issue. The faculty of the Farmers' College of Ohio, through their journal, credited the zealous endorsement and advocacy of the Morrill Act by the farm press with responsibility for its passage. The widespread support thus generated helped put the squeeze on many Democratic congressmen. The journalists likewise agitated for state appropriations for agricultural schools, societies and clubs, and for the establishment of state boards of agriculture and agricultural experiment stations. Their concern was for reform in practice, not in theory, and they ignored the objections based on possible political repercussions. In the process, the Ohio journals prepared a generation of Ohio farmers to view agricultural education with a specific set of expectancies.[29]

Norton S. Townshend, later a member of the first board of trustees of the Ohio Agricultural and Mechanical College and the school's first professor of agriculture, was a good example of the Ohio reformer who chose farming as his chief field of endeavor. A native of England, Townshend's family immigrated to Ohio in 1830, when he was fifteen years of age. At the age of twenty, he was

28. Ibid., p. 69.
29. Ibid., p. 69.

teaching in Lorain County, but the following year, in 1837, he began the study of medicine. He studied at Starling Medical College in Columbus and also attended the Cincinnati Medical College. In 1840, he received his degree from the College of Physicians and Surgeons in the University of New York. Upon graduation, he went to Europe to study in the hospitals of Great Britain and France. He also went as the delegate of the Temperance Society of the College of Physicians and Surgeons to the temperance societies of Great Britain and Ireland.[30]

In addition, because of his standing in the movement, he was commissioned by the antislavery society of Ohio to represent it at the World Antislavery Convention in London. He returned to America in 1841, and practiced medicine at Avon until, in 1848, he was elected to the Ohio legislature by the antislavery men of Lorain County. Townshend found himself among the small minority of abolitionists in the legislature who held the balance of power between the Whigs and the Democrats. They first used their position to repeal the infamous black laws of the state, and later to elect an antislavery man, Salmon P. Chase, to the United States Senate.[31]

In addition to reform interests in temperance and abolition, Townshend likewise advocated the establishment of an asylum for imbecile youth, and later served for twenty-one years as a member of the board of trustees for the asylum established by the legislature to serve this deprived class of citizens.[32]

In 1855, however, Townshend's interest in agricultural reform manifested itself in the establishment of an agricultural college for Ohio which the state farm press, oblivious of developments in Michigan, dubbed the first agricultural college in America. Townshend modeled his school after the medical colleges with which he was familiar, and he, together with the president of Oberlin College, a professor from Oberlin, and a doctor from Cleveland, constituted the first faculty. They taught agricultural science and practice in winter sessions of three months' duration for two years at Oberlin

30. Norton S. Townshend, *"Farm and Fireside,"* February 1, 1887, X, no. 9, 146.
31. Ibid., p. 146; Mendenhall, op. cit., p. 68.
32. *Farm and Fireside*, February 1, 1887, X, no. 9, 146.

and a final year at Cleveland. Financial difficulties curtailed the
effort, although Townshend sought to enlist the support of the
Ohio State Board of Agriculture to prevent its closing. The passage
of the Morrill Act in 1859, though vetoed by President Buchanan,
gave promise of a more feasible prospect for financing such endeavors.[33]

By the 1860's, however, the farm press and agricultural reformers
such as Norton S. Townshend were no less sure of the steps to be
taken to bring their reforms to fruition than were the abolitionists
and the temperance crusaders. They had a commitment to a
practical reformation of the daily life of the farmer, insulated from
the academic irrelevance of men who would chloroform bees, and
devoted to meeting the farmer where he was, at the common school
level, with a system of rural education. Perhaps eventually the
farmer would accept the city and the host of benefits to be derived
from the modern life. But first of all, he had to be freed from the
soil and given cause not to feel envious or distrustful of his city
brethren. The settlement of the problem, however, was considerably
more complicated.

The changing nature of the state's population, the emergence of
industry and commerce on an economic equality with farming, the
rise of new cities and the concomitant rivalry for political and
economic dominance, and the emergence of this element of com-
mited agricultural reformers all at the same time created strong
centrifugal forces which did not augur well for a new university.

In the Ohio of the 1860's, there existed over 11,000 manufacturing
establishments which produced nearly $123 million worth of prod-
ucts. The state's industrial production was thus roughly equal in
dollar value to its total agricultural production and was gaining
steadily.[34] An emerging clothing industry, one hundred and sixty
distilleries in fifty-six counties, and a multimillion-dollar-a-year meat
packing business indicated the widespread industrial development
of the state.

The state's factories produced annually several million dollars'
worth of castings, machinery, and utensils. A growing farm ma-

33. Mendenhall, op. cit., p. 68.
34. *Fourth Annual Report of the Commissioner of Statistics to the Governor
of Ohio, 1860* (Columbus, 1861), pp. 25–27.

chinery industry created new towns and cities from older villages like Dayton, Springfield, Canton, and other interior towns. Hundreds of new industries appeared, and every decade the state's industrial production doubled. In Ohio, a cross section of prosperous agriculture coexisted with developing industry.[35] As the state's statistician saw it, Ohio was not only an emerging industrial power but was also the great natural gateway between East and West, presiding as it were over the very intersectional life of the nation. "Every increase of harvest in the West, or of trade and manufactures in the East," he observed, "increased traffic and business in Ohio."[36] That, plus easy access to the South via the Ohio and the Mississippi River system, and a foreign trade with Canada that doubled every decade, gave Ohio an enviable position. The prosperity of Cincinnati, fed by the Mississippi River valley, and that of Cleveland, fed by the lakes and the Erie Canal, gave Ohio two natural holds on the internal commerce of the nation, and gave the state two rivals for dominance in state politics. Furthermore, the National Road, which cut from Zanesville through Columbus and Springfield to Indiana, fostered a series of prosperous communities which, by presiding over another of the nation's main arteries, sought power by balancing the north of the state with its south.[37]

The tonnage of foreign shipping in the harbors at Cleveland, Sandusky, and Toledo more than doubled in less than a decade. Shipbuilding on the Ohio River, but primarily on Lake Erie, ranked Ohio fifth in the nation in competition with all of the maritime states. Cleveland, Ohio's "forest city" of 17,000 people in 1850, had grown to 43,000 by 1860, and a decade later was the fifteenth largest city in the nation. Columbus, central in the state and central on the National Road, with the assets of the state government and increasing railroad connections, was growing with equal rapidity.[38]

New industry and new cities pointing toward new distributions of population, wealth, and political power thus characterized the

35. Ibid., p. 28.

36. Ibid., pp. 30, 31.

37. Ibid., p. 31; see also Balthaser Henry Meyer (ed.), *The History of Transportation in the United States Before 1860*, (Washington, D. C.: Carnegie Institution, 1917).

38. *Fourth Annual Report of the Commissioner of Statistics*, pp. 24–25, 124 ff.

state in the latter half of the nineteenth century. The demands of the emerging cities for new kinds of educational facilities and opportunities in contrast to the demands of the organized farmer for practical and specific agricultural reform clashed in the debates about how to use the Morrill Land Grant fund in Ohio. Given these fairly equally balanced factors, it was not difficult to recognize the need for delay and patience in disposing of the land grant in Ohio. Since such factors more or less canceled each other out, inaction became the wiser course.

CHAPTER 1

The Cannon Act

Although the newspapers and the public in general paid little attention to the Morrill Land Grant College Act, the act did attract some attention. There were many interested parties who petitioned the Ohio legislature concerning the state's acceptance and use of the proffered assistance. Both Miami University at Oxford and Ohio University at Athens expressed immediate interest.[1] The State Board of Agriculture memorialized the legislature on the great opportunity which the Act provided. Various and sundry other educational institutions throughout the state made representations about the possible use of the grant.

The Act, by providing what was for the time a very handsome endowment, quickened the interests of men devoted to the traditional college concept, those zealous for a more utilitarian view of higher education, and those who envisioned for Ohio a great state university committed to research and scholarship. All who may have entertained some idea of educational or agricultural reform were interested. The Act brought many men with divergent purposes and objectives to the point of considering what might be done with so handsome a grant. And, in ensuing decades, a confusion of purposes and activities tumbled one upon the other in Ohio's effort to create a land grant institution. The Act itself did not provide

1. Thomas N. Hoover, *The History of Ohio University*, (Athens, Ohio: Ohio University Press, 1954), p. 126.

great detail in prescribing the kinds of colleges that should be supported by the federal largesse. In fact, the legislation was deliberately somewhat vague in order to have as broad an appeal as possible.

Eventually, the Ohio land-grant netted more than $340,000 for the support of higher education under the terms of the Morrill Act, although most observers had expected the proceeds to exceed a half million dollars before the actual sale of the state's land grant. In Ohio that was an unbelievably rich endowment and none of the score or more of colleges in the state possessed such a handsome foundation. Ohio University's endowment was $80,000, and Miami's approached $100,000. Ohio Wesleyan, Oberlin, and Kenyon were the most comfortable, with endowments only one-half the size of the land grant fund, or slightly more than half. Under the circumstances, the fund, though small by later standards, represented the largest single educational endowment in Ohio in the 1860's.[2]

In November of 1862, Governor Tod reviewed the Morrill Act provisions with a special meeting of the State Board of Agriculture, and it recommended overwhelmingly that the state accept the grant. In January of 1863, in his annual message to the Assembly, the governor recommended acceptance, while the State Board of Agriculture advised the legislature about wise use of the grant.

Opposition to the acceptance, however, was voiced by the state auditor. He saw in the grant a burden to the state, and a drain on state resources rather than an educational opportunity. Although the Act was designed to establish an educational institution, he said, the state was required to absorb the cost of marketing the land scrip, and was prohibited from spending the proceeds for the construction of buildings. Furthermore, if the endowment should be lost, the state was obligated to replace it. As the Act stood, in other words, the expenditures for getting an educational institution underway and housing it would be the responsibility of the state, and the auditor felt that the costs were too great. He reflected the opinion of a large number of people in the state and in the legisla-

2. For a discussion of comparative endowments, see Hoover, op. cit., pp. 130–31; for a readily available summary of the Ohio land-grant sales, see Thomas C. Mendenhall, *The History of the Ohio State University*, I, (Columbus, Ohio: Ohio State University Press, 1920), 8–13.

ture. The fears which he expressed were not at all uncommon. In the final disposition of the problem, the legislature enticed the counties to raise the funds to house the new institution in return for its location and put the original land-grant fund into the state treasury from whence it could never be lost.[3]

In the Fifty-fifth General Assembly, five measures were introduced to accept and make use of the federal grant. None passed, but those introduced indicated the diversity of views concerning the uses that might be made of the 630,000 acres which comprised Ohio's grant. One bill would claim the benefits of the act and create an agricultural bureau. Another would establish the Ohio State College of Arts. Still a third accepted the Morrill grant and established Farmers' College in Hamilton County as the Agricultural and Mechanical College of Ohio. A fourth would establish the Ohio Agricultural, Military, and Mechanical College as a separate and new institution at a place to be determined. Overwhelmingly, however, the legislators favored procrastination and voted to postpone action. The fifth effort to dispose of the Morrill grant was suggested in the Senate and it was important in indicating the ultimate direction of legislative action. The Senate proposal required simply that the state accept the grant, leaving all other questions to be resolved later.[4]

Delay was the will of the legislature, however, in this case as in the others. Further delay allowed other interested groups the necessary time to determine their course of action. On September 28, 1863, the trustees of Ohio University, for instance, met in a special session to discuss the implications of the Morrill Act for that institution's dire financial situation. They appointed a special committee to act in concert with a similar committee from Miami University to get the General Assembly to divide the grant between the two older institutions whose boards of trustees were state appointed.[5] Petitions from the trustees of the two institutions were presented to the legislature early in 1864. The State Board of Agriculture, however, still firmly advocated that the grant not be

3. Ibid., pp. 4–5, 7.
4. Ibid., pp. 5–7.
5. Hoover, op. cit., p. 126.

divided, that it be used to establish one new state institution, and that it be specifically designated to promote the teaching of agricultural and mechanical subjects.

In an effort to equal the Agricultural Board's voice in the legislature, the trustees of Miami and Ohio universities sought to organize public opinion in their behalf through the state's newspapers. The members of their special committees, in addition, functioned as lobbyists in Columbus during the session of the legislature pressing the claims of the two older state-created institutions. The opposition of the Board of Agriculture, however, was unrelenting.[6]

When the Fifty-sixth General Assembly convened, action to dispose of the land-grant issue was taken quickly and with little delay. On January 7, Representative Columbus Delano, later a member of the United States Congress but in 1864 a member of the Ohio Board of Agriculture, introduced a bill which resembled the Senate bill of the previous session. It authorized the state to accept the grant, and to indicate that it would be used in a manner consistent with the provisions of the Morrill Act, but contained no stipulation about the allocation of the proceeds. Delano's bill appeared on the heels of a unanimous resolution of county agricultural societies urging immediate acceptance of the grant. They asked for action, and the legislature complied, but sidestepped the more crucial issue of the use of the grant.[7]

Obviously, the legislature had decided to settle the crucial issues raised by the Morrill Act one at a time. The first, whether to accept or not, was resolved by the Delano bill. A fundamental issue, and one upon which agreement was not possible at the time, concerned the use which the state might make of the fund. The first bills introduced in the Assembly to establish an agricultural bureau or to establish an Ohio state college of arts defined the two extremes. The first did not purport to be an educational institution in the usual sense at all; rather, it was an agency for direct service to farmers in the field and a direct response to the main demands of the agricultural reform movement. The second did not purport to

6. Ibid., pp. 126–28.
7. Mendenhall, op. cit., pp. 6–7.

provide agricultural education but established instead a traditional type of educational institution under state auspices ignoring the desires of farmers and industrialists alike.

The legislature continued to avoid a decision about the nature of the new institution and took the next logical step, that of authorizing the sale of the land scrip. It also sidestepped the more fundamental question, politically, concerning the specific location of the institution. Instead it directed the governor to appoint a commission of five men to report on a suitable location for a college or colleges, and on any inducements which various localities might be prepared to offer to secure the establishment of the institution in their midst. As a result of this action, in the spring of 1865, the sale of land scrip was commenced and the commissioners began a study of locations. Later that year, the commissioners returned a majority report advocating the division of the land proceeds between two institutions. The first, Miami University, would receive half of the fund and would be reorganized as an agricultural and mechanical college. The other half of the fund would be used to endow a college in the northern part of the state.[8]

A minority report advocated giving the entire fund for an agricultural and mechanical college at College Hill near Cincinnati where Farmers' College was located. Neither report was adopted by the legislature, however, and for five more years the questions of location, a division of the fund, and the nature of the program to be offered remained unresolved. Various proposals were considered during each legislative session but agreement was not possible and succeeding assemblies merely reconsidered proposals made earlier.[9]

The state commissioner of education suggested dividing the fund between one centrally located, professional institution and three colleges in different corners of the state which would offer training in agriculture and science. Presumably, Ohio University, Miami University, and an institution in the northeastern section of the state would have been included in this plan. The objective was commendable, and the plan would have satisfied most sections of

8. Ibid., pp. 5, 16, 17.
9. Ibid., pp. 17–21.

the state, particularly the growing urban industrial areas in the southwest and the northwest. It was doubtful, however, that the funds available would have been sufficient to carry out such a grandiose plan. Furthermore, the State Board of Agriculture was as irrevocably committed as ever to opposing such a division of the land grant fund. This then was the impasse: farmers' organizations wanted one new institution which fully reflected the agricultural reform movement, but people in each section of the state sought access to the fund to meet local educational needs.[10]

It was understandable that proponents of an undivided fund and those who advocated a centralized state university should seek to undermine the claims of existing institutions. The claims of Ohio University and Miami were decidedly weakened during the years of procrastination by agitations against sectarian influences at the two older colleges. A professor of mathematics who had been asked to resign at Ohio University published a defense charging that various Methodists were chiefly responsible for his ouster. The *Ohio Statesman*, a newspaper in Columbus, took up the cause of another professor who, the paper claimed, had also been forced to resign under suspicious circumstances. The paper questioned the right of the Ohio Conference of the Methodist Church to control the institution to the degree that it obviously did, and demanded that the legislature make a thorough investigation of the school, its administration, and its board of trustees.[11]

The influence of the Methodists at Ohio University had grown increasingly strong. Originally, the school had been dominated by Presbyterians and, unable to dislodge them, the Methodists had founded Ohio Wesleyan University at Delaware, Ohio. Ultimately, however, because of the strength of the Methodists among the people in southeastern Ohio, and the institution's complete dependence upon its environment for sustenance, the Methodists won control. In 1865, in addition to the president of the institution, a majority of the faculty were ordained Methodist ministers. Furthermore, the board of trustees was dominated by Methodists, and a majority of the honorary degrees which the school awarded were given to Methodist ministers. The Baptists of Ohio, in particular,

10. Ibid., pp. 13–14.
11. Hoover, op. cit., pp. 133–37.

resented Methodist ascendancy at the Athens institution, and did not view favorably efforts to divide the Morrill grant proceeds with the institution.[12]

Miami University, however, was as much controlled by the Presbyterians of the state as Ohio University was by the Methodists. As early as the 1830's, Ohio parents considered the school a safe Presbyterian influence on their children. A majority of the faculty members were Presbyterian clergymen, and the trustees generally reflected the same sectarian commitment. There was here the same Methodist-Presbyterian conflict which occurred at Ohio University and which raged throughout Ohio in the 1840's, but at Miami, the Presbyterians maintained control. On more than one occasion, however, the community was thrown into turmoil by the appearance of a Methodist circuit rider bent upon reforming the Calvinism of the area.[13]

In 1867, having been rebuffed by the legislature in an appeal for funds, President Robert Livingston Stanton of Miami sought direct aid from the Presbyterian church as the school had done on other occasions. It was proposed this time that control of the university be conveyed directly to the denomination if its financial support was to reach the proportions envisioned by Stanton. The plan was abandoned, however, when it was realized that such a transfer could not be accomplished without a statewide referendum. Somewhat earlier, Ohio's Presbyterians had offered to endow four chairs at the Oxford institution provided the church could name the occupants. The trustees of the institution, having given up hope of ever attaining such generous support from the state, entertained the proposition seriously, but a movement among the denomination's synods to support a school which in fact belonged to them gained the upper hand. Gradually, the movement among Presbyterians to establish Wooster College turned the denomination's financial assistance away from Miami altogether. The Presbyterian influence at Miami, however, no less than the influence of the

12. Ibid., p. 136; Henry Clyde Hubbart, *Ohio Wesleyan's First Hundred Years*, (Delaware, Ohio: Ohio Wesleyan University, 1943), p. 10.
13. Roscoe Huln Eckelberry, "A Study of Religious Influence in Higher Education in Ohio" (Masters thesis, Ohio State University, 1923), pp. 31 ff; James H. Rodabaugh, "The History of Miami University from Its Origin to 1885" (Ph.D. diss., Ohio State University, 1937), pp. 119–46.

Methodists at Ohio University, undermined support for the institution in its hope for funds from the Morrill land grant. Any proposal which seemed in one way or another to enrich or endorse one church denomination, immediately elicited opposition and competitive bills in the legislature. In the general melee, the position of the State Board of Agriculture, advocating a single, new institution was strengthened.[14]

A free-for-all session, showing lawmakers at their log-rolling best, occurred in January of 1867, and illustrated the extreme variety of opinions which the legislature reflected. A resolution was introduced in the House instructing the Committee on Agriculture to prepare a bill distributing the funds among Miami and Ohio universities and the Western Reserve College. Immediately, there was an amendment to include Oberlin, popularly called the people's college because of its democratic ideas, and shortly thereafter another to include Methodist Mount Union. A substitute motion was then offered giving the entire fund to Episcopal Kenyon College. The resolution, amendments, and the substitute motion were all referred to the Agricultural Committee.

The same day, another resolution was offered directing that the funds be parceled out to establish professorships in several existing institutions for the teaching of agricultural and mechanical subjects. Another substitute motion was introduced, however, putting the House on record as favoring one college centrally located. Debate then focused on the phrase "centrally located" and the limitations which it placed on certain county ambitions. Finally, the House agreed to strike the word "centrally" and to use instead the word "accessibly," which implied good road and railroad connections and not mere geographic placement. The resolution passed the House but failed to pass in the Senate. The lower house, however, had correctly assessed the tenor of public opinion and had indicated the reasonable solution of the issue. Though the decision would be three more years in coming, its essential outlines had emerged in the House debate.[15]

14. Ibid., pp. 119–20.
15. Mendenhall, op. cit., pp. 19–20.

The state legislature had been given a nearly impossible task of reconciling extreme differences of opinion about the disposition of the proceeds of the grant. The claims of Miami and Ohio universities were not unopposed. The efforts of representatives from Cincinnati to secure the fund for Farmers' College excited the jealous opposition of interested parties in other sections of the state. The claims of the northeastern part of the state and the city of Cleveland were difficult to ignore, and the first commission assigned the duty of locating the school or schools had returned a rather pragmatic proposal for dividing the funds between the desires of Cincinnatians and those of Cleveland spokesmen. Representatives from Columbus and the central part of the state, however, backed the position of Springfielders who advocated legislation insisting that the institution be centrally located near an industrial city.[16]

In light of the total situation, the plan of the State Commissioner of Education seemed the most astute and the one best designed to satisfy all parties, all except the farmers. A school at Athens, one near Cincinnati, one near Cleveland, and one near the center of the state appeared to him to be the price of progress. The funds were obviously insufficient, though they exceeded the endowments of most institutions in the state at the time. But the plan was politically wise. It outlined, essentially, the state system of higher education which ultimately emerged after the turn of the century, and it indicated the directions of the settlement ultimately reached in 1870.[17]

Only the farmers would have objected, and their viewpoint was increasingly important. The state farmers' organizations insisted that the fund not be divided, that it be designated for the support of one new, centrally located institution, and that the study of agriculture be a primary objective of the institution. Their position strengthened the proposal of Franklin County enthusiasts, because location near the state capital became increasingly the only viable alternative that would satisfy the groups who could not obtain the institution for themselves.

16. *Daily Republic* (Springfield, Ohio), March 10, 1870.
17. Mendenhall, op. cit., pp. 13–14.

Finally, in 1870, the legislature passed four important acts which settled the crucial issues involved in expending the land grant. Rutherford B. Hayes, governor of the state, took an active interest in the disposition of the issue. With a penchant for compromising diverse viewpoints he set about to move the state from dead center. He thought it sheer folly for the state to forfeit the Morrill grant merely because it was unable, for eight years, to agree upon the details of its use. He had told the legislature in his message in January that unless action were taken soon, the deadline date would pass, and the state would be obligated to return the proceeds of the land sale to the federal government. Already Congress had twice extended the original deadline date, but Hayes urged that conflicting interests be compromised. It would be dangerous, he thought, to trust that a further extension of time would be forthcoming.[18]

As the Fifty-ninth General Assembly convened, however, the political balance was somewhat disturbed. Representatives from Cincinnati presented themselves to the Assembly as a Reform party unwilling to join either the Republican or the Democratic caucuses. By this maneuver, the Hamilton County delegation held the balance of power in the legislature and could enable either party to control the Assembly depending upon its decision to support one or the other. The editor of the Springfield *Daily Republic* was concerned about this effort of Queen City politicians to strengthen their slipping hold on state power, and wondered how high the bid would go before the "fourteen" sold out to one party or the other.[19]

The wielding of this new power by the Cincinnati group had important implications for the disposition of the Morrill Act funds. A major objective of Cincinnati policy was to obtain authorization for the city to assume trusteeship over a variety of small educational endowments within the city as a foundation for a municipal university. None was sufficient to establish a great municipal uni-

18. "Annual Message of the Governor of Ohio to the General Assembly," *Executive Documents, Message and Annual Reports for 1869 Made to the Fifty-ninth General Assembly of the State of Ohio at the Session Commencing January 3, 1870*, Part I, Columbus, 1870, pp. 336–37.

19. *Daily Republic* (Springfield, Ohio), January 3, 4, 1870.

versity by itself and all together would adequately support a beginning. Citizens of the Queen City, oblivious to the ambitions of
Miami University and the nearby Farmers' College, sought state
legislation that would enable them to proceed with the establishment of the University of Cincinnati. Opposition to such legislation
throughout much of the rest of the state had prevented such legislation previously.[20]

The Assembly then constructed an effective four-part compromise
which after eight years settled the argument about the Morrill land
grant. The first part of the accommodation was an act which
authorized municipalities such as Cincinnati to organize, support,
and control institutions of higher education. This legislation made
agreement upon a central location for the land-grant college easier
to obtain by providing a means for other outlying sections of the
state to solve their own educational problems. A second act authorized the investment of the funds received from the sale of the
land scrip by making them part of the irreducible debt of the state,
with interest to be paid to the benefiting institution at the rate of
6 percent per year. Thus, the state's responsibility for the safe-
keeping of the original fund was discharged regardless of the ultimate designation of the beneficiary. There was thus very little
chance of its being lost and fiscal conservatives were satisfied. The
third act authorized counties to raise funds with which to secure
the location of the new institution by the selling of bonds. This
measure opened the competition to more counties and provided
a means whereby the buildings for the new institution could be
provided without an expenditure of tax revenues. The fourth act
was the Cannon Act, the charter act of the Ohio State University.[21]

20. Roscoe Huln Eckelberry, *History of the Municipal University in the
U. S.*, U. S. Department of Education Bulletin No. 2 (Washington, D. C.: U. S.
Government Printing Office, 1932), pp. 87–90.

21. The Act making land grant funds a part of the permanent or irreducible
debt of the state was passed first. On March 22, 1870, the Cannon Act, or An
Act to Establish and Maintain an Agricultural and Mechanical College in Ohio
passed 75 to 24 in the House and 25 to 12 in the Senate. An Act to Enable
Cities of the First Class to Aid and Promote Education was then enacted on
April 16 by a unanimous vote of the House and with only 4 dissents in the
Senate. The way was then cleared for the passage two days later of an act
authorizing the counties to raise funds to bid for the new college authorized in
the Cannon Act. For a brief account, see Mendenhall, op. cit., pp. 20–23 and

When the Cannon Act was first introduced, its supporters had more than enough support to pass it and to defeat all amendments. Amendments offered by opponents to reduce the desirability of the bill were soundly defeated. Friends of the measure, feeling added strength, insisted upon the passage of the bill without any changes at all. One amendment, offered by friends of the bill, would require that the board of trustees take into consideration the facilities of any location for the teaching of the mechanical arts. This amendment reflected the insistence of the industrial interests of the state that Ohio not establish a mere farmers' college. The amendment received a great deal of support but was defeated by a slim majority. Such an amendment would have restricted the trustees, many thought, to a choice of Springfield or Columbus for the new institution's location. A spokesman from Columbus observed that the change was probably designed to strengthen the claim of the wide-awake manufacturing town of Springfield but that it was a good amendment and one which the friends of the legislation should permit.[22]

Nevertheless, the Cannon Act was passed by both houses without amendment. The act created a powerful board of trustees empowered to locate the Ohio Agricultural and Mechanical College permanently on a tract of not less than one hundred acres suited to the wants and purposes of the institution, reasonably central in the state and accessible by railroad. The board was to give due regard to the healthiness of the area, and to the money, land, or other property offered by the county to secure its location. Duties of the board outlined in the act included the power to elect, fix the compensation of, and remove, the president and professors, teachers, and other employees of the institution; to fix and regulate the course of instruction; and even to prescribe the extent and character of any experiments conducted at the university. It was

---

Roscoe Huhn Eckelberry, *History of the Municipal University in the U. S.* pp. 87–90. While the Journals of the Ohio House of Representatives and the Ohio Senate for 1870 give the outline of proceedings, they, unfortunately, are totally devoid of descriptive and elaborative data. They do reveal key maneuvers and votes.

22. *Daily Republic* (Springfield, Ohio), March 10, 1870.

a broad and sweeping delegation of authority which made the Ohio board of trustees a model for the clear and unequivocal assignment to trustees of a definite role in the governance of higher education. Although the immediate concern was for the location of the institution, and the board was clothed with adequate authority for that purpose, the ultimate concern was for the permanent establishment of the college, and here also the board's authority was clear and inclusive.[23]

The Cannon Act called for a nineteen-member board of trustees, one representing each congressional district in the state. The posts were to be filled by the governor with Senate confirmation. This scheme of representation provided a voice for every part of the state in the further deliberations about the location of the college and the nature of its program. Hopefully, this arrangement, coupled with the broad and sweeping authority of the board, would transfer from the halls of the legislature, where the issue had floundered for eight years, to the board of trustees the crucial decisions yet to be made. In effect, the legislature had transferred to the new board the thorny problems of determining both the school's location and its nature and governing philosophy. The board the act created was unquestionably strong enough to get that job done.[24]

As the editor of the *Ohio State Journal* soon lamented, however, the transfer was not absolute, and the legislators retained a directing interest and the ultimate power. A quarter of a century later, William Oxley Thompson, as president of the university, observed that the state could not and should not relinquish the voice of the people in the affairs of their college. In 1870, however, with the precedents of the establishment of Miami and Ohio universities, editor James M. Comly's original expectation seemed wholly justified: the future of the new institution apparently had been

23. John J. Corson, *Governance of Colleges and Universities* (New York: McGraw-Hill Book Co., 1960), pp. 49–50.

24. "An Act to Establish and Maintain an Agricultural and Mechanical College in Ohio," *Ohio Laws and Statutes: General and Local Laws and Joint Resolutions Passed by the Fifty-ninth General Assembly*, LXVII (Columbus, 1870), 20–23.

placed securely in the hands of its board of trustees.[25] Thus, from 1862 to 1870, from Morrill and Wade to Hayes and Cannon, the emerging institution had been nurtured on politics. Now, it was assumed the political phase of the institution's development had ended.

25. *Ohio State Journal* (Columbus, Ohio), September 12, 1870; William Oxley Thompson, "The Influence of the Morrill Act Upon American Higher Education," *Proceedings of the Twenty-sixth Annual Convention of the Association of American Agricultural Colleges and Experiment Stations, Atlanta, Georgia, November 13–15, 1912* (n.p., n.d.), p. 24.

CHAPTER 2

A Preliminary Consensus

Rutherford B. Hayes quite naturally approached the task of creating a university politically, with keen appreciation for the importance of political balance and perspective. He was not an educator but a politician, although one with a better developed philosophy of education than most. He argued for organizing the new school's board of trustees on the basis of congressional districts because in that event the chances were exceedingly good for Republican control. Such organization would also dramatize the national as opposed to the state nature of the land-grant system. It would achieve both of these things while at the same time being rationally and politically defensible.

Nevertheless, Governor Rutherford B. Hayes wanted a "capital board," as he described it, one comprised of sound men who would make the new school an institution of great importance. He did not get all of the men he wanted, but he succeeded ultimately in obtaining most of those he really wanted. He tried to appoint a Republican from those congressional districts which had elected a Republican to Congress, and a Democrat from those which had elected a Democrat; and he wanted to include a leading figure from each party in order to get the school off to a good, bipartisan start. George H. Pendleton, however, a leading Democrat and that party's candidate for vice-president in 1864, refused to serve. When

Pendleton declined, Hayes allowed former Republican Govenor Willian Dennison to decline also. After having met these requirements of political etiquette, then, Hayes proceeded to construct a Board that would take a broad view of its function, being neither too narrowly traditional nor too narrowly utilitarian.[1]

Joseph Sullivant of Columbus also refused a post on the board. Hayes, however, would not permit him to decline. In the battle for confirmation of his appointees in the Senate, Sullivant's nomination received the greatest opposition and though he was approved, it was by a vote of nineteen in favor and eleven against. He said that he expected to be opposed by some because he was too progressive and too much imbued with modern ideas concerning education. He was not prepared, however, to be misrepresented as he felt he was. His knowledge of, and interest in, agriculture and collateral sciences had been deliberately deprecated, he felt, by those who thought he might resist efforts to manage the institution in favor of the narrower, agricultural college concept. They knew he would not be a tool of that self-appointed clique that expected to manage things, he said. After the bitter Senate debate, however, he told Hayes that his sense of self-respect prohibited his accepting the troublesome and thankless post. Hayes would not relent, however, precisely because of Sullivant's progressive and modern ideas, and insisted upon his serving.[2]

Ralph Leete, another preferred Hayes' appointee, met stiff opposition in the Senate, but he took it differently. He told Hayes that he wanted to serve, "especially as there was a strong opposition in the Senate to my confirmation." His, too, was a broad view of agricultural and mechanical education. He thought that the agricultural and mechanical arts were innumerable, and that every branch of science was, therefore, rightfully involved in the insti-

1. Rutherford B. Hayes to R. C. Anderson, March 18, 1870; Hayes to V. B. Horton, March 18, 1870; Hayes to Sardis Birchard, March 20, 1870; Hayes to William Dennison, March 22, 1870, Hayes Papers, The Rutherford B. Hayes Library, Fremont, Ohio.

2. Hayes to Dennison, March 22, 1870; Sullivant to Hayes, April 15, 1870, Hayes Papers; Sullivant to Hayes, March 23, 1870, miscellaneous letters, Ohio Historical Society Library, Columbus, Ohio.

tution's program whether the senators and the farmers they represented thought so or not.[3]

Ralph Leete was caustically and rather undiplomatically outspoken about the status of higher education in Ohio anyway, and his views did not strengthen his chances for confirmation. Not all men agreed with him when he observed, "There are no intellects of high order in her numerous colleges, nor in any manner connected with her educational system."[4] Most of the professors in Ohio colleges, he elaborated, were bitter sectarians and not infrequently, narrow-minded country politicians. "As a class," he observed, "they are generally incompetent." Leete's bitterness derived in large measure from his opposition to sectarian control of Ohio University and from his vision of better things. The day would come, he was convinced, when public instructors would rank with jurists and statesmen, and when institutions of higher education bred thinkers and discoverers who could apply their thoughts and discoveries to the concerns of everyday life.

Ralph Leete's thinking was in keeping with that of many educational reformers who would transform American higher education in ensuing decades, but his thinking was as incompatible with that of the farmers of Ohio as it was with that of the leaders of the state's denominational colleges. "For the improvement of agriculture and mechanical arts," he observed, "we are indebted to Lord Bacon and Joseph Priestley more than any who preceded them, yet neither is a farmer or a so-called practical man." Ohio needed a great, modern university superior to anything which it already had, not so much in facilities as in men, he said. It needed great scholars and teachers committed to inquiry and progress, and when she had that, agriculture and the mechanical arts and all the other interests of the people of the state would be enhanced and elevated.[5]

By the eleventh day of May, 1870, the board of trustees of the Ohio Agricultural and Mechanical College was completed and the

3. Ralph Leete to Hayes, April 27, 1870, Hayes Papers.
4. Mendenhall, op. cit., pp. x–xi.
5. Ibid., p. xl.

nineteen Hayes appointees met in the governor's office in Columbus. Twelve of the nineteen were formerly members of the state legislature, and three had served in the national Congress. Seven were lawyers, and three were gentlemen farmers with inherited estates. There were several businessmen and industrialists, including Cornelius Aultman and John R. Buchtel, the developers and maufacturers of the Buckeye mowers and reapers in Akron.[6]

Four of the trustees were members of the State Board of Agriculture. The four included William B. McClung of Troy, who was appointed superintendent of the college farm, Norton S. Townshend, a pioneer in agricultural education who was appointed professor of agriculture, Henry P. Perkins, one of the gentleman farmers who managed a large, inherited estate, and Joseph Sullivant, of Columbus, a gentleman farmer and patron of the arts who was more concerned about the establishment of a state university than he was about training farmers.[7]

Fewer than half of the trustees had attended college themselves, and those who did attended such institutions as Woodward, Kenyon, Denison, and Marietta colleges in Ohio, Ohio University, Centre College in Kentucky, and the Harvard and Yale law schools. As a group, the trustees constituted an able body of men as much identified with politics as any church college board was with the ministry, and very obviously unrepresentative of the industrial classes from the standpoint of dirt farmers and rank and file mechanics. Many, however, had begun life as farmers, blacksmiths, carpenters, millwrights, and schoolteachers. John R. Buchtel, who, by the time he was appointed to the board, was a wealthy industrialist with a fine library and an enthusiasm for education, had been barely able to write his own name at the age of twenty-one. Although there were many from more privileged backgrounds, the number of self-made men of humble beginnings was substantial. Significantly, however, they considered themselves to be members

6. The summary of information here presented is based upon biographical sketches of the original trustees given in Mendenhall, op. cit. 25–30.

7. Opha Moore, *History of Franklin County, Ohio* (Indianapolis, Ind., and Topeka, Kan.: History Publishing Co., 1930), I, 102; Mendenhall, op. cit., p. 27.

of the industrial classes—that is, those who were helping to create the industrial society.[8]

The board, at its organizational meeting, elected Valentine B. Horton, who was president of the Ohio University board of trustees, to be its first president. Joseph Sullivant was elected treasurer, and Richard C. Anderson, secretary. The trustees spent a fairly casual evening meeting in a general discussion of what the college ought to be, and authorized an address to the people of Ohio setting forth clearly and persuasively the aims, purposes, and needs of the new college. Two paramount issues faced the nineteen trustees. They were charged with the responsibility for locating the institution, and they would have to agree upon the nature of the school's program before very much more could be done in establishing it. In their first discussions, the divergence of philosophy which characterized the group was apparent and it became inseparable from the more specific question of location.[9]

Interest in securing the college developed in Champaign, Montgomery, Franklin, and Clark counties, and campaigns were launched from Urbana, Dayton, Columbus, and Springfield to persuade the voters to authorize bond issues to raise the funds necessary to secure the college. The two chief competitors were Springfield and Columbus, and the residents of the two cities were not strangers in combat. Since 1862, Clark and Franklin counties had been in the same congressional district. In that year, the Republican legislature had gerrymandered a new district that would match the strong Republican Samuel Shellabarger against the vociferous Peace Democrat Samuel S. Cox of Columbus. Since that year, district nominating conventions had pitted Shellabarger's Springfield supporters against Samuel Galloway's Columbus backers. In 1870, as the trustees prepared to select a site for the new college, the two counties were again engaged in a battle for the district's congressional nomination. For the district's seat on the

8. Ibid., p. 30.
9. *Record of Proceedings of the Board of Trustees of the Ohio Agricultural and Mechanical College and the Ohio State University*, May 11, 1870–June 25, 1890 (Columbus, Ohio: Ohio State University, n.d.), pp. 3–5; Mendenhall, op. cit., pp. 23–24.

board of trustees, however, Rutherford B. Hayes had selected Joseph Sullivant of Columbus.[10]

Nevertheless, Springfield was a very strong competitor for the new college. Everything seemed to be developing at the right moment to dramatize the city and to publicize it throughout the state at the very moment that the trustees were making their decision. Clifton M. Nichols, editor of the Springfield *Republic,* had secured the convention of the Ohio Editors' Association for the winter of 1870, and the County Agricultural Association and the businessmen of the city courted the editors assiduously during their stay.[11]

As a result, most newspapers in the state carried reports of the convention and a description of the agricultural and industrial achievements of the city. In addition to being a very rich agricultural area, the stories generally observed, the city's factories produced 13,000 reapers and mowers annually, not to mention plows, cider mills, grain drills, grass seed sowers, a variety of mowers, and an improved sulky cultivator. Nowhere in the state, the publicity indicated, were the interests of the farmer and the mechanic more appropriately combined than in Springfield and Clark County. The implication which the city's boosters emphasized was that here of all places the utilitarian program which the Morrill Act envisioned was safe.[12]

Shortly before the editors' convention, Springfield had achieved another strategic victory which served to dramatize its appropriateness as the home of the new institution. By action of the State Board of Agriculture, Clark County had been selected as the site for both the 1870 and 1871 state fairs. In fact, when the committee of the board of trustees was to visit Springfield to inspect the farms being offered for the location of the new school, they were obliged to come at fair time when the agricultural interests of the state were gathered there.

One development, however, served to weaken the county's claim. Residents of Cleveland, disappointed in the selection of

10. *Ohio State Journal* (Columbus, Ohio), July 12, August 31, 1870.
11. *Republic* (Springfield, Ohio), February 23, 25, March 7, 1870.
12. Ibid., March 7, 1870.

Springfield as the site for the state fair for two consecutive years, announced plans to conduct a rival state fair in northeastern Ohio. The annual conflict over the location of the fair, which the agricultural board had sought to relieve by picking one centrally located city for two years in a row, was becoming increasingly acrimonious as the agricultural interests in various areas, including the implement industries, weighed the costs of losing to a competitor. Ultimately, the State Board of Agriculture had to decide that the only acceptable permanent solution was to locate the fair in the state capital.[13]

The case for locating the Agricultural and Mechanical College in Franklin County was strengthened by the inherently sound argument that such state activities should be located at the state capital. Columbus was emerging as a self-conscious community eager for advancement and progress, and sensitive about its lack of adequate educational facilities. Columbus and Franklin County had earlier supported the establishment of Capital University and shared membership on the board of trustees with representatives of the supporting churches. In 1854, however, fearful of losing control, the church forced a rather liberal president out of office, pushed non-Lutherans off the board of trustees, and soon thereafter moved the institution out of town.[14]

Now almost two decades later, as a result of improved transportation facilities and a slight decline in state provincialism, the city was being increasingly regarded as a more important city and, by some, a logical place for the new state college. There was also emerging a class of citizens, typified by Joseph Sullivant, a descendant of a pioneer Franklin County family, and James M. Comly, the influential editor of the *Ohio State Journal* who envisioned for Ohio a great state university located at the capital. "No intelligent person," Comly editorialized, "professes now to believe that a purely agricultural college . . . would be of any particular benefit to the state" or to farmers. Just as surely as enthusiasts for the Springfield location emphasized a practical agricultural and me-

13. Ibid., January 25, March 25, 1870.
14. David B. Owen (ed.), *These Hundred Years: The Centennial History of Capital University* (Columbus, Ohio: Capital University, 1950) pp. 33–69, 64, 76.

chanical concept of what the institution should be, the Columbus enthusiasts advocated the broad and inclusive program of a state university.[15]

The model for the great university which Sullivant and Comly envisioned was Cornell University in New York, an institution which they considered the most successful and most prosperous of all the land grant institutions. Their choice of models was consistent with some of the prevalent notions in Ohio about what higher education should be like. The school was fundamentally a private institution, in the eastern tradition, established out of the generosity of Ezra Cornell. In addition, the institution had received New York's land grant under the Morrill Act, and the state agricultural and mechanical college was incorporated with a traditional college. There were, in 1870, five hundred and fifty students at Cornell, Comly told his readers, and he published for their edification the commencement exercises of the eastern institution. Bear in mind, he advised, that, in voting for the bond authorization in Franklin County, citizens voted for a great state university. The school would not be a traditional, old line, denominational college nor a mere utilitarian institute for farmers and mechanics but a full-fledged state university to serve all of the people in all of the state.[16]

The farmers of Ohio, however, did not share the Franklin County dream of Cornell in Ohio. They saw the model agricultural college in those located in Michigan and Iowa, both of which had been established separately from, and independently of, the state university. If the farmers had their choice, they would select a site at Urbana, a farming community and the county seat of Champaign County, and their preference was not unknown to members of the state legislature.[17]

The dream which Sullivant had and which Comly endorsed, however, was appealing to many in the state and to many on the Hayes-appointed board of trustees. Others added to Sullivant's plan the idea of securing the endowments of the Ohio and Miami uni-

15. *Ohio State Journal* (Columbus, Ohio), July 8, 1870.
16. Ibid., July 20, 28, 29, October 4, 1870.
17. Ibid., September 12, 1870.

versities to give added support for a great state university at
Columbus. With the Morrill grant to finance the agricultural and
mechanical departments, and the earlier congressional grants for
Ohio and Miami universities to support the remainder of the
university, Ohio's school would soon rank with the best endowed
institutions of the country. Comly had suggested merging the three
in 1869, and felt that support for the idea was growing. He continued to push the idea and, in an editorial, added the idea to
Sullivant's more circumspect public statement. The editor felt
certain that a majority of the trustees of the agricultural college
would favor the plan, and rather prematurely he predicted legislation to that end in the next legislature.

Sullivant enlisted top leaders of the state administration to support his plan, and to support Franklin County's bid for the location
of the Ohio Agricultural and Mechanical College. He appealed to
the voters of Franklin County to approve so large an offer that no
other county could hope to compete, thus assuring that no other
county could frustrate the plan for a state university.[18]

Advocates in Springfield and Columbus courted the farmer's
vote and talked in language that implied overwhelming support for
securing the college. The votes taken in Clark, Franklin, and Montgomery counties, however, demonstrated the almost total apathy
which characterized the farmers. The Montgomery County authorization passed by a wide majority, but twelve of fifteen townships
showed a majority opposing the bond issue. Only three townships
had supported the issue, and these were in or very near the city
of Dayton. Clark County experienced a similar result. The issue
passed by a two-to-one vote in an election characterized by a
fairly light turnout at the polls, but the issue had not received the
vote of the rural districts. In Springfield, 1,462 favorable votes were
cast to a negligible 37 opposed, whereas county farmers opposed
the measure by better than two to one.[19]

The astute James Comly failed even to publish the total vote
in Franklin County, so revealing was it of farmer disinterest. He
did observe that the city had passed the issue 1,259 to 69 in an

18. Ibid., July 7, 8, 28, 29, September 22, 1870; Mendenhall, op. cit., p. 31.
19. *Republic* (Springfield, Ohio), July 25, September 16, 1870.

extremely light vote which, he confessed, indicated that there was little real interest in the issue. He told his readers that he had heard that at least three of the rural townships had voted in favor, but the rest had opposed it.[20] In all three elections, it was obvious that the voters were not overwhelmingly excited about the location of the new college, and that farmers were the least concerned of all.

A letter to the editor of the Springfield *Republic* before the election had raised the question of whether the winning county might not be obligated thereafter to provide annual sustenance. The voters, the correspondent observed, were probably not going to favor a perpetual obligation. In Columbus, Comly had assured taxpayers among his readers that the tax would be almost painless, and that never would the county have another opportunity to obtain so valuable an asset at so cheap a price.[21]

On September 6, the board of trustees met in the rooms of the State Board of Agriculture to consider the bids of the various counties. They decided not to delay any longer but to allow additional counties to submit bids if they wished. They then proceeded to consider the three offers before them from the counties of Franklin, Clark, and Champaign. Montgomery County's bid came a week later, and its receipt was objected to by spokesmen from the other counties. Anyone could make a larger offer, they observed, if he submitted his bid after all the others were known. Springfield had increased its bid and ranked close to Columbus in its total offer, but Montgomery County had topped Columbus by $100,000.[22]

At this point, some members of the board wanted an interpretation of the phrase, "reasonably central" used in the Cannon Act. The feeling was that both Dayton and Urbana failed to qualify on the basis of that terminology. The stipulation that the location selected be accessible by railroad likewise favored Franklin and Clark counties and further weakened the claim of Urbana. One railroad line

20. *Ohio State Journal* (Columbus, Ohio), August 15, 1870.

21. *Republic* (Springfield, Ohio), July 21, 1870; *Ohio State Journal* (Columbus, Ohio), July 8, 28, 1870.

22. *Record of Proceedings of the Board of Trustees*, pp. 6–11; Mendenhall, op. cit., pp. 30–32; *Ohio State Journal* (Columbus, Ohio), September 7, 1870.

serving both Springfield and Columbus offered to donate $28,000 to the institution if it were located in either one of the two places.[23]

On September 8, the trustees visited Springfield to view the sites offered there. During their visit, the Springfield Street Railway Company told the trustees that, if they selected the Cooper farm north of Springfield or the Warder farm to the east, the company would build a streetcar line to the campus entrance.[24] Editor Nichols of the *Republic* was disappointed that the trustees had appeared unexpectedly; but he felt that they were very much impressed with the Springfield offer, and he was optimistic about the city's chances. The increased offer, the proffered gift from the railroad, and the promise of the streetcar line combined with the obvious value of the Warder and Cooper farms, he concluded, made the county's inducement a strong one indeed.[25]

From Springfield, the trustees proceeded to Urbana from whence they returned to Columbus on the ninth to view sites in Franklin County. They then adjourned to meet in Springfield on September 15. By this time, General Comly was becoming increasingly uncertain of the results of the board's deliberations. He told his readers that there was a most serious danger of losing the college to Urbana. He complained of a formidable combination, apparently supported from within the legislature, that sought to force Urbana upon the trustees. Of all the possible cities, Urbana obviously had greater appeal for the farm element. The Columbus editor lamented, however, that the transfer of the question from and legislature to the trustees by means of the Cannon Act was supposed to eliminate such political maneuvering. He felt, however, that the plan had not worked, and intimated that a split among the trustees themselves on the nature of the institution provided the opportunity for outside elements to exploit its indecision.[26]

23. *Republic* (Springfield, Ohio), September 21, 1870.

24. Ibid., September 7, 8, 1870.

25. Ibid., September 8, 1870.

26. Ibid., September 14, 1870; *Ohio State Journal* (Columbus, Ohio), September 12, 1870.

On September 20, however, the board met in Columbus to take final action. They listened to the presentations of large delegations from Montgomery, Franklin, Champaign, and Clark counties concerning the relative merits of the various proposed sites. Joseph Sullivant presented the proposition of Franklin County, and his argument was buttressed by former Governor Dennison. Dennison assured the trustees that it would be a mistake to locate the state college outside of Franklin County and away from the state capital. He advised them to locate it in the capital, where it would have "the sympathy and cooperation of the legislature and the state government." There was no question, he insisted, but that continuing assistance would be required by the new institution, and its location would have a bearing upon the sympathies and the interest of the legislature.[27]

Clark County was represented by a large delegation including the leading industrialists of the community. They made clear their interest in preserving the strength both of the agricultural and the mechanical aspects of the institution's program. That night, while the session was recessed, spokesmen for the Springfield group wired home for authorization to raise their bid by another $50,000. They were confident of winning, they said, if the additional funds could be authorized.[28]

The following day, the board met again and proceeded to ballot for the selection of the county in which to locate the college. They cast twenty-six ballots before a final decision was reached. After a number of votes were taken without result, the board agreed to drop the lowest county on subsequent ballots, and to declare that county selected that received the highest number of votes. Confirming farmers' suspicions about the sympathies of the board, Champaign County was dropped on the very next ballot. Shortly thereafter, Montgomery County was dropped, and the contest narrowed to Franklin and Clark. After several ballots, Franklin County was designated as the location for the institution.[29]

27. Ibid., September 21, 1870; *Republic* (Springfield, Ohio), September 19, 21, 22, 1870.

28. Ibid., September 21, 1870.

29. Ibid., September 22, 1870; *Ohio State Journal* (Columbus, Ohio), September 22, 1870; Mendenhall, op. cit., p. 32.

Three weeks later, however, the board seemed unable to agree upon a specific site within Franklin County. Interested parties in Springfield were advised by a member of the board that they should resubmit the county's offer. "We are locked and cannot locate here," the informant advised. "Send your offer and try us."[30] The county did renew its offer, and, on October 11, felt that success was almost within reach.

At this stage of the deliberations, however, Rutherford B. Hayes reentered the picture and used his influence to persuade a majority of the board to agree upon the Neil farm just north of Columbus as a suitable site. Hayes said later that he worked hard to get the university located there and that his insistence was justified by the fact that the university property was soon worth twice as much as the land grant fund itself.

Finally, on October 13, the trustees voted not to reconsider their earlier decision to locate in Franklin County and proceeded to vote on the various sites offered within that county. Up to the next-to-the-last ballot, several trustees held out for the Warder farm in Clark County. The specific issue over which the board was divided was the size of the farm on which to locate the school. Agriculturists who had lost in the effort to locate in Urbana and who later advocated the Clark County site were now concerned lest a site be selected that was entirely too small to accomodate an experimental agricultural college at all.[31]

When the board first decided upon Franklin County in September, James M. Comly had been delighted; and as soon as the vote was known, he raised the issue of the character of the proposed institution. He strongly reemphasized the plan to combine the resources of Ohio and Miami universities with the new institution, and he attributed the plan to Ralph Leete, an outspoken member of the board of trustees from Ironton, Ohio. In that event, Comly was certain that the state would have not a mere farmers' college but a grand state university. "We would have more faith in a bull-

30. *Republic* (Springfield, Ohio), September 24, October 11, 1870; *Ohio State Journal* (Columbus, Ohio), October 13, 1870.

31. Rutherford B. Hayes to William Henry Smith, November 27, 1887, Hayes Papers; *Ohio State Journal* (Columbus, Ohio), October 13, 14, 1870; *Republic* (Springfield, Ohio), October 11, 1870; Mendenhall, op. cit., p. 33.

calf and castor-oil beans business," he gloated disparagingly, "if we could find . . . one cattle-breeding and crop-raising institution that had been successful."[32] While the trustees remained deadlocked over the proper location in Franklin County, with some of them holding out for a tract larger than 300 acres, Comly thought the issue irrelevant. This was the chief objection to the Neil farm. "The Board will find on farther reflection," Comly lectured them, "that a smaller body of land than three hundred acres will answer the purposes which the friends of liberal education and true learning have in view."[33] Nevertheless, efforts were made to secure additional lands adjacent to the Neil tract in order to quiet opposition. The editor's attitude however was not designed to win the support of the large number of communities and the great host of farmers who counted themselves the losers in Franklin County's victory.

Nevertheless, Comly continued to press for the state university idea and provided his subscribers with detailed information about his model, Cornell University. He reported to them on Cornell's "wonderful growth, its present condition, its future prospects," and he hoped that his own enthusiasm would be contagious.[34] But the rest of the state turned its attention to the solution of its own educational problems.

The trustees of the Ohio Agricultural and Mechanical College moved on to the consideration of the character of the institution over which they were to have charge, but their selection of a site had fairly well revealed their direction. Ralph Leete set forth his views for a broadly conceived institution, which were countered by Norton S. Townshend, who spoke for those who advocated a less ambitious program. The board appointed a committee composed of Valentine B. Horton, Joseph Sullivant, Norton S. Townshend, Thomas C. Jones, and John R. Buchtel to propose a curricular plan. Horton was president of the board; Sullivant, an outspoken proponent of the state university idea; Townshend, an agricultural reformer committed to a program that would be of practical importance to the farmer; Jones, a leading state Republican favoring a

32. *Ohio State Journal* (Columbus, Ohio), September 22, 1870.
33. Ibid., September 22, 1870.
34. Ibid., September 29, 1870.

general and classical institution; and John R. Buchtel, an advocate of a broad program who later contributed generously to establish Buchtel College in Akron.

The committee reported a plan of organization for the institution consisting of ten departments, which duplicated the plan submitted by Joseph Sullivant shortly after the board was first organized.[35] The college would be broadly conceived as a state university encompassing departments of agriculture, mechanical arts, mathematics and physics, general and applied chemistry, geology, mining and metallurgy, zoology and veterinary science, botany, horticulture and vegetable physiology, English language and literature, modern and ancient languages, and a department of political economy and civil polity. The advocates of a broad gauge institution, patterned after Cornell and located in the state capital, had won a complete success, though it proved to be a pyrrhic victory. They proposed to offer a program unduplicated in breadth by any other institution in the state. Its emphasis upon science, mechanics, and agriculture marked it as unique. The glaring weakness, however, was that in all that the trustees had wrought they counted on obtaining the endowments of Ohio and Miami universities to support their great university. In addition, relying upon the assurances of former Governor Dennison, they fully expected the ongoing support and interest of the state legislature. The failure to obtain either seriously crippled the enterprise from the beginning.[36]

35. *Record of Proceedings of the Board of Trustees*, pp. 27, 28.
36. *Ohio State Journal*, July 29, September 20, 21, 22, 1870.

CHAPTER 3

A Vanishing Enthusiasm

The individuals and the groups who lost out in Ohio's great land-grant sweepstakes were still faced with serious unmet educational needs once the institution had been awarded to Franklin County. Their participation in the competition had been not so much an exhibition of parochial pride as a manifestation of local need. Securing the new institution had been tremendously important to all who had participated in the great debate. Now that the issue was resolved, the institution located, and its nature more clearly defined, all but one of the competitors still faced their own unresolved educational problems. For the state's growing urban centers, the problem was a local one, and the needs of a central state institution, by comparison, became increasingly irrelevant.

The first reaction to victory in Columbus, as expressed by James M. Comly in the *Ohio State Journal*, reflected the spirit of local need that had motivated all the contenders. Each group had seen its own needs without seeing them as a part of a statewide need. As a result, the perception of Franklin County's victory seemed to be that Columbus had won its college and that other communities had now to devote themselves to harder solutions. Comly himself complained of a common belief growing in the state that the city of Columbus and the county of Franklin were "great leeches on the body politic" because they had prevailed.[1] He said that he heard the idea ex-

1. *Ohio State Journal* (Columbus, Ohio), September 24, 1870.

pressed so often and so generally that he was convinced that there was a general prejudice against the city throughout the state. The attitudes which Comly assessed were those of envy and jealousy, and they had great implications for the future of Franklin County's college.

The industrial community of Springfield, for instance, was not about to be deterred in its quest for higher educational facilities geared to the agricultural and mechanical needs in its own area. The trustees' decision to locate in Columbus merely turned the Springfield representatives in other directions. Following the trustees' original decision to accept the offer of Franklin County, the editor of the Springfield *Republic* observed stoically that the town's boosters had done their best. Immediately, however, he published a feature story with the caption: "A Good Word for Wittenberg: Ought Not Springfield to Make It A Great University?"[2]

Wittenberg College had been located in Springfield since 1845. In the first twenty-five years of its history, it had struggled with financial weakness and the opposition of Lutherans who opposed the school's English language emphasis and its Americanized Lutheranism that contenanced revivals.[3] Not long before editor Nichols' proposal to make it great, however, Wittenberg had faced the choice of moving out of town and selling its building and forty acres to the Presbyterians or of remaining and competing with that more numerous body for limited local support. Unable to agree upon a fair price for the Wittenberg campus, however, the Presbyterians considered the alternative of taking over the Miami University instead, but in the end founded Wooster College at Wooster, Ohio.[4]

Editor Nichols' proposal, however, provided a new problem for the Springfield institution. It certainly would have given the community what it wanted, but it showed little regard for the desires and the purposes of Wittenberg's founders. The editor recommended that the community add $50,000 to the school's endowment

2. *Republic* (Springfield, Ohio), September 22, 1870.

3. William A. Kinnison, "The More Toil, The More Grace", *Wittenberg Alumnus*, vol. XIV, no. 7 (January, 1963).

4. Ibid., pp. 8–9; Eckelberry, "Religious Influence on Higher Education in Ohio," pp. 31 ff.

to establish three new professorships: one for agriculture, another for mechanics, and a third for political economy. "An agricultural college, at best, is but an experiment," the editor observed, referring to the Columbus institution, but "Wittenberg is not an experiment." He advised the residents of Clark County to take better care of what they already possessed. "Let us foster Wittenberg College," he advised, "and make it a better institution than the agricultural college in Franklin County can ever be."[5] Editor Nichols emphasized, however, that since the county would provide the increased endowment, the county would certainly have the privilege of deciding what the new professorships would be and who would fill them.

The following day, Nichols suggested a general public meeting to discuss the Citizens' Endowment Fund proposal and to stir up enthusiasm for it. He was certain, he told his readers, that it would be far easier to enlarge the scope, usefulness, and general importance of Wittenberg by adding to its endowment than it would be to establish a new institution no matter how large the endowment fund. He proposed that the community form a partnership with Wittenberg. with the city contributing money and the institution contributing its established reputation and public confidence. Such a merger of resources, he insisted, would provide the kind of modern educational opportunities which the community needed.[6]

At this point, however, Nichols learned that there was yet a chance that the trustees would be unable to agree upon a site in Franklin County, and he dropped the Citizens' Endowment Fund proposal temporarily in order to urge a renewal of the county's bid for the Morrill land grant college. Once the decision in favor of Franklin County was reaffirmed, however, the editor revived his proposal. "Now for old Wittenberg," he headlined his renewed appeal. The Agricultural and Mechanical College was out of the question for Clark County he advised and the best policy was to give all possible encouragement to the institution already in its midst. He scaled down his proposal, however, suggesting that

5. *Republic* (Springfield, Ohio), September 22, 23, 1870.
6. Ibid., September 23, 1870.

thirty to forty thousand dollars and two professorships might satis-factorily remake the local institution in the city's image.[7]

The unwillingness of the Wittenberg directors to consider such a drastic change in its institutional purposes, however, put an end to speculation about a citizens' endowment. The decision did not, however, strengthen relationships between the institution and the industrial leaders of the community, and resulted in the renewal of the institution's lonely struggle for funds. Within the decade, the institution once again considered relocation as the only alternative to poverty.[8]

In addition, the city's sense of loss in not remaking Wittenberg to better serve its needs reemphasized its failure to win the land grant college. The loss festered for a decade and emerged in a vociferous opposition to the Ohio State University in the columns of a fast-growing Springfield agricultural journal entitled *Farm and Fireside*. By the end of the century, *Farm and Fireside*, which claimed a readership of over a million, had been acquired by the publishers of *Colliers' Weekly*, and its critical interest in Ohio ag-ricultural education gave way to broader national coverage. Never-theless, in the 1880's, the magazine featured farmer criticism of the Franklin County institution, and undermined its financial support. The magazine played an important role in bringing about Ohio State's capitulation to Ohio farm interests in 1887.[9]

The supporters of Miami and Ohio universities were no more eager to surrender their existence to the new institution in Colum-bus than other cities were to surrender their ambitions. Miami University closed its doors for want of support and students in

7. Ibid., September 24, October 11, 14, 1870.

8. Harold Lentz, *A History of Wittenberg College* (Columbus, Ohio: The Wittenberg Press, 1946), pp. 129–32.

9. Frank L. Mott, *A History of American Magazines* (Cambridge, Mass.: Harvard University Press, 1938–57), IV, 337, 468, and Theodore Peterson, *Magazines in the Twentieth Century* (Urbana: University of Illinois Press, 1956), pp. 133, 135. One could almost select at random an issue of *Farm and Fireside* in the 1880's and find a representative article deprecating the agri-cultural college at Columbus; the *Farm and Fireside* "crusade" reached its peak in late 1886 and early 1887 and then subsided, giving way to strong support of the institution as it changed its emphasis on agricultural education; see issues for December 15, 1886; January 1, 15, February 15, March 1, 15, April 1, 15, 1887.

the year that the Ohio Agricultural and Mechanical College opened, but the trustees were not inclined to move the foundation to Franklin County.[10] Ohio University resisted the siren song of Columbus for two decades, and, though it lost board members and presidents to the new institution, it preserved its independent existence with dogged determination. The first president of the Ohio Agricultural and Mechanical College Board of Trustees had been a member of the Ohio University Board of Trustees for twenty-six years, and was chairman of the committee charged with the responsibility for representing Ohio University's claim to the Morrill Act funds. The Athens County institution's president, William H. Scott, later became president of the Ohio State University.[11]

Both Miami and Ohio universities renewed their appeals to the legislature for ongoing financial support as legitimate wards of the state, and fought vigorously the idea of union in Columbus. Occasional appropriations beginning in the 1880's for isolated and inexpensive necessities were made, but nothing resembling a state recognition of its responsibility. The conflicting interests of the three sets of trustees seriously weakened their efforts at cooperative lobbying in the legislature.

The idea of combining the resources of the state's three land grant institutions received greatest consideration following the five-year depression, which began with the panic of 1873. By 1880, William Henry Scott, president of Ohio University, was favorable to the proposal of union. He wrote Edward Orton, president of the Ohio State University and an ardent supporter of the idea, suggesting that the trustees of their schools appoint committees to discuss the idea, and that the trustees at Miami be encouraged to join in the discussion. A bill had been introduced in the legislature to effect the union and had the strong support of President Orton.[12] The trustees of the Columbus institution were quite amenable to growth by merger and union on their own terms. A few years later they assented eagerly to a proposal that the endowments of Antioch

10. Rodabaugh, op. cit. p. 368.
11. Hoover, op. cit., pp. 132, 157.
12. Ibid., p. 145.

College, temporarily closed, be used to support professorships at Ohio State University over which both sets of trustees would have control.[13]

But at Ohio University, the trustees were not interested in Scott's ideas of union. Within a short time, Scott submitted his resignation from "a charge in some respects uncongenial" as Ohio University began a building program which precluded any notion of union. After Scott left Athens to become president at the Ohio State University, the Ohio University trustees directed their committee on legislation "to resist and oppose any and all schemes of consolidation that in any way would curtail or restrict the course of study in the Ohio University," or impair its status as a university or its location at Athens.[14]

Scott's long association with the Athens County institution, however, had convinced him that it could not compete with the Ohio State University, and that one state institution might receive adequate support where three separate ones would not. Miami University, which had closed its collegiate department from 1873 to 1885, likewise was not interested in merger. Its trustees used its annual income to pay its debts and to build an endowment fund in anticipation of its reopening in Oxford.[15]

One proposal to correlate the three universities sought to distribute the state's educational efforts among them, making Miami the state's academical and classical college, Ohio University its normal college, and the Ohio State University the state's center for scientific and industrial studies. The plan assumed that law and medical schools would remain virtually independent institutions and that appropriate graduate work would be offered, if necessary, at each of the three state universities. Alexis Cope, secretary of the board of trustees, and William Henry Scott, president of the university, were appalled by the proposal. All Miami had, said Scott, was a $9,000 annual income and an isolated location. Cope said the plan might work if a normal school were located at Athens and a

13. *Record of Proceedings of the Board of Trustees*, p. 214.
14. Hoover, op. cit., p. 157.
15. Ibid., pp. 156–57.

preparatory academy were established at Oxford and everything else centered at Columbus. A true consolidation which gave Ohio one great state university was highly desirable, said W. H. Scott, but anything else destroyed the benefits of having a state university at all and hopelessly divided the future interests and efforts of the state. The interinstitutional bickering and competition seriously hampered the growth of state support for any of the three and established a tradition of suspicion and ill will.[16]

In Cincinnati, too, there were other concerns than Franklin County's agricultural college. The Queen City moved forward to meets its educational needs in such a way as to render its people fairly independent of state activities whether at Columbus or at Athens. The success of the Cincinnati experiment, however, proved too much for nearby Miami, with the combined impact of the opening of the University of Cincinnati and Ohio State closing that institution for twelve years. For over a decade, the Queen City had looked forward expectantly to the establishment of a real university that would be symbolic of the cultural, social, and economic achievement of the city. In 1858, a civic-minded benefactor, Charles McMicken, left his estate to endow a school for Cincinnati. In McMicken's plan, the school was to have a decided vocational emphasis, and was to be a real city college. Law suits by McMicken's heirs, the Civil War, demographic shifts within the city which affected real estate values, and postwar inflation had delayed the start of McMicken College and had diminished the value of the fund available. It soon became apparent that the bequest would be insufficient to achieve all that was desired, and a movement to unite various educational trusts in the city developed and gained strength.[17]

In 1868, while the state legislature pondered the disposition of the Morrill grant, the city council of Cincinnati submitted a bill to authorize the city to set aside grounds for a university, and to endow and otherwise maintain a university of colleges by accepting as

16. William Henry Scott to R. B. Hayes, January 2, January 9, 1888; Alexis Cope to R. B. Hayes, February 2, 1888, Hayes Papers, The Rutherford B. Hayes Library, Fremont, Ohio.

17. Eckelberry, *History of the Municipal University*, pp. 82–87.

trustees a variety of existing educational foundations. Under the plan, McMicken College, Cincinnati College, and the Woodward and Hughes funds would be consolidated. This proposal would solve Cincinnati's problems in higher education.[18]

Finally, in 1870, an act to enable cities of the first class to aid and promote education passed by a unanimous vote in the House of Representatives and with but four dissents in the Ohio Senate. It was part of the compromise package that resolved the Morrill fund stalemate. The wording of the act restricted such activity to any city with a population of 150,000 or more, and, in the Ohio of 1870, there was only one city of that size and that was Cincinnati. Nevertheless, by 1873, the population requirement was lowered to 31,000.[19]

The idea of municipal higher education, however, caught the interests of many people in Ohio. In 1875, a movement began in Toledo which ultimately resulted in the Municipal University of that city. Jessup Scott, eager to provide practical education related to the emergence of Toledo as a railroad hub, provided the funds to establish Toledo University of Arts and Trades in 1872. Actual municipal control of the Toledo institution did not occur until 1884 when the Scott trustees turned the institution over to the city.[20]

In 1872, John R. Buchtel of Akron provided the resources which enabled the Universalists to establish Buchtel College, which served the growing community of Akron as a private college with close community orientation. The Akron institution, by 1913, had become a municipal university. Also by that date, three of the nation's seven municipal universities were located in Ohio. Counting the institutions at nearby Louisville and at Detroit, the city college movement, with the exception of New York City, appeared to be concentrating in the Midwest in a narrow belt between the East, with its emphasis on private education, and the West, with its emphasis upon the state university.[21]

18. Ibid., pp. 88–89.
19. Ibid., pp. 90, 105.
20. Ibid., pp. 104–5.
21. Ibid., pp. 6–7; Charles B. Galbreath, *History of Ohio* (New York and Chicago: American Historical Society), I, p. 492.

The establishment of the Case School of Applied Science in 1880 was consistent with the Ohio trend toward the solution of educational problems in expanding urban areas. Although Leonard Case did not establish a municipal institution, he did establish one that was nonsectarian and committed to practical education, readily available to the sons of a particular community. Case's will, drawn in 1877, called for the establishment of a school of applied science to teach mathematics, physics, engineering, mechanical engineering, civil engineering, chemistry, economic geology, mining, natural history, drawing, and modern languages. The establishment of the Case School of Applied Science, together with the successful efforts of Clevelanders to move the Western Reserve University from Hudson to Cleveland, represented the efforts of the citizens of Ohio's Forest City to meet their educational needs.[22]

In other towns and cities where the population was insufficient to qualify under the municipal education act, efforts were made to encourage the establishment of new private and denominational institutions. In the 1870's and the 1880's, new institutions were encouraged particularly in the northern and northwestern parts of the state. At the same time, in other places like Youngstown, Dayton, and Cleveland, educational efforts were launched under the auspices of Young Men's Christian Associations, which later emerged as YMCA colleges seeking to meet specific local needs. The YMCA schools were education for the industrial classes in a real sense. Nationally, by 1890, there were 162 YMCA educational clubs providing commercial, industrial, technical, vocational, cultural, and grammar school courses on a part-time basis in the evening for working city youths. Out of these programs grew several colleges, law schools and commercial colleges.[23]

22. Ibid., p. 481.

23. George B. Hodge, *Association Educational Work for Men and Boys* (New York: Association Press, 1912), pp. 7–30, 246. Perhaps the first of the YMCA institutions which ultimately emerged as an independent college was Fenn, established in 1881 under YMCA sponsorship; the establishment of new institutions included Wilmington College in 1870, the forerunner of Ohio Northern in 1871, McCorkle College at Sago in 1873, Rio Grande in 1876, Ashland in 1878, Findlay in 1882, Defiance in 1884, and St. Ignatius in 1886. In addition, St. Mary's School for Boys, later Dayton University, began awarding degrees in 1882 and in that same year Western Reserve University was enticed to move to Cleveland by the munificence of a Cleveland benefactor.

While communities worked individually to meet their own higher educational needs, representatives of the older established colleges drew closer together for mutual assistance and protection. Common problems drew them into dialogue. The problems of Civil War, the changing nature of preparatory work in the new high schools, and the need to appraise the meaning of the Morrill Act brought college representatives together informally for several years at meetings of the Ohio Teachers' Association and similar gatherings. By 1860, the informal meetings had become regular; and in 1866, the assembled group appointed a committee to propose a plan for a more formal organization of the state's colleges. The faculty of Ohio University provided more than token interest in this development and in fact took the lead in bringing the established schools together.[24]

On July 2, 1867, representatives of Marietta, Farmers' College, Mount Union, Western Reserve, Ohio University, Urbana College, Wittenberg, Kenyon, and Antioch met in Springfield to organize the Association of Ohio Colleges. President Howard of Ohio University served as temporary chairman while the group heard a report by Professor Tappan of Ohio University concerning a plan for organization. In a session following the afternoon session of the Ohio Teachers Association, the college representatives adopted a constitution establishing a permanent association, and then elected the Reverend Samuel Sprecher, President of Wittenberg College, as the Association's first president. President Howard of Ohio University who had been a leading light in bringing about the organization was elected vice-president.[25]

The purpose of the organization was to promote an interchange of opinions among college officers, and to adopt common rules governing the definition and conduct of higher education in the state. Membership was open to all presidents and professors at Ohio colleges, and the governor, the commissioner of common schools, and the president of the Ohio Teachers Association were

24. John M. Ellis, "Historical Sketch of the Association of the Colleges of Ohio," *Transactions of the Twenty-first Annual Meeting of the Association of Ohio Colleges, 1889* (Oberlin, Ohio: Ohio College Association, 1890), p. 54.
25. *Daily Republic* (Springfield, Ohio), July 3, 1867; *Weekly Republic* (Springfield, Ohio), July 4, 1867.

named members ex officio. The annual meeting was scheduled in conjunction with the OTA Convention but several years later was moved to the Christmas holiday season.[26]

By 1877, twenty-three colleges were participating in the association's deliberations. The Ohio State faculty was at first cool to the invitations of the association to participate, but eventually assented and ultimately assumed a very active role. The organization, in some ways, appeared to circumscribe the state institution's autonomy and in others served to undergird Ohio University's dogged independence. The association deliberated on high school–college relations, teaching methods, the lecture system, the proper role of scientific studies in the college curriculum, modern versus ancient languages, the responsibility of the college for the teaching of English, and the merits of elective systems and original research in the undergraduate program. As early as 1868, the association proposed an examination of the curriculum in each Ohio college, and, by 1875, had established standards which member institutions had to meet. The association stipulated (1) that a member college must have four regular classes: the freshmen, sophomore, junior, and senior levels of work; (2) that it must require "four years of solid work with fifteen recitations per week" for the awarding of a degree, and (3) that it must maintain minimum admissions requirements which included the common school English curriculum, two to three years of Latin learned in a program requiring daily recitations, two years of Greek in a program requiring daily recitations, and algebra up to quadratic equations. These requirements for membership in the association, adopted before the Ohio Agricultural and Mechanical College was fully organized, later placed the Ohio State University faculty in a tenuous position between the standards of their peers and the demands of the state's farmers and legislators. Not until 1890 was the university able to boldly proclaim a different standard.[27]

In 1873, the year the Ohio State University opened, the association began a three-year debate concerning a board of examiners

26. *Daily Republic* (Springfield, Ohio), July 3, 1867; Ellis, "Historical Sketch," pp. 54–55.

27. Ibid., pp. 55–57; Minutes of the Faculty, The Ohio State University, University Archives, II, pp. 410, 411.

for the State of Ohio with power to examine and certify for graduation the candidates for academic degrees in the various colleges.
In 1876, however, the association decided against an outside agency
for such purposes, and proceeded to define for its members the
requirements for their own variously awarded degrees. They outlined requirements that members should maintain for the bachelor
of arts and bachelor of philosophy degrees but decided against
setting standards for the bachelor of science degree. So few Ohio
institutions awarded the degree, they said, that the standards for
it were of no concern to the group as a whole. The association
further stipulated, however, that no member college would confer
the degree of doctor of philosophy without a specific program of
postgraduate work.[28]

Thus, before the state university was sufficiently well established
to provide any degree of leadership, a score of Ohio colleges, including rival Ohio University, had organized and set standards for
the protection of the academic program of its members. In concert,
they exhibited a rather conservative tendency and a strong bias
for the methods and the studies approved by past experience,
and they established a bulwark against radical innovation. They
excluded the institutions which refused to maintain similar standards and defended one another from agricultural, urban, and
industrial pressures for change. That at least was their intention,
and, though they did not entirely succeed, they did slow down
and stabilize the process of change.[29]

Because Ohio was late in establishing a state university, the
standards set were those mutually agreed upon by the private institutions. Miami University was closed at the time, the Ohio State
University was in its infancy, and Ohio University took the same
viewpoint, fundamentally, as the private and denominational colleges. Because the new state university was also the institution for
industrial education, and was expected to advocate the modification of older views, it was at first denied an effective position of
leadership in the standard-setting body.[30]

28. Ellis, "Historical Sketch," pp. 58–61, 65.
29. Ibid., p. 58.
30. Ibid., pp. 58–61.

Thus, the older institutions became increasingly aware of a need for mutual cooperation; and Cincinnati, Toledo, Akron, Cleveland, and smaller towns proceeded to meet their educational needs locally. Both developments proceeded without regard for the fledgling state university in Columbus or any legitimate role which that institution might have served in establishing collegiate standards or meeting the needs of urban, industrial Ohio. The creation of the new institution in Franklin County was a part of the new spirit of urgency in higher education in Ohio, but it was not a leader of the movement.

The older and newer private institutions ignored agricultural education, relegating that responsibility to the Columbus institution. Some gave greater emphasis to commercial and mechanical subjects. Some institutions broadened their offerings in response to the kinds of pressures which industrialists had exerted on Wittenberg College in Springfield.

The preoccupation with educational resources closer at hand seriously crippled the ambitions of those who would make the Ohio Agricultural and Mechanical College a great university. The state university idea in Ohio thus became enmeshed in the problems related to an emerging urban and industrial economy, and those related to the establishment of standards by the private institutions. The stout defense of their independent existence by the trustees of Ohio and Miami universities eliminated one of the two sources of additional endowment which Dennison, Comly, and Sullivant had counted on to build the University. The eclipse of their plan and the weakening of their leadership in the institution's foundation accompanied the demise of their second hope for support: legislative appropriation.

It was natural, perhaps, that the interest of local communities in local educational opportunities would lessen the concern of many legislators for the institution north of Columbus. Furthermore, the apathy and disinterest of rank-and-file farmers spoke more convincingly to legislators than the fulminations of the agricultural reformers. The farm press had long acknowledged that the farmer was interested not so much in broadly scholastic agricultural theory as he was in practical, down-to-earth, "muddy-shoe" experimentation. Not until the rise of disseminating agencies such as experiment stations and the farm extension program could the alliance between agricultural theory and life on the farm be made effective. In the meantime, the farmers brought little pressure to bear on their representatives to support the Agricultural and Mechanical College.[31]

To make the situation worse, the farmers and most other people in the state became increasingly preoccupied with the hardships of depression. The panic of 1873 cut like a knife into the prosperity that had followed the recession of 1869 and ushered in five years of hard times. Economic adversity affected all the colleges and universities, both old and new, and the general hardships made it increasingly unlikely that financial support for the Ohio Agricultural and Mechanical College would be forthcoming.

The economic contraction was part of a worldwide readjustment to a decade of wars in North and South America, Europe, and Africa. The demand for funds in Europe precipitated a contraction of credit in America. Jay Cooke and Company, for instance, began a series of debt settlements which shook the delicate financial structure of the overbuilt and overexpanded railroads. In addition, the hard money policies of the Grant administration had precipitated a deflationary cycle based upon a contraction of the currency. United States industry had borrowed extensively abroad and was hampered by heavy interest charges and an unfavorable balance of trade, and the demand for settlement from Europe was too much for the American money market to withstand. Debt in America had increased 50 percent since the Civil War, but the circulating currency had increased less than 8 percent. Many critics had voiced the fear that, when crisis came, the dollars in circulation would never cover the debts to be settled. Farmers and laborers had long resented fiscal policies which required them to repay debts in a currency dearer than the war-time inflated currency which they had borrowed. In the depression of 1873, all America experienced

31. *Farm and Fireside*, August 1, August 15, 1887; Demaree, op. cit., pp. 51–55.

the same burden. The depression, however, strengthened the resolve of the industrial classes to pursue more directly, through farmers' and labor organizations, a recognition of their condition.[32]

By the winter of 1874–75, the nation experienced long bread lines and soup lines. Salaries were cut for those who were still working, and luxury businesses virtually ceased to exist. Thievery grew rapidly, and the nation experienced general social unrest. Strange economic doctrines, such as those espoused by Henry George, and more traditional socialist concepts, received a wider hearing than ever before. In 1876, in the contested Hayes-Tilden election, some politicians spoke of bringing armed men to Washington (one called for 100,000) to see that justice was done. Former Congressman Shellabarger of Ohio and others feared that the nation was to be "Mexicanized" with two rival presidents. The masses of the unemployed were viewed with fear and suspicion, and a spirit of defensiveness and conservatism grew. Native-Americanism revived as American workers sought to protect themselves from the increasing numbers of immigrants who, they claimed, took what few jobs there were by working for lower wages.[33]

The reaction of the industrial classes to hard times was varied. They revolted against the corruption in government which was manifested in the Crédit Mobilier scandal in which millions of dollars had been siphoned from the Union Pacific Railroad project into the pockets of speculators while Congressmen, salved by gifts of Crédit Mobilier stock, were less than cautious in their oversight of the federal investment in the road. Federal and state extravagance and manipulation, as represented in the infamous Tweed Ring of New York City, were widespread and costly. In one state, the entire

32. For a balanced account of the economic crisis in its historical setting, see Allan Nevins, *The Emergence of Modern America* (New York: Macmillan, 1927); Arthur M. Schlesinger, *The Rise of the City* (New York: Macmillan, 1933); and, Ida M. Tarbell, *The Nationalizing of Business* (New York: Macmillan, 1936); Arthur Schlesinger, Sr., and Dixon Ryan Fox (eds.), *History of American Life Series*, vols. VIII–X (New York: Macmillan Co., 1927); see also Henrietta M. Larson, *Jay Cooke, Private Banker* (Cambridge, Mass.: Harvard University press, 1936).

33. See Paul Leland Haworth, *The Hayes-Tilden Disputed Presidential Election of 1876* (Cleveland: Burrows Bros., 1906), and Comer Vann Woodward, *Reunion and Reaction: The Compromise of 1877* (Garden City, N. Y.: Doubleday, 1956).

land grant fund had disappeared, and in Ohio there was strong belief among farmers that the Ohio fund had been misappropriated and applied to a use not consistent with the Morrill Act.[34]

Farmers and laborers alike came out of the depression with less respect for government, embittered by big business and big industry, and educated by such organizations as the Patrons of Husbandry and the Knights of Labor to cooperate to achieve their goals. The ritual of the Patrons of Husbandry incorporated the enthusiasm of agricultural reformers for lifting the level of living for the farmer by self-improvement. Though the order officially eschewed politics and preached the fraternal doctrine of self-improvement, the Patrons in their local Granges learned to influence elections and legislators and to ask specifically that they act in ways beneficial to the farmer. After 1878, as the nation began to recover economically, the farmers of Ohio were much more militant in their demands; and politicians, eager to win their support, were much more ready to please them if they could.[35]

The demands of the farm element concerning the Ohio State University, after 1878, therefore, were more specific, more militant, and better focused by legislative power than previously. The farmer no longer ignored the state's agricultural college, as he had been inclined to do earlier, but proceeded to press his demands for its reorganization. He insisted upon withholding or diverting funds from its general program and directing them specifically toward agriculture. The editors of *Farm and Fireside*, published in Springfield, hinted broadly that the Morrill funds in Ohio had been deliberately misappropriated and brought pressure to bear on the legislature to award the Hatch Act funds not to the university but

34. For a review of the Grant administration and the politics of postwar America, see William B. Hesseltine, *Ulysses S. Grant, Politician* (New York: Dodd, Mead and Co., 1935), and Matthew Josephson, *The Politicos, 1865–1896* (New York: Harcourt Brace, 1938); Allan Nevins, *Illinois,* (New York: Oxford University Press, 1917); Clarence Paul Slater, *History of the Land-Grant Endowment Fund of the University of Illinois* (Urbana: University of Illinois, 1940).

35. Solon J. Buck, *The Granger Movement: A Study of Agricultural Organization and Its Political, Economic and Social Manifestations, 1870–1880* (Cambridge: Harvard University Press, 1913); and Solon J. Buck, *The Agrarian Crusade: A Chronicle of the Farmer in Politics* (New Haven: Yale University Press, 1920).

to the Agricultural Experiment Station. With Ohio's older institutions more alert, more responsive, and better organized for action through the Association of Ohio Colleges and with major population centers preoccupied with the newer institutions, the need for the Ohio State University to gain the farmers' support became increasingly important.[36]

In 1873, however, upon the opening of the new institution in Franklin County, the income from the Morrill land grant fund, though not extravagant, was sufficient for a beginning. It greatly exceeded the assured income of all other Ohio institutions who augmented their operations with student fees and tuition. As time passed, however, and expenses mounted, the chances for increasing the income of the institution decreased. Governor Dennison's assurance that a Franklin County location would suffice to keep the institution's needs before a sympathetic legislature was not borne out. The legislature, cognizant of hard times, was not at all sympathetic, and, while the industrial classes in general balanced their budgets by eliminating the many luxuries to which a wartime economy had accustomed them, the legislature eliminated from consideration such luxuries as higher education.[37]

There was another factor working to the disadvantage of the new institution. Rutherford B. Hayes, as governor, had directed the intricate procedures which compromised state disunity about the Morrill grant and created the new institution. He had helped to engineer

36. *Farm and Fireside*, January 15, 1887, p. 129; February 15, 1887, p. 161; March 15, 1887, p. 197; April 15, 1887, p. 231.

37. Legislative appropriations for the University from 1871 to 1881 were as follows:

1871	$ 4,500.00
1872	. . .
1873	2,000.00
1874	. . .
1875	. . .
1876	. . .
1877	4,500.00
1878	. . .
1879	15,800.00
1880	8,500.90
1881	1,350.00

All such appropriations were for specific and limited purposes and not until 1891 did the legislature provide an annual tax levy for the school's support; see Mendenhall, op. cit., pp. 52–57, for a succinct summary of state aid to the institution.

its location and he had given it a board of trustees delicately balancing the advocates of a broad-gauge state university and the advocates of the indispensible program of industrial education for farmers and mechanics. His hope was that both would triumph. As his term as governor ended, however, a strong hand for balance was removed and the machinery could be tipped one way as well as the other.

CHAPTER 4

Men and Ideas

Rutherford B. Hayes hoped for a state university with a broad educational program and he appointed a board which gave representation to a broad view of what the Morrill Act should accomplish. He sidestepped the narrow sectarianism of the old line college and without minimizing broad cultural programs, insured a strong utilitarian program in industrial education. Perhaps he did not pay sufficient attention to the religious views of a population which had nurtured so many sectarian colleges, but his enthusiasm for progress in industrial education was his primary motivation. The unique industrial feature, he said, was the new institution's major distinction among all other institutions and was the one feature which would eventually bring popular support to the school. If there were a dominant reason for the passage of the Morrill Act, this for Hayes was it.

Hayes believed that one of the crucial issues in America between the Civil War and the turn of the century was the emerging industrial system and the rank and file workmen of the farms and factories. "Capital and Labor is the burning question," he later told Alexis Cope, secretary of the board of trustees, and he was convinced that once a boy had been educated in skilled labor he could never despise labor or the laborer. It was important that the state university provide this kind of experience for all of its students.

Rich and poor alike should experience industrial education. This
was the role for a land grant college in a state like Ohio and it could
never be fulfilled by an institution which merely tolerated industrial
education, or in one which excluded everything else. In Hayes' view,
the state university would provide the basis for progress and unity
in the modern industrial state. This at least was his hope, although
conflicts among men and ideas hampered his progress and created
disunity.[1]

This was true because the early years of the Ohio State University coincided with a period of transition in American higher
education and a period of conflicting ideas about educational purpose. There were educational giants throughout the land during
the era including Charles W. Eliot of Harvard, Noah Porter of Yale,
Frederick A. P. Barnard of Columbia, James McCosh of Princeton,
Daniel Coit Gilman at Johns Hopkins, Andrew D. White at Cornell,
James B. Angell at Michigan, and John Bascom at Wisconsin. There
were no comparable educational giants in Ohio, however. Such
men were for the most part the leaders of institutions with established reputations, such as an Eliot at Harvard, or were men at
places like Johns Hopkins and Cornell where a wealth of ideas and
of resources were brought uniquely together. Ohio had neither a
Harvard nor the making of a Cornell or a Johns Hopkins. Even
later when two Ohioans like John D. Rockefeller and William
Rainey Harper combined forces, it was not in Ohio but at a
struggling denominational college in Chicago. The giants, nevertheless, outlined the dimensions of educational philosophy and gave
leadership to educational development; but they were not in agreement. Conflicting opinions about the nature and the purpose of the
American university was inherent in this era of growth.[2]

In general, divergent philosophical views could be classified in
four categories, and in Ohio one was dominant. The first embodied

1. R. B. Hayes to Alexis Cope, February 7, 1891, R. B. Hayes Correspondence, Manuscript Collection, Ohio State University Library.
2. For a general view of the period see Frederick Rudolph, *The American
College and University: A History* (New York: Knopf and Co., 1962); a more
specific treatment of philosophical differences appears in Laurence Veysey,
The Emergence of the American University (Chicago: University of Chicago
Press, 1965); also helpful are the biographies of individual educational leaders.

the nature of the old-time, traditional, and mostly denominational college. It was devoted to a concept of higher education as disciplining man's faculties, both mental and moral, and transmitting classical truth from the ancient generations to the modern. No institution was completely devoted to any one philosophical position although generally the smaller the faculty and the more orthodox the controlling denomination the less likely it was that a divergent philosophy would survive. The small denominational colleges for the most part were devoted to the philosophy of mental and moral discipline. Miami and Ohio Universities, likewise, were basically oriented in this direction. Thus, almost without exception, Ohio institutions were devoted to this old-time college view or were moving very gradually from it in the direction of the second general orientation, liberal culture.[3]

This second orientation viewed higher education as a matter of liberal culture and general education. This, too, was an essentialist position, insisting that there were ancient truths, or at least ancient values, which ought to be transmitted from one generation to the next. The view was related to the position of mental and moral discipline but had abandoned faculty psychology, moderated sectarian enthusiasms to some extent, and sought to incorporate itself with more modern trends by providing a basic education antecedent to further specialization.[4]

The third general classification of views regarding higher education was that which saw education as basically utilitarian. This orientation embraced such concepts as the equality of all knowledge, the principle of free election, the societal obligation of an educational institution, and the validity of industrial education. Advocates of the utilitarian position opposed the old-time, traditional college with its classical curriculum and its Whiggish tendencies. They were not particularly disposed to accept the notions of liberal culture either but were less emphatic in their opposition. Institutions

3. For a recent outline of philosophical positions in higher education and some analysis of the development of current positions, see *Modern Philosophies and Education: The Fifty-fourth Yearbook of the National Society for the Study of Education*, Part I, ed. Nelson B. Henry (Chicago: University of Chicago Press, 1955); Veysey, op. cit., pp. 217–18, 257–58.

4. Veysey, op. cit., see chap. i, "Discipline and Piety" and chap. iv, "Liberal Culture."

such as the industrial university projected by Jonathan B. Turner of Illinois, and the agricultural college in Ohio which Norton B. Townshend conducted with President Fairchild of Oberlin were representative of the utilitarian doctrine applied.[5]

The fourth philosophical orientation was that of research and scientism. Basically, it was the German university idea which focused this group of ideas. Advocates of research and science were not entirely hostile to utilitarian views of higher education although many deplored their narrowness. Relationships with advocates of mental and moral discipline, however, were virtually non-existent. The incorporation of the sciences and the attitudes related to scientific inquiry into the program of liberal culture made for less conflict between these two positions.[6]

There was no institution in the Ohio of the 1870's, however, devoted to the sciences and to the scientific method applied in other fields. There were individual men who leaned in that direction, such as Edward Orton, first president of the Ohio State University, and Thomas C. Mendenhall, a professor of physics, at that institution. At no institution, however, had the German idea become paramount, nor was it likely that such a view would characterize the new land grant institution in Franklin County.[7]

The Morrill Act itself excluded none of these philosophic orientations. While it specified that a main objective should be utilitarian education, it did not require the exclusion of liberal culture. It did leave open to interpretation the degree to which the spirit of mental and moral discipline or the spirit of scientific research should motivate the institution. While the founders of the land grant institutions could debate this, and could debate how liberal culture and utilitarian education might be combined, they could not question the fact that the two were to be combined. Essentially, then, the

5. Edmund Janes James, *Origin of the Land-Grant Act of 1862 (The So-called Morrill Act) and Some Accounts of Its Author: Jonathan B. Turner* Urbana-Champaign: Illinois University Press, 1910).

6. Veysey, op. cit., chaps. ii and iii, pp. 21–262; Charles Franklin Thwing, *The American and the German University: One Hundred Years of History* (New York: Macmillan Co., 1928), passim.

7. It is Laurence Veysey's conclusion that in the 1870's research played no important role in American higher education at all. He denotes a definite change in the 1880's and, by 1890, characterized American universities as having a dominant concern for research; Veysey, op. cit., pp. 174–75.

Morrill Act authorized an institution that would not exclude liberal culture but which would embrace as a leading object utilitarian kinds of education. In the Ohio of the 1870's, this meant a different kind of institution for Ohio than it meant for Nebraska or Iowa or somewhere else. For Hayes and most of those whom he had appointed to a board of trustees, it meant more than a farmers' college.

Of a score or more of men who most influenced the beginnings of the land grant college in Ohio, Joseph Sullivant perhaps entertained as diverse a view of university purpose as any other. He was one of the oldest of those involved and the son of one of the early families in the county. His brother, William, was a botanist and one of the leading bryologists of his day, while another brother, Michael, was a very successful farmer with large holdings in Illinois. The family was active in Columbus banking circles and in horticultural and agricultural organizations. Joseph Sullivant himself was described as a man of leisure and letters with keen interest in art, literature, and science. He was active in the support of education and served on the Columbus Board of Education. He collected a large cabinet of shells, fossils, and minerals and published a catalog describing his collection.[8]

Indicative of his broad interests, he also published a monograph on hog-feeding and pork-making, and studied the problem of a water supply for the city of Columbus. He traced the early boundaries of Franklin County and wrote a genealogy of the Sullivant family preserving much detail about the town of Franklinton and the early life of the county. He was well aware of the dimensions of the agricultural reform movement and associated closely with M. B. Bateham, editor of the state's most influential prewar farmer's magazine, the *Ohio Cultivator*.[9]

8. Moore, op. cit., p. 102; Osman Castle Hooper, *History of the City of Columbus, Ohio, from the Founding of Franklinton in 1797 through the World War Period to the Year 1920* (Columbus and Cleveland: Memorial Publishing Co. [1920]), pp. 19, 248; Joseph Sullivant, *An Alphabetical Catalog of Shells, Fossils, Minerals and Zoophites in the Cabinet of Joseph Sullivant* (Columbus, Ohio: Cutler and Pilsbury, 1838).

9. Joseph Sullivant, *Hog-Feeding and Pork-Making* (n.p., 1870); *Historical Sketch Relating to the Original Boundaries and Early Times of Franklin County* (Columbus, Ohio; Ohio State Journal, 1871); *A Genealogy and Family Memorial* (Columbus, Ohio: Ohio State Journal, 1874); Hooper, op, cit., p. 41.

In addition, Joseph Sullivant hoped for the establishment of a college in Columbus and deplored the absence of a real state university in Ohio. As a result, he worked hard to secure the location of the land grant college in Franklin County and without hesitation intended to make it a state university. His plan for the institution was not well thought out and written down in detail, but his appeal to the citizens of Franklin County to raise the funds to secure the school's location, his outline of a program of instruction and the school's departmental structure, and his actions as a member of the board of trustees indicate his philosophical orientation.[10]

Giving vent to his interest in the artistic, he designed a college seal which provided an elaborate expression of his educational philosophy. He had the seal engraved and presented to the board of trustees which accepted it as the official insignia of the institution.[11] To signify the fixedness and perpetuity of the institution, he used the geometric form of a pyramid representative of durability. The base of the pyramid represented agriculture as the chief occupation of man underlying and supporting human knowledge. Above agriculture, Sullivant represented the arts, both mechanic and polite, as having developed after agriculture and before science and as only artificially separable. Next, rising in the pyramid, he located science, including philosophy and all systematized and classified knowledge. Then, as the outgrowth of all before it and the mark of a nation's refinement and intellectual achievement, he placed letters, including all language and literature. Above his pyramid, he placed the lamp of knowledge to signify that the Agricultural and Mechanical College was a light on a high place to illuminate all within its sphere.[12]

Thus, graphically, Sullivant revealed his educational philosophy. The seal was that of a state university, illuminating all, devoted to a

10. Joseph Sullivant, *Address in Behalf of the Location of the Ohio Agricultural and Mechanic College in Franklin County* (Columbus, Ohio: n.p., 1870); *Ohio State Journal* (Columbus, Ohio), July 28, 1870; Joseph Sullivant, *Schedule of the Departments Proposed by J. Sullivant to Serve as a Basis, in the Organization of the Ohio Agricultural and Mechanical College and School of Applied Science* (Columbus, Ohio: n.p., n.d.).

11. *Record of Proceedings of the Board of Trustees*, p. 30.

12. Mendenhall, op. cit., pp. 37–38.

liberal culture of language and letters, recognizing the importance of all systematized and classified knowledge, and embracing both the polite and the practical and utilitarian arts of man. Sullivant's representation did not include the religious emphasis of the traditional American college. His drawing was also more descriptive of knowledge to be taught than of that to be discovered. Like his friend, James Comly, who endorsed Sullivant's plan for the University, the model institution after which this new one was to be patterned was Cornell in New York.[13]

For those like Ralph Leete of Ironton who wanted to give greater emphasis to the role of research and discovery in higher education, however, the Cornell model was quite sufficient. It was not buildings and land that would benefit farmers and mechanics, Leete said, but rather an institution that bred thinkers and discoverers of unknown truths. Even in advocating progress based upon research, however, Leete displayed the lack of precise allegiance to philosophical positions that characterized men in education. Humanistically, he put his emphasis upon the men who would teach and the men who would apply discovered truth, and insisted that the purpose of all education was the moral and intellectual development of men. Teaching, he emphasized, was the highest calling of man but the content of instruction should surely incorporate moral truth and not be restricted to the intellectual alone.[14]

This represented a slightly different emphasis from the German idea as instituted at Johns Hopkins where method predominated over content and discovery over transmission. At Johns Hopkins, the doctor of philosophy degree became the specific goal and objective of the program. The lecture to replace the recitation and the seminar to train scholars in the independent investigation of an important problem were the means to that end. An entirely new emphasis upon the library and the laboratory emerged to aid researchers. The concern, through it all, was with competence more than breadth and well-roundedness.[15]

13. *Ohio State Journal*, July 29, 1870.
14. Mendenhall, op. cit., pp. x–xi.
15. Thwing, op. cit., pp. 109, 114–15, 120, 130.

Norton S. Townshend would not have disagreed fundamentally with Leete. His emphasis would be different, and he would have implied different things even though he used similar words. With Leete's insistence upon moral development, Townshend would have agreed, being careful to specify that this did not include denominational indoctrination or compulsory exposure to specific doctrinal views of what was moral. Townshend had taken moral stands on alcohol, slavery, and the improper care of dependent persons such as the mentally deficient, and was convinced that the moral strength of the nation that would correct such evils should be fostered. But he was a Unitarian and conscious of the evils inherent in sectarian intolerance. His views concerning the restrictions he would impose on the purpose of moral training would not have been unacceptable to Ralph Leete, but Townshend was more inclined to insist that they be specified.[16]

Similarly, Townshend would not have disputed with Sullivant concerning the breadth desirable in the new institutional program, provided, of course, that sufficient resources were available to do it all. He was insistent, however, that the school do what other institutions had failed to do and that it undertake whatever practical instruction would make the labor of any class more successful and more elevating. He would have placed greater emphasis upon Sullivant's depiction of agriculture as the base of the entire superstructure, and the mechanic arts as next in importance. It was apparent that, while Sullivant focused upon the apex of his pyramid, Townshend focused upon the base. Both were willing that the total structure exist, but Townshend saw the upper portions as enhancing the success of the industrial classes and elevating their lives and not as goals in and of themselves.[17]

On more than one occasion, Townshend took issue with institutional critics among farmers, and defended the coexistence of utilitarian education and liberal culture. He saw the two as complementary with liberal culture augmenting the more utilitarian programs which were the primary programs of the institution. From

16. *Farm and Fireside*, February 1, 1887, p. 145.
17. Ibid., February 1, 1887, p. 146; Mendenhall, op. cit., p. 35.

the very beginning, Townshend's concept of agricultural education was greatly influenced by his associations with several medical schools. He was involved in the professional assessment of medical education and approved the trend away from practical training by means of the apprenticeship to more formal education drawing upon the basic sciences. He had a similar perception of agricultural education but insisted upon different admissions requirements that would enable a college of agriculture to meet the farm boy where the rural school systems left him. Spokesmen for farmers in general viewed this as a crucial problem. The non-utilitarian programs were geared to the preparatory programs of private academies and urban high schools, and, in the absence of special consideration, the broader program tended to shut out the farmer and to deprive him of a degree.[18]

The difficulty facing the first Board of Trustees, therefore, was much more tactical than it was philosophical. There was no certainty that all of Sullivant's pyramid could be built at once, and, if not, there was no consensus about what should be done first. Even Sullivant was certain that resources were not sufficient to do everything, and that some choices would have to be made.[19] For those most inclined toward a utilitarian view, however, Sullivant's pyramid was realistically descriptive, and they wanted to begin at the base and add other sections later on. For others, particularly those devoted to the idea of a state university, the seal was a figurative representation, and they would begin with all objectives at once even if none could be fully developed until later.

There was no fundamental disagreement on the first board about the breadth of the program desirable. Sullivant's list of ten basic departments was approved with but one dissenting vote. Less unanimity prevailed as the board implemented programs and committed resources. The closest division came on the chair of ancient languages which was preserved by a mere one vote majority, 8 to 7.

In general, however, the board of trustees seemed to favor a broad program aimed in the direction of establishing a great state university. In 1871, by direction of the board, the executive com-

18. *Farm and Fireside*, April 15, 1887, pp. 231, 235.
19. Mendenhall, op. cit., p. 36.

mittee, of which Dr. Townshend was chairman, traveled in the east visiting other institutions with a view toward gaining increased insight for the board's work in Columbus. One of the first institutions visited was Cornell University with its liberal and utilitarian programs. Ezra Cornell had said that he wanted a school in which any person would pursue any subject, and the Cornell program sought to fulfill that goal by offering both the traditional and the new. The executive committee then visited six other institutions, all in Massachusetts. They visited the Massachusetts Agricultural College, Amherst, Harvard, Lawrence Scientific School, which Edward Orton had attended, the Museum of Zoology at Cambridge, and the Polytechnic Institute at Boston.[20] The itinerary indicated very clearly where the Ohio board of trustees was looking for guidance. The great preponderance of their time was spent in Boston, and the breadth of the Ohio dream was encompassed in the variety of institutions they visited.

Ohio also looked east for a president after a former Ohio governor indicated that he was not interested. They found the man to be president at the Ohio Agricultural and Mechanical College in a former professor at Dartmouth College. James W. Patterson, whom the trustees elected by a two to one majority over Norton Townshend, had been a professor at Dartmouth for several years before entering politics. He and Townshend both had combined political careers with education, and Patterson was, at the time of his selection, a senator from New Hampshire. Immediately following his selection, however, the corruption of the Grant administration erupted in the Crédit Mobilier scandal, and all of Congress lay under a cloud of suspicion. Patterson, who owned Crédit Mobilier stock, immediately released the board of trustees from its commitment because of the embarrassment involved for the fledgling institution.[21]

The trustees then elected Edward Orton, a professor of geology and president of Antioch College at Yellow Springs, Ohio, to be the first president of the Ohio Agricultural and Mechanical College. Orton, who had been ordained a Presbyterian minister, and was the

20. *Records of Proceedings of the Board of Trustees*, p. 28, 31, 44, 61.
21. Ibid., p. 56; Mendenhall, op. cit., pp. 39–42.

son of one preacher and son-in-law of another, by the age of thirty had been charged with heretical views, threatened with a heresy trial, and driven from his position as a professor of natural sciences at the New York State Normal School.[22]

For six years after his resignation from the State Normal School for his heterodox views on theology, Orton served as principal of a small academy in Chester, New York, and furthered the geological studies in which he was becoming increasingly interested. In 1865, his friend, the Reverend Austin Craig of Bloomington Grove, New York, acting president of Antioch College, persuaded Orton to go to Yellow Springs, Ohio, as principal of the preparatory department of the college. Shortly thereafter, he became professor of geology, zoology, and botany at the school. His father considered his association with the Unitarian establishment in Ohio a final form of apostasy and was alienated from his son for many years. In 1872, Orton was elected president of Antioch College. He had also been selected by Governor Rutherford B. Hayes to be second assistant in the Ohio Geological Survey. In 1873, at the age of forty-four, Orton was offered the presidency and a professorship in geology in the newly created Ohio Agricultural and Mechanical College in Columbus. In addition, he retained his place on the Ohio Geological Survey as well.[23]

In his inaugural address, Edward Orton defined what education for the "industrial classes" meant to him, and further emphasized the broad view of the institution which had been taken by its founders. Education for the industrial classes, he said, was real education at a collegiate level available to the great mass of the American people. It was to be liberal, however, as well as practical. Such persons, he felt, should not be denied access to the study of Greek any more than they should be denied access to the study of

22. Ibid., pp. 44–45; Samuel C. Derby, "Edward Orton," *Old Northwest Genealogical Quarterly*, III (January, 1900), pp. 1–14; Allen Johnson and Dumas Malone (eds.), *Dictionary of American Biography*, vol. XIV (New York: Charles Scribner & Sons, 1928–37; Pollard, James E., *History of the Ohio State University: The Story of Its First Seventy-five Years, 1873–1948* (Columbus: Ohio State University Press, 1952), pp. 31–49, hereinafter cited as *History of the Ohio State University*.

23. Derby, op. cit., pp. 1–14; Francis P. Weisenburger, *Ordeal of Faith: The Crisis of Church-Going America, 1865-1900* (New York: Philosophical Library, 1959), pp. 58–60.

mechanics and agriculture. The land grant was to provide liberal culture for the masses just as surely as it was to elevate the practical and utilitarian pursuits of life to a university standard.[24]

Later, in 1878, in addressing the new school's first graduating class, Orton presented a much more specific statement of his definition of the industrial classes. "The term can by no means be limited to the classes that live by manual labor," he said. It was a mere division of labor that separated the man who grew corn from those who transported it or sold it in the market. Nor would he exclude the manufacturer, the merchant, the builder, the engineer, or the banker from the industrial classes. While these had been gathered from the fields and, having been found faithful in a few things, were made rulers over many, he said, they indisputably carried the heavier end of the nation's industrial life. The industrial classes in essence embraced nearly all of American society, he argued, and to defend a kind of education based upon divisions within the industrial classes was indefensible. If the Land Grant Act assumed a division of the people on the basis of rich and poor or cultivated and industrial, said Orton, and established education solely for the poor and industrial classes, then it would train them for a narrow sphere and hold them there. Such an objective, he said, was utterly repugnant and totally inconsistent with the true nature of the Morrill Act. The act declared its purpose to train the industrial classes "for the several pursuits and professions of life," observed Orton. The new university was to train a modern generation for the new industrial world and older and more narrow definitions of terms would not suffice. His view of the purpose of the Ohio State University agreed remarkably with that of Rutherford B. Hayes. The University would promote the basis for progress and unity in the modern industrial state.[25]

24. Mendenhall, op. cit., pp. 103–4; for the complete address see, "Industrial Education, Its Character and Claims," Inaugural Address of Edward Orton, in *Third Annual Report of the Trustees of the Ohio Agricultural and Mechanical College to the Governor of the State of Ohio* (Columbus, 1874), pp. 10–26.

25. Mendenhall, op. cit., pp. 104–5; for the complete address, see Edward Orton, "The Liberal Education of the Industrial Classes: An Address Delivered in the Chapel of The Ohio State University at the Graduation of its First Class, June 19, 1878," in *Eighth Annual Report of the Board of Trustees of The Ohio State University to the Governor of the State of Ohio, for the Year 1878* (Columbus, 1878), pp. 71–79.

Orton's view of the meaning of the Morrill Act and the purpose
of the new Ohio school fitted well with Sullivant's plan and the
general tenor of the board's opinion. He was committed to a broad
state university program emphasizing a liberal culture which en-
riched the whole man and a utilitarian emphasis which ran the
gamut from the humblest to the highest of man's vocations. The
Ohio State University was to incorporate the genius of emerging
urban, industrial America, and in higher education in passing to
introduce the farmer to that new America.

As a geologist, Orton was also sympathetic to the research orientation of the German university. He was an active scholar both
while president and afterward, and an active participant in scholarly
organizations. In addition, he was a very busy consultant during
his career in several states making his scientific knowledge and skill
available to the industry of the nation. There were two kinds of
research and Orton approved of both. In the one instance, the
scholar pushed back the frontiers of knowledge in his field, in the
other, he made that new knowledge available and useful for man-
kind.[26]

Orton also reflected the liberal religious views which characterized the original board of trustees and the faculty. He did not
follow the general custom among colleges of his day and hold daily
religious services on the campus. Opposition to such a stand did
not reach great proportions, however, until 1877, when the board
was reorganized. In that year, the Board of Trustees took official
notice of the situation. The executive committee instructed the
faculty to establish religious services because of mounting objections to the godlessness of the state university. Nevertheless, after
a lengthy discussion by the board of the executive committee's
order and the faculty's response, the board condemned the action
of its own executive committee and changed the order to a recommendation that such services ought to be established as soon as
feasible.[27]

26. An attempt to construct an Orton bibliography including all his scientific and educational publications appears with Derby's memorial to Orton in
the *Old Northwest Genealogical Quarterly*, III (January, 1900), 11–14.
27. *Record of Proceedings of the Board of Trustees*, p. 142.

In his address to the school's first class of graduates in 1878, Orton decided to speak directly to the religious issue as he had to a narrow definition of the industrial classes. The school had no right to involve itself in denominational creeds and religious concepts, he said. The Ohio State University served a people whose voices in religion were as various as were the tongues at the Pentecostal Feast, and since the college belonged to all the people, it should not take sides. Even so, he said, the land-grant colleges brought "glad tidings to the poor" and served the underprivileged classes of society and did not deserve to be condemned as godless.[28]

The churches of America, however, were themselves in a period of great crisis. The theories of Darwin about the origin of man, the spectacular discoveries of geologists about the origin and the age of the earth, and the higher criticism of the Scriptures that challenged accepted beliefs about the origin and the meaning of the Bible had led to serious repercussions in the churches. The trends of research and scholarship seriously challenged orthodox theology, both Protestant and Catholic. At that time, the religious community in America rather generally accepted the Bible as divinely inspired and divinely preserved in its every detail, and its explanations of the origin of the earth and the origin of man were, therefore, felt to be incontestable.[29]

But the new scholarship challenged accepted views of the authorship and the authority of Scripture, the creation of the world, and the creation of man. Its spirit fostered interest in the study of comparative religions in which men sought to analyze the similarities and the differences in various religious heritages presuming some truth and error in all. Within the churches, this particular product of modern Biblical scholarship undermined the important missionary zeal, and led to violent disputes among church leaders about the validity of the enterprise and the orthodoxy of its participants. The full effect of the new trend in theology as responsive to the new scholarship was to precipitate crisis after

28. Mendenhall, op. cit., pp. 104–5.
29. Weisenburger, Francis P. *Triumph of Faith: Contributions of the Church to American Life, 1865–1900* (Richmond, Va.: William Byrd Press, 1962), p. 24.

crisis within the churches. The Presbyterian church, tied to its historic professions of faith, was less equivocal than most on matters of Biblical authority, and liberals were tried for heresy, as was Orton in New York, for their views.[30]

For many church-goers in Ohio in the 1870's, the Ohio State University represented the embodiment of liberal and heretical views in institutional form. Governor Hayes, who appointed the first board of trustees, and T. C. Mendenhall, one of the institution's leading professors, belonged to no church at all. President Orton and Norton S. Townshend were Unitarians, and Orton had been accused of heretical views by the Presbyterian church. The denominational colleges were themselves suspected of harboring heretics, or at least liberals, and they, too, in many cases, became involved in serious theological disputes. The new institution in Franklin County suffered the same pressures that the denominational colleges suffered but was, at least for the time being, more able to resist.[31]

Religious opposition to the Ohio State University in its early years derived basically from the heterodoxy of its faculty, and the general crisis in which the beliefs of church-going America were questioned. Most of the denominational colleges were not opposed to the new institution, generally. The trustees of the Episcopal Theological Seminary at Kenyon purchased one-third of all the bonds sold by Franklin County to secure the location of the new institution, thus entrusting $100,000 of their institution's endowment to that one source. Somewhat later, the trustees of Antioch College offered to use the income of its endowment to support faculty at the Ohio State University in the studies related to liberal culture. Several denominational colleges conferred honorary degrees upon faculty members of the new institution. Furthermore, the Association of Ohio Colleges never failed to invite the new school's representatives to its meetings, and, on occasion, made special efforts to secure the participation of the new institution. The grow-

30. Weisenburger, *Ordeal of Faith*, pp. 110–11, 90–98.
31. Some of the individual histories of denominational colleges adequately reflect the controversies over orthodoxy; Lucy Notestein's *Wooster of the Middle West* provides a good picture of the orthodoxy controversies at that institution.

ing closeness between the association and the state university lent
credence, perhaps, to the fears of the more orthodox that even
their own denominational institutions needed closer scrutiny. In
any event, the sharper antagonisms between the denominational colleges themselves and the Ohio State University arose later, in the
late 1890's.[32]

In his address to the Ohio State University's first graduating class
in 1878, Orton spoke directly about the creeds and confessions of
the denominations which restricted the freedom of conscience and
freedom of inquiry of liberal theologians. The land grant colleges,
he said, "have not much to say about the Council of Trent or the
Synod of Dort . . . they do not nail to their doors the Augs-
burg Confession, the Westminster Catechism, or the Thirty-nine
Articles, and, above all, they do not establish compulsory religious
worship. . . ."[33]

Most liberal theologians recognized, however, that the great
masses of the people were not ready to accept the new theology.
There was an immense problem of communication involved, and
there needed to be discretion in deciding how such revisions were
to be incorporated. Views such as Orton's presented a problem for
the liberals. Most could not take so advanced a view immediately
but needed time to make a more gradual transition. It was not so
much a question of what the new scholarship meant theologically,
although there was considerable lack of agreement on that itself,
as it was a question of how fast the people could be reeducated to
accept the newer views. Those who moved too fast found themselves outside the church, branded as heretics, and subject to
immense social pressure.

Coincidentally, religious conservatism and argricultural displeasure with the new institution touched the same people. One
member of the board of trustees reflected the fact in his observa-
tion that the new institution was as far from God and agriculture
as it could get. His feelings, compared with those of Orton, indi-

32. *Record of Proceedings of the Board of Trustees,* pp. 35, 214; Minutes
of the Faculty, I, 109, 110; Mendenhall, op. cit., pp. 65–73.

33. Ibid., p. 76; for the complete address see *Eighth Annual Report of the
Board of Trustees,* pp. 71–79.

cated clearly the nature of the division. A traditional view of agriculture and religion held by the constitutents of a majority in the legislature conflicted with a newer view of what constituted the industrial classes and the new theology. Different perceptions of what the Ohio State University should be resulted. The sublety of the real difference was lost, however, in the emotionalism which the religious issue elicited. The leadership and faculty of the university preferred liberal culture to the more traditional mental and moral discipline of the old line denominational college, and they preferred a broader view of industrial education than the idea of an agricultural college. Quite clearly, the basis of their preference was an inclination to incorporate in their thinking the product of modern research and scholarship.[34]

Members of the legislature, however, dependent upon the suffrage of the people, could not ignore public displeasure with the new university. Most were not concerned with the philosophical issues, however, but were part of that mass of church-going Ohioans who were uneasy even about their denominational colleges. Legislators, therefore, sought more practical solutions to the problem. To give the appearance of having acted seemed much more important under the circumstances than trying to explain the intricacies of the administrative and philosophical issues involved. For one thing, a failure to appropriate funds was a very obvious attack upon the "Godless place." For another, the legislature could reshuffle the board of trustees.[35]

The Republicans and the Democrats conveniently had different ideas about the nature of the board. Thus, every time the state government changed hands, there was excuse for the board to conform with party views. Governor Hayes appointed a nineteen-member board in 1870. The Democrats, in 1874, established a five-

34. Mendenhall, op. cit., p. 458. A reading of the faculty minutes of the university throughout the period 1870 to 1887 reflects something of the spirit of the faculty; see particularly the records of discussions concerning compulsory chapel, military drill and the curriculum, Minutes of the Faculty, I, 300–301, 315–17, 337; II, 27.
35. Mendenhall, op. cit., p. 105.

member board which abolished tuition, authorized a manual labor system, and created a chair of political economy and civil polity.

The Act reorganizing the board also enlarged the powers of the office of board secretary, and in a move of crucial importance for the further development of the institution made the occupancy of that office subject to the annual approval of the governor of Ohio.[36]

In 1877, however, the Republicans regained control of the state government and created a board of twenty members again based upon Congressional districts. The new trustees reduced faculty salaries by 10 percent and stipulated that the reduction would continue until enrollment reached 200. The new board also authorized the faculty to establish a special program which permitted young men aged eighteen or older to take courses in the college not aimed at a degree. They were to be subjected to no entrance examinations and were to be exempted from military drill. Defensively, the faculty agreed to offer the program provided thirty men would indicate a willingness to enroll in such a course. The trustees insisted that the quota be reduced to twenty.[37]

About a year later, with Democrats again in control of the state government, the twenty-member board was replaced by a seven-man body, and the institution's name was changed to the Ohio State University. The new board replaced Joseph Sullivant as secretary, a post he had held for eight years, rescinded the 10 percent pay reduction, accepted the resignation of T. C. Mendenhall, and considered the resignation of Edward Orton. Orton submitted his resignation following his commencement address, but it was not accepted. The board also designated a faculty member to serve as bursar on the campus.[38]

36. Ibid., p. 108, implies that each party made just enough changes to justify appointing a new board of trustees and that their commitment was to change itself more than to any particular theory of organization; for the immediate sequence of actions taken by the new board in 1874 see *Record of Proceedings of the Board of Trustees*, pp. 79–87.

37. Ibid., pp. 132–35, 144.

38. Ibid., pp. 147–60; Mendenhall, op. cit., pp. 107–8.

Prior to the reorganization of 1878, the faculty had considered the problem of constant reorganization at great length, and appointed a committee which included Norton Townshend and Thomas C. Mendenhall to present the faculty's views to the legislature. The faculty submitted three proposals. The first called for a nine-man board on which there would be three representatives of mining, agricultural, and manufacturing interests of the state, three state officers, and three representatives at large. The second proposal was that the president of the institution have a seat but not a vote on the board. The third was that the law include a provision that the trustees be empowered to undertake any investigation that the General Assembly requested provided the assembly offered sufficient funds for its successful completion. The faculty proposals were pragmatic, aimed directly at solving some of their on-going problems, but they were virtually ignored by the legislature. The resignations of Mendenhall and Orton particularly reflected the sense of futility which pervaded the faculty.[39]

Regardless of board size and irrespective of philosophical orientation, however, all four of the institution's boards had pursued policies aimed at enhancing the institution's appeal and broadening its support. The chair of political economics, it was hoped, would appease the industrial and business community. For a similar reason, a Department of Metallurgy and Mining was added in 1877. The abolition of tuition, the promotion of a manual labor scheme, and the creation of a special nondegree program would, it was assumed, please the farmers. Recommendations about daily chapel were made to appease religious critics. All such actions, however, worked on tactics and externals but failed to attack the basic philosophical differences. In the final analysis, appeal was not enhanced and support was not broadened. With the exception of a few small and specific appropriations, the legislature was tight-fisted with its university.[40] The church-goers of the community were unappeased, and the farmers insisted, in spite of what the trustees might do or say, that they were not welcomed at the farmers' college.

39. Minutes of the Faculty, I, 149–50.
40. Mendenhall, op. cit., p. 107.

CHAPTER 5

Freedom and Tenure

By June of 1880, Edward Orton had decided to press his long-standing resignation. He had first submitted it in 1878 but had remained in office at the insistence of the board. "During the past two months," Orton told the faculty on June 3, "I have made my demand as imperative as the case would allow." He took that occasion to read a formal paper to the faculty outlining his thinking concerning the change of presidents. He recognized the faculty's great interest in the matter of his successor but said that he thought there was no profit in the faculty's discussing it. While individuals might act personally, he said, the faculty as a faculty would probably not be a factor in the choice. He saw another element of particular concern to the faculty which he said was based upon facts patent to all. "The appointment of a president," he said, "will probably involve some changes in our present force and work," and he regretted that the resignation which he so desired would have such repercussions. His resignation, he thought, might well precipitate the unseating of others, but he saw no alternative. "I can see no way by which I can free myself. . . . " he confessed. The best interests of the college, he added, demanded a new incumbent because of his growing distaste and increasing sense of inadequacy for the duties and responsibilities of the office.[1]

1. Minutes of the Faculty, I, 251–52.

In 1881, the board finally accepted Orton's resignation but retained him as professor of geology. The resignation was accepted in part because they had found in the Reverend Walter Quincy Scott a man they felt would institute the board's recommendations concerning daily chapel services and other changes. The university acknowledged Edward Orton's work on its behalf during his eight year administration by awarding him an honorary degree. The state recognized him by promoting him to director of the State Geological Survey. For seventeen years then, he continued his scholarly work primarily in the area of economic geology and served with distinction on the faculty in teaching and in committee service. He was an authority on gas and petroleum resources in Ohio, Kentucky, Indiana, and New York and an outspoken proponent of conservation. His career as teacher and scholar spoke well for the judgment of those who first selected him for president. He represented well the great state university which they sought to build.[2]

If Orton's confidential talk with the faculty in June of 1880 had heightened their anxieties about the change of administrations, however, Walter Quincy Scott's inaugural address allayed their fears. "The transition from one administration to the next in civil government," he said after two or three perfunctory and introductory sentences, "is often characterized by arbitrary changes in officers and methods." This occurred, he said, to satisfy the demands of patronage and the requirements of policy. He then added, "an institution of learning cannot properly be subjected to such a form of administration." Educational administration, he said, should be inconspicuous and subservient to the "organic elements and spirit exhibited in the instruction and culture of the young." He recommended that the tree of knowledge be pruned only for better growth, and that it should occur as a result of the vicissitudes that occur in individual lives. In government, he asserted, the machinery of politics was so dominant that the people confused politics with the principles for which government itself was ordained, but a similar fate should not befall education. "This university cannot hope to develop the great and complicated ideas embodied in its organization without substantial continuity of its trustees and

2. Derby, op. cit., pp. 1–14.

faculty," he observed. President Scott was thus attempting to forestall two developments. The first, which Orton foresaw and other
faculty members feared, was the change of faculty with the change
of administrations. The second was the political reorganization of
the board of trustees which had already occurred three times in the
short history of the institution.[3]

In a second part of his inaugural Scott then devoted attention to
those "great and complicated ideas" which he said were embodied
in the establishment of the institution. In this middle portion of
his address his utterances became increasingly disquieting particularly to many who looked for changes in the personnel and
the direction of the university. "The people of this generation," said
Scott, alluding to the recent Civil War, "are too near the triumph of
the nation over the states, and too much absorbed in the amazing
progress of all industries under its sovereign power, to appreciate
the perils to free institutions which lie stored up in the national
idea itself." He alluded to an arrogance of power and said that a
nation was always in greatest danger of decline when it was powerful and its neighbors weak. "When the eagle is a fool," he quipped,
"the sparrows can avenge themselves." Scott reserved his major
criticism, however, for the corporations which, he said, clothed
in the authority of the nation itself, encroached upon local legislation and "the rights and liberties of classes of citizens."[4]

Scott, a forceful speaker who commanded attention, then landed
with full force upon the traditional conservatism of his listeners:

> We have wiped out the compromise line between the civilization
> of free labor and the civilization of slavery; we have dissolved the
> partition lines of the sovereignties of states; but we have laid down
> lines of continental transportation and lines of continental tele-
> graphic communication, to which we are adding lines of shipping
> and of cables extending across the seas—all in the hands of private
> corporations. To these we are adding boundaries around the agri-
> cultural and mineral products of the natural divisions of our soil,
> and around the areas of service occupied by public buildings and
> fortification. All these things, while suppressing territorial sectional-

3. "Inaugural Address of Walter Quincy Scott," in *Twelfth Annual Report
of the Board of Trustees of the Ohio State University to the Governor of the
State of Ohio for the Year 1882* (Columbus, Ohio: G. J. Brand, 1883), p. 156.
4. Ibid., pp. 157, 161.

ism of the North and the South, and of the East and West, tend to
develop the selfish interests of classes of the people and are fraught
with the perils of antagonism between the upper and the under
classes.[5]

This, he said, explained the origin of the land-grant colleges for
the industrial classes. "Because the nation apprehended peril to itself
from its people, from their growing up in ignorance of its moral
organism and true nature," the nation in the midst of Civil War
provided for the higher education of the whole people. He cited
the provisions of the Morrill Act and insisted that there was no
mistaking the intent. In the Morrill Act, he said, the nation laid
hold upon higher education in order to accomplish what had not
been done and, furthermore, what secretarian and private endowments could never do. Wars seemed usually to be joined, he said,
with great educational movements, and the nationalizing Civil War
in America had directed the national spirit into higher education
by means of the Morrill Act. Out of the War came the nation and
the instrumentalities to educate its people. The Ohio State University, said Scott, originated in this national idea of education,
and the state was thence forward forever indebted and forever
pledged to maintain and support the liberal and practical education
of all the youth of the state. Even then, however, Ohio was not the
sole beneficiary. "The nation itself," he said, "claims the entire
ultimate benefit of her bounty to the states."[6]

The national idea of education, Scott continued, was nonetheless
implemented in a particular place, and thus became commingled
with a state idea of education. Thus, in Ohio, the meeting ground of
varieties of peoples and a highway and battleground for ideas, the
Morrill Act was embodied in a specific setting. It was a setting, Scott
insisted, in which no more serious problem existed than the imper-
fection of its system of public instruction from the lowest to the
highest level.

At this point then, in what must have been a rather stunning as
well as stimulating address, Scott turned to a third and final portion

5. Ibid., p. 162.
6. Ibid., pp. 157, 162–63.

of his address involving the science-religion controversy. He told his listeners that the scientific controversies of the Age of Newton had centered in ideas of space and had emphasized the littleness of man's place in nature. It forced a reconstruction of traditional views and tempted man to exert his power over space. The newer controversies of the Age of Darwin, he added, were centered in ideas of time and ideas which terminated in man's nature. "Man's origin must be pushed back to a place as little as it is remote," said the new president.

Scott's views seriously impaired efforts to allay public fears about the godlessness of the state university. He insisted that natural sciences, mathematics, astronomy, physics, chemistry, geology, and botany had wrought great changes in industry, commerce, social, civil, and ecclesiastical polity and that they made the Miltonian cosmogony a childish superstition.

Hastening then to conclude his inaugural remarks, Scott confessed that any system of education which ignored the moral conduct and religious nature of undergraduate youth was fundamentally defective. But, he insisted, while the state university should be concerned with the morality and religion of Christian civilization, it should be nonsectarian.[7]

At each point in his narration, Scott had antagonized some element of public opinion. But his radical views concerning corporate enterprise and religion actually camouflaged the fundamental idea which, for Scott, justified the broad, liberal, and demanding educational program which he envisioned for the Ohio State University. The sweep of the 1870's, Scott implied, in science, in politics, and in religion was toward a new nationalized and industrialized age, an age for which the land grant college was specifically created:

> . . . great organizers are coming to be needed more and more, he said. The rapid communication of innumerable minds, and almost equally rapid exchange of powers and products among the dense populations of the globe, are demanding and developing the highest orders of executive genius and philosophic wisdom ever displayed in the history of man. Surely the state is called upon

7. Ibid., pp. 163–65, 173–75.

everywhere to provide for the education of the masses, but all the
stars of heaven and all the souls of men call for all degrees of
liberal education reaching to the highest.[8]

Walter Quincy Scott had not been argumentative. He was not
condemnatory even in his observations about corporations and the
concentration of economic power. He was discussing his scholarly
observations about the setting of the modern university. He sought
to evaluate the origin and the purpose of the land-grant college, and
he projected the implications of his findings onto the Ohio situation.
He saw its origins in the growing national spirit, and its purpose in
providing all men with a breadth of education that would enable
them to understand and cope with the dawning age. While his
contemporaries were disturbed by his observations, however, the
students under his tutelage caught a glimpse of the new generation
that was to be theirs, and admired him for telling them what life
was "really" going to be like.[9] Scott's economic and religious views,
however, were not as acceptable to his peers as his vision of tomor-
row was to his students. And between the two sets of views, a
majority of the trustees soon found themselves in disagreement with
their president.

In January before Orton had resigned, the trustees had instructed
the president and the faculty to hold a daily assembly of students in
the university chapel but allowed that the nature and the time of
the exercises should be under the control of the faculty. A week
later, the action was temporarily suspended after President Orton,
as he had done earlier, apprised the board of the difficulty of execut-
ing the order.[10] At its next meeting, after Scott's election and before
his inaugural address, the board of trustees reaffirmed the resolution
of the previous January with the full expectation that President W.
Q. Scott would carry it into effect. They added a stipulation that
Scripture reading and prayers were to be included in the exercises.
The question of daily chapel services was, therefore, considered in
the very first faculty meeting over which President W. Q. Scott

8. Ibid., p. 174.
9. Ibid., p. 161.
10. *Record of Proceedings of the Board of Trustees,* pp. 211–12.

presided. After discussion, however, the faculty created a committee to consider the advisability and feasibility of having Sabbath morning services rather than daily exercises. The intense feeling of the faculty on the subject is illustrated by the faculty's reluctance even to ask the president to hold memorial services for the assassinated James A. Garfield; instead they asked for a committee to make whatever arrangements the occasion required. Scott's reluctance to initiate chapel services reflected the general hesitancy of the faculty to involve the school in such activities, its refusal to be responsible for directing such services and its insistence that it not require someone else to establish such services.[11]

Three months later the board discovered that President Scott and the faculty had not complied. The trustees asked the attorney general of the state for a ruling concerning the legality of their requiring daily chapel since there were many who were insisting that it would not be legal for a governmental agency to require attendance at religious services on a state campus. The Attorney General replied that such action was clearly within the scope of the authority granted by the legislation establishing the board of trustees. He did not speak to the broader issue of church-state relations but restricted himself to an interpretation of the charter act of the institution. The delegation of authority to the board of trustees had been broad and inclusive, and their instruction concerning chapel did not exceed the authority granted.[12]

The trustees evidently assumed that this would settle the matter and that the president and faculty would comply with the requirement of daily chapel, but they did not. The faculty failed even to consider the board's instructions until three months after the attorney general's report, and then it laid the matter on the table. The faculty passed a resolution that the board stay proceedings upon the matter pending further study. A faculty committee studied the problem of how to comply with the trustees' request without violating the faculty's convictions concerning the role of religious services on the campus. They suggested a voluntary Sunday after-

11. Minutes of the Faculty, I, 300–301.
12. Record of Proceedings of the Board of Trustees, p. 220, 225.

noon program of religious education as a possible alternative. In November of 1882, the trustees expressed surprise that no chapel had been established. It was the unanimous wish of the board, they informed the faculty, that its request be carried into effect at once. The faculty complied, setting a time and place for the required services but placing responsibility for the act upon the board of trustees. They also again suggested the Sunday afternoon voluntary and educational alternative.[13]

While some members of the board of trustees viewed President Scott's failure to institute chapel services immediately upon taking office as obvious insubordination, others were increasingly concerned with his "unsound and dangerous" economic views. Theological liberalism which entertained the higher criticism and comparative religion also fostered the social gospel movement and economic views of varying degrees of unorthodoxy. Even the mild-mannered Edward Orton advocated effective measures to protect the public welfare in matters of health, and opposed the reckless wasting of natural resources. The Reverend Washington Gladden, who had just accepted a call to First Congregational Church in Columbus, typified a more direct example of the young liberals in the church. In 1876, he published a book entitled *Working People and Their Employers,* further illustrating the economic perspective of the liberal theology. In this work, Gladden, who was later denied the presidency of the Ohio State University, recognized the right of labor to organize, and advocated cooperative negotiation between capital and labor. For the 1870's, this was a decidedly forward position.[14]

Scott's religious and economic views were likewise typical of the trend nationally among religious liberals. Furthermore, it was a well-known fact that, at the time he was elected president he would not shrink from a public defense of his position. Immediately prior

13. Minutes of the Faculty, I, p. 337; *Record of Proceedings of the Board of Trustees,* p. 242; seven weeks later the faculty considered a ten minute morning chapel service, but finally approved taking fifteen minutes away from military drill time for such purposes; Minutes of the Faculty, II, 27; Pollard, op. cit., pp. 84–86.

14. *Dictionary of American Biography,* XIV, 63; VII, 326.

to his coming to the Ohio State University, he had been involved in a dispute at Wooster College from which he was ousted in 1881 because of suspected religious heterodoxy. At Wooster, in two years, he had become a popular citizen and a provocative teacher with a wide following on campus and off. He so taught students that they thought in ways they had never dared to think before, and he jolted them from popular and accepted prejudices. His teaching method sought to demolish previous prejudices in order that new commitments might be constructed rationally. He caused his students to think and their parents and pastors to write letters to the president complaining about his teachings. Students at Western Theological Seminary in Pennsylvania, hearing of his lectures, wrote Wooster's president demanding that Dr. Scott be removed for heresy. By the end of his first year on the faculty, the trustees were convinced that they had to do something. They suggested that he make a clear statement of his orthodox views on doctrine in order that his students understand his solid Calvinistic foundation.[15]

Scott refused to take the suggestion seriously and felt that it was an unwarranted interference with his teaching method. During his second and last year of teaching, Scott failed to issue the statement of his faith and continued to provoke students to rethink their own. University officials blamed him for a growing infidelity among the students, although one student observed that the unrest was more the result of the removal of unorthodox books from the library by the administration than it was of Scott's teaching. Nevertheless, the following July, the trustees requested Scott's resignation. He defended himself for two hours before the board but lost an 8 to 4 decision.

The local community was disturbed about the outcome. In the final analysis, Scott's orthodoxy seemed to have been vindicated, and the only remaining complaint seemed to be his provocative teaching methods. The local press carried articles concerning the injustice of the decision, and criticized the trustees and the narrow

15. Lucy L. Notestein, *Wooster of the Middle West* (New Haven, Conn.: Yale University Press, 1937), pp. 101, 102, 104.

sectarianism of the institution. A local citizens' committee was formed to express community views to the school's administration. A lurking sentiment in the community that the school was not as interested in the city and its needs as it was in its own orthodoxy reinforced the ill feeling.

Students as well as townsmen took the professor's side in the dispute. When Scott returned to Wooster from a trip East, he was met at the station by 150 students. They planned to include a brass band in the welcoming ceremonies, but Scott, learning of their plan, dissuaded them from doing so. Later, the senior class called at Scott's home, and, later in the same week, the lower classmen tendered him the same respectful attention. He preached in the First Presbyterian Church and responded to a petition of citizens to deliver once again a popular lecture.

As the fame of the teacher spread, he was invited to Columbus to preach and addressed a crowded house. Increasingly, he was considered a martyr to his pedagogic convictions and an early defender of the professor's freedom to teach in a way which he considered effective. Within a year, he was president of the Ohio State University, and his friends at Wooster were delighted. Within two more years, however, he had been dismissed as president at the state university, and once again partisans and opponents were vociferous in their consideration of the merits and demerits of the provocative Dr. Scott.[16]

In view of the Wooster affair, the trustees at the Ohio State University ought not to have been too surprised when his provocative teaching of political economy aroused opposition. Nor should they have been too surprised when his notions about church-state relations and personal freedom precluded compulsory chapel. In his inaugural address, he had candidly removed any lingering doubts about these matters that any of them might have held.

Scott lectured on campus and elsewhere in Ohio, and was charged with proclaiming views similar to those of Henry George, the author of *Progress and Poverty*, with advocating a single tax on land, and with opposing the individual ownership of land. He had described capitalism as a kind of robbery, claimed his opponents, and had

16. Ibid., pp. 102–6.

referred to stock dividends as theft.[17] The one set of lectures toward which most criticism was aimed had been delivered at a farmers' institute in January of 1883. All lectures had been taken down in shorthand for publication in the *Ohio State Journal,* but the scribe, whom Scott claimed was a student, was unable to catch all of Dr. Scott's words. Scott, who was known as a rapid speaker, said he did not have time to rewrite the lecture for publication. The *Ohio State Journal* did not, therefore, publish the address, but other Columbus newspapers did.[18]

When the board of trustees met the following June they refused to reelect Scott as president or to retain him as a member of the faculty. Under the provisions of the Cannon Act it was customary procedure for the board to rehire all of the faculty annually, being free to refuse reelection as well. On this particular occasion, all of the faculty except Scott were reelected, and the decision not to continue him in office passed by a six to one vote. Later, faced with the problem of an impending commencement without an official presiding officer, the board rescinded its action on the condition that Scott resign immediately following the ceremony.[19]

When the news of Scott's ouster reached the campus and the community, there was shock and surprise. "His preeminent social qualities have made him an honored and delightful guest among the best homes of this city," observed one journalist. He had occupied the pulpits of many of the churches in the community, and was widely known and appreciated as a lecturer. He was "a ripe scholar and fearless investigator of truth," observed the *Ohio State Journal,* and was so received among the people of Ohio.[20]

William Henry Scott, president of Ohio University, was elected president *pro tem* to serve until another official could be designated. Within a year or so, however, the temporary nature of the appoint-

17. Mendenhall, op. cit., p. 79; in an extended footnote, pp. 70–84, Mendenhall provides a detailed explanation of Scott's disagreements with the trustees, but minimizes the matter of economic views and emphasizes the chapel issue. It appears, however, on balance, that the two issues together account for the decisiveness of the Board's action.

18. Ibid., p. 81; *Ohio State Journal,* June 25, 1883.

19. *Record of Proceedings of the Board of Trustees,* pp. 254, 255; Mendenhall, op. cit., p. 82.

20. *Ohio State Journal,* June 21, 1883.

ment was changed by the Board of Trustees. The two Scotts had much in common, observed the *Ohio State Journal*. Both had the same surnames, both were presidents of universities with names almost identical, both were noted for boldness and original thought, and both had been on trial for heresy. There was at least one difference, however, and it was an important one.[21]

James M. Comly, an ardent supporter of the university, and former editor of the *Ohio State Journal*, and now publisher of newspapers in Toledo, Ohio, said that he believed that Walter Quincy Scott was a Communist and, therefore, ought to be removed from the presidency of the university. "Believing him to be a Communist," he wrote the new editor of the Columbus *Journal*, "I approved the determination of the trustees to make a change. . . . " The religious question, Comly felt, was a false issue. He opposed campus chapel services himself and supported Scott's efforts to prevent sectarianism on the campus. Comly also reported that T. Ewing Miller, president of the board of trustees, disagreed with him on the religious issue but agreed heartily on the economic one. Miller, said Comly, "regretted that President Scott was running off into unprofitable and objectionable views with relation to the rights of property in lands, the receipt of dividends where capital assisted labor and the like." The whole question, said Comly, turned on the question of whether Scott taught the communistic doctrines which he was said to teach and, since he did not deny it, the board had to accept that as an admission of guilt.[22]

There was a great lack of precision in the 1880's about the meaning of the word *communist* and similar ephithets like nihilist and socialist. Rutherford B. Hayes once observed that these words were used by some to describe what William Dean Howells would call justice and that some who were so labelled were merely espousers of the doctrines of the Declaration of Independence and the Sermon on the Mount. Nihilism, Hayes finally decided, was a good word for such a philosophy as opposed the "money-piling tendency" which changed laws, government and morals to serve the rich

21. *Record of Proceedings of the Board of Trustees*, p. 255; *Ohio State Journal*, June 21, 1883.
22. *Ohio State Journal*, June 29, 1883.

while creating a wretched flood of poverty and crime. Hayes himself deplored the new tendency toward "a government of the rich, by the rich, and for the rich," but he, like most others, was more circumspect than Walter Quincy Scott in his public statements.[23]

The editor of the Marietta *Register* described Scott's utterances on economic questions as "like an electric shock." The chairman of the board challenged Scott about the furor over his views in January, six months before his ouster, but Scott replied that he could not be responsible for what reporters wrote about him. A day later, however, Scott published an open letter in the Columbus *Dispatch.* "The student who made the report," he said, "doubtless meant well, but the misuse of terms and ideas has utterly misrepresented me." He denied that he entertained the slightest sympathy with any form of communism or socialism, and described them as foolish and abhorrent doctrines. So far as his views concerning land ownership were concerned, he added, they were neither new nor radical.[24]

When the ouster came in June, William Isaac Chamberlain, secretary of the State Board of Agriculture, provided the most vociferous defense for the beleagured Scott. "The method of President Scott's dismissal endangers the very genius of college and university life and government," he told Columbus readers in an open letter to the *Ohio State Journal.* Chamberlain then outlined a defense of academic freedom, declaring it essential to the life of a university. He justified his right to make the observations: "Reared in a college town," he said, "myself a college graduate, and for several years a college teacher, acquainted with college men and methods all over the land, I assert that the history of college government . . . gives no precedent or resemblance to this unparalleled outrage." Chamberlain was keenly interested in college government and in the Ohio State University. He later served as president of what was then called the Iowa State Agricultural College at Ames, Iowa, and resigned to become president of Ohio

23. Charles R. Williams (ed.), *Diary and Letters of Rutherford B. Hayes,* 5 vols. (Columbus: The Ohio State Archaeological and Historical Society, 1922–26), pp. 435, 556.

24. *Dispatch* (Columbus, Ohio), January 22, 1883; Pollard, *History of the Ohio State University,* pp. 82–84.

State University but was passed over by the trustees. Then, in 1892, he himself became a member of the University board of trustees.[25]

Chamberlain asked his readers in Columbus if they could imagine the trustees of Yale, Harvard, Cornell, or Michigan deposing their presidents without warning or without notification of the reasons for their action. Chamberlain's assessment of the situation was in complete accord with the emerging concept of academic freedom. His attitude coincided entirely with the self-consciousness and the self-confidence that was growing in a national, academic community. Appointment to a university faculty, he insisted, was for life. Removal from a faculty could be justified only for reasons of immorality or incompetence clearly proved and with full warning in advance and a chance for the accused to defend himself. The issue, he said, was not whether Dr. Scott was the best possible man for the office; that was a question to be answered prior to his call. The issue was whether a man of unblemished reputation and broad attainment, regularly chosen and installed, could be secretly and suddenly dismissed.[26]

As the storm about Scott's dismissal grew in intensity, the trustees implied that one important reason for their action was Scott's lack of executive ability and administrative competence. He failed to forward important communications to them, they claimed. At issue here was Scott's retention of correspondence addressed to the trustees concerning faculty appointments, and his insistence that the faculty ought to be involved in the hiring procedure. The board which was considering the creation of a chair of agricultural chemistry planned, in the process of establishing the chair, to fill it as well. It was Dr. Scott's opinion that the board should create the chair and then fill it after considering the views of the faculty about the incumbent.[27]

To Chamberlain, the accusation that Scott was a poor administrator was a false charge aimed at hiding other reasons for the action. The students, said Chamberlain, had branded that charge

25. *Ohio State Journal* (Columbus, Ohio), June 25, 1883; Earle D. Ross, *History of the Iowa State College* (Ames: Iowa State Press, 1942), p. 107; Mendenhall, op. cit., p. 166.

26. *Ohio State Journal* (Columbus, Ohio), June 25, 1883.

27. Ibid., June 25, 1883; Mendenhall, op. cit., pp. 79, 483–84; *Record of Proceedings of the Board of Trustees*, pp. 258–59.

as "infantile" and "imbecile." Chamberlain described Scott's two year administration as "brilliant and most successful." Under Scott's leadership, students had begun to flock to the university, appropriations were secured from the legislature, new buildings had been started, the agricultural department had more than doubled in efficiency, and an agricultural experiment station and meteorological bureau had been established. "Dr. Scott was not the choice of the farmers," said Chamberlain, "their opinion was not asked." And yet, he added, in the two years of Walter Quincy Scott's administration, the university grew into the hearts and the hopes of the farmers of Ohio more than in all the years that had gone before.[28]

It was obvious, felt Chamberlain, that the trustees' action in deposing Scott was aimed at least in part at his evident proagricultural policy. Taking several board actions together, he said, you could see what looked like "a deliberate thrust at the agricultural interests of Ohio." The board that failed to renew Dr. Scott's contract had also appointed a second professor of ancient languages and failed to create the chair of agricultural chemistry.

In Chamberlain's long recital of the issues involved in Scott's dismissal, he also made reference to the economic issues. He said that he had "more than once heard the lecture which raised this wind." He did not deny that Dr. Scott had expressed the views that his critics alleged, but, he said, "I declare that they are in no sense communistic views nor subversive of just property rights." They were the philosophic views held by John Stuart Mill and Herbert Spencer, he observed, and others of the ablest political economists and social writers on both sides of the Atlantic. They were legitimate subjects for discussion, he concluded, and "If my lands or my railroad stocks are endangered by a free discussion of the general principles of political economy, then let them go." That was a far better alternative, he concluded, than gag-rule and a political inquisition.[29]

Chamberlain, however, was not content to spell out the dimensions of academic freedom. He also had a plan of action to suggest. The trustees were doing, he said, what the faculty should be doing,

28. Ibid., June 22, 25, 1883.
29. Ibid., June 25, 1883.

and the board was functioning improperly in excluding the president from its deliberations. He suggested that the trustees read the increasing number of articles in national publications regarding the governance and administration of universities to provide them with better background for their actions. For the immediate situation, however, he advocated that the Governor demand an explanation of the recent action from the trustees, because their action was "a grievous wrong to our state university and its President, and to the cause of higher education." In the meantime, he suggested, the newly elected president *pro tem* should not accept his office. "I do not see how," he observed, "any man of ability and self-respect can consent to accept a position from which the last occupant has been thus summarily and insolently ejected."[30]

Chamberlain's immediate, public, and detailed response to the ouster of Dr. Scott was of crucial importance. As secretary of the State Board of Agriculture, he was desirous of extending the influence of the agricultural community at the university, and progress seemed to be resulting from Dr. Scott's administration. His championing of the emerging concept of academic freedom, and his recognition of a national academic community with its own customs and standards for educational administration was something of a revelation for many Ohioans. Coupled with Chamberlain's extended discussion of the issue, however, four of the leading bankers and businessmen of Columbus called for Scott's reinstatement pending a legitimate hearing before the board concerning their objections to his performance as president and faculty member.[31]

Pressure increased upon Governor Charles Foster, much of it aimed at getting another reconstruction of the board of trustees. The governor asked the trustees to give him an accounting of the reasons for their recent action, and he interviewed Dr. Scott and

30. Ibid., June 25, 1883; Chamberlain referred the trustees specifically to an article on "College Presidents and the Power of Appointment," in *Century Magazine*, vol. XXVI, no. 3 (July, 1883), in which the emergent role of the president in the appointment of faculty was emphasized.

31. *Ohio State Journal* (Columbus, Ohio), June 25, 1883; W. G. Deshler, M. M. Greene, P. W. Huntington and Alfred Thomas signed the letter asking for Scott's reinstatement and indicating that they had interviewed both the former president and the president of the board of trustees before issuing their open letter.

the trustee who had voted to sustain him. It was the governor's opinion, however, that it would be useless to reinstate a man for an investigation conducted by the trustees who had already once fired him, and he viewed the clamor for reinstatement as an appeal for reconstituting the board itself.[32]

Many, including the students and the Columbus alumni, called upon him to dismiss all of the trustees, to appoint new ones, and then to reinstate Scott for his hearing. Foster, however, sought to avoid this alternative. Friends of education in the state hoped to prevent another reorganization for political reasons, and Scott himself had decried political reorganization in the life of the university. The governor was not eager to stir up the delicate political balance within the state by ousting the five Democrats and two Republicans who had been appointed to the board of trustees by his Democratic predecessor. The state's electorate had been erratic during recent elections, switching party with the change of economic conditions, and the pulse of corruption as revealed from Washington exposés. The Governor said he would not reorganize the board unless there were clear and sufficient causes, and unless he had some assurance that his action would be confirmed by the Senate.[33]

Governor Foster emerged somewhat unexpectedly as the champion of stability in the university. He suspected that the furor raised was aimed more at reorganizing the board of trustees than at regaining Scott's position, and he resisted the pressure. Though a Republican when the first normal vacancy occurred, he reappointed the Democrat whose term had expired to a second seven year term. Foster appealed to state pride in its university to justify support of it, and was the first governor to do so. On that basis he asked for appropriations for the university and in spite of the unfortunate situation, he got some. It was Foster also who helped obtain the Virginia Military District land cession for the university, and, although it brought unexpected difficulties to the institution and only gradually added to its financial strength, it ultimately provided an endowment fund half the size of the original land-grant

32. *Record of Proceedings of the Board of Trustees*, pp. 258–59; *Ohio State Journal* (Columbus, Ohio), June 26, 1883.
33. Ibid., June 22, 26, 27, 1883.

fund itself. Foster reflected a concern for the university throughout his administration, and he acted, during the crisis over Scott's ouster, to uphold one of Scott's own cardinal principles: the elimination of political reorganization of the school's governing board. For the most part, the precedent set by Foster endured.[34]

As the dispute over Scott's dismissal continued, however, the real basis for disagreement became increasingly clear. The real issue, said the editor of the *Ohio State Journal,* was the discrepancy between the law of the state as it applied to the university, and the customs and usages developing in the academic world so ably identified by William I. Chamberlain. Legally, the board of trustees was within its rights, and, in fact, was to the best of its ability, fulfilling the requirements of the state legislature. The board, said the law, had power to adopt by-laws and rules and regulations for the government of the college: it elected the president, determined the number of professors and tutors, elected them, and fixed their salaries. The board was authorized to remove the president or any professor or tutor "whenever the interests of the college, in their judgment, shall require." Even beyond that, the board had the power to fix the course of instruction and to prescribe the extent and the character of experiments conducted in the school. It was a "wonderfully wide breach," said the editor, between modern academic custom and state law. The delegation of authority to the board by the legislature had been extensive and unequivocal; it provided no accommodation whatever for developing academic customs.[35]

As the students had done at Wooster, the students at Ohio State University ardently defended Dr. Scott. News of his resignation came upon them like a thunderclap, observed the newspapers. Although many had gone home for the vacation, those remaining and those living in Columbus called a meeting of protest. The student meeting was lively and reflected the indignation of the students. Expressions of strong personal liking for Dr. Scott were balanced by equally strong declarations of dislike of the trustees. Dr. Scott's departure, said the students in a set of resolutions, was

34. Mendenhall, op. cit., pp. 112–13.
35. *Ohio State Journal* (Columbus, Ohio), June 25, 26, 1883.

an irreparable loss to the university resulting from "infantile" and "embecile" actions of trustees. The students marched in a body to Scott's residence and expressed their esteem for him and their sorrow at his leaving. He responded by thanking them for their kind wishes, but he urged them to stand by the Ohio State University and not to let personal feelings affect their loyalty to their alma mater. The *Ohio State Journal,* whose editor disapproved of the student actions, characterized Scott's address as "marked by good taste."[36]

The *Ohio State Journal* deplored such direct and unorderly student action. An indignation meeting by a "small minority of students" was certainly not the best method for settling the matter, counseled the editor. The students, he said, should have addressed a request to the governor or to the board of trustees through some gentleman of standing. Such a procedure, he advised, would have resulted in a statement of the causes which led to the action. He felt that the students were too eager to take direct action, grow excited, and to use hard words and slanderous epithets.

Originally, however, the editor of the *Journal* had said that the students should not have demonstrated because such actions might well force the board to reveal the real reasons for its action. Dr. Scott's reputation would be better served, he implied, by silence. General Comly, in Toledo, himself felt that the matter should be dropped with a simple announcement of the change, but he later changed his mind and issued a long statement. The *Journal* editor suggested that Comly revealed too much by his statement and should have been more circumspect.[37]

Comly, however, was goaded into making further statements by student-originated charges that the real cause for Scott's ouster was that he had refused to doctor the examination grades of Comly's son and the son of the president of the board of trustees. The added circulation which William I. Chamberlain and other Columbus newspapers gave the accusation prompted Comly to say more and brought a great many of the issues out into the open. "Things are stated on the street and in the papers," said Chamber-

36. Ibid., June 22, 26, 1883; Mendenhall, op. cit., p. 83.
37. *Ohio State Journal* (Columbus, Ohio), June 22, 26, 1883.

lain, that were believed by the people. It was either true, he said, that the sons of two of Dr. Scott's most active enemies had trouble in passing their examinations and that Dr. Scott would not consent to favoritism in their behalf, or it was false and should be publicly denied. Chamberlain felt that sufficient evidence should be presented to answer such an accusation and to provide the real information behind the ouster. The theory current, said Chamberlain, was that Albert Allen, the secretary of the Board of trustees and a Democratic politician desirous of getting Scott's place for a fellow Democrat, had whipped up the personal pique of Comly and Miller and other trustees by either the chapel issue or Scott's economic views, whichever was more effective.[38]

Comly, however, immediately denied the charge that his son's grades had affected his position, and made the complete report of the reasons for the board action as he saw them in which he labeled Scott a Communist. It was in this statement that the Columbus editor thought Comly went too far. The situation in Columbus was not as serious as Comly had been led to believe, said the editor, and he did not need to defend himself quite so thoroughly. Nevertheless, Comly admitted that his son would not be returning to the Columbus campus. He was "too young for his classes," said his father, and would be better off "out of school entirely for the present." For the students, the reasons that had been given for Scott's ouster did not seem valid, and the suggestion that a student's grades were involved seemed much more likely. Besides, the Comly boy had left campus several weeks before the end of the term, "ordered out by his physician," said his father, and that was conclusive evidence so far as other students were concerned.[39]

Actually, during Walter Quincy Scott's two year administration, the faculty had toughened examination procedures considerably, and had set standards to determine who should remain in school and who should not. They established minimum loads for all students and required them to pass examinations in better than half their courses or lose their standing in the university. Even a com-

38. Ibid., June 29, 1883.
39. Ibid., June 22, 29, 1883.

muting student from Columbus was required to carry a minimum load, or secure permission of the faculty to reduce it. Students in difficulty were given an additional term in which to pass half or more of their examinations. If they then failed to do so, they were dismissed. Overall, the admissions standards, the examination procedures, and the requirements within course programs were toughened during Scott's brief administration. One of his critics dismissed the whole conflict between Scott and his board as a "curricular" matter and it was to these changes that he had reference. The fact that Scott could advocate a toughening of the school program and yet at the same time retain the overwhelming and enthusiastic confidence of his students and show an increase in enrollment was an unnoted achievement of his short administration.[40]

With summer vacation underway, concerted student activity was impossible to sustain. Columbus journalists advised the people to remain calm, view the controversy objectively, and concede the legality of the board's action if not its wisdom. The governor agreed with this line of reasoning and behaved in such a way to diminish controversy.

Furthermore, the institution's supporters thinking of the university's prosperity, were beginning to fear the repercussions of the affair. The alumni had "respectfully demanded" that Walter Quincy Scott be reinstated, and that the trustees be removed from office "unless a better way be provided." And it seemed, perhaps, that a better way was to let the matter ride quietly. Comly had said in the beginning of the dispute that it was a matter which should be dropped "right where it is," and he advocated as amicable a settlement as possible. Everyone, including the faculty, evidently, was willing to let the matter drop; everyone, that is, except the students. The summer vacation delayed any further action on their part, but they would be the last to let Walter Quincy Scott be forgotten.[41]

In a less public way, some of Walter Quincy Scott's other friends remembered him too. He accepted a post in Worthington and, according to Washington Gladden, the ouster from the Ohio

40. Minutes of the Faculty, I, 315–17.
41. *Ohio State Journal* (Columbus, Ohio), June 22, 27, 1883.

State University did not affect his standing among those who knew
the details of the affair. William I. Chamberlain recommended him
for a professorship of history at Adelbert College of Western Reserve University, recently moved from Hudson to Cleveland.
Rutherford B. Hayes, one of the new trustees of the Western Reserve University, served on the committee seeking to fill the faculty
vacancy. Chamberlain advised that he was an admirable choice
for the chair with good character, intelligence, competence, thorough scholarship, youthful vigor, and an effective manner of speech.
Gladden also recommended him without qualification. Scott's capacity for inspiring young men with an enthusiasm for learning,
said Gladden, made him an admirable choice for a college professorship.[42]

Others, too, took note of Scott's qualifications and his availability.
The trustees of Phillips Exeter Academy in Exeter, Massachusetts,
felt that fresh blood was needed at their institution and they looked
west to find it. Dr. Nicholas E. Soule, a trustee who lived in Cincinnati, recommended that they select Walter Quincy Scott. Scott's
dash, power, and freedom from convention seemingly promised
to provide for Exeter what the trustees felt that it needed. They
hired him at a salary higher than that he had received as president
of Ohio State University, and 33⅓ percent higher than the salary
of his succesor. In addition, the trustees provided him with a home
on the school grounds.

At Exeter, Scott emphasized the sciences over the classics, attacked the hallowed traditions of the institution, began awarding
diplomas, and based all official distinctions on academic rather
than social achievement. By 1889, though enrollment was up and
new buildings had been built, Scott resigned. His breezy western
manner and contempt for the traditions of the eastern academy
had won him little support even among the students. His seeming
lack of interest in increasing the number of his pupils who gained
admission to the select eastern colleges appeared increasingly in-
appropriate. His insistence that student decorum off the school

42. H. E. Lee to R. B. Hayes, March 24, 1884; George H. Ely to John C.
Lee. April 10, 1884; George H. Ely to R. B. Hayes, April 29, 1884, Hayes
Papers, Rutherford B. Hayes Library, Fremont, Ohio.

grounds was the responsibility of the community itself led to the use of police power to curb student enthusiasms, and further tarnished the image of the western headmaster in an eastern academy.[43]

Scott then held pastorates in Albany, New York, and Elmhurst, Pennsylvania, and from 1902 to 1912, taught church history and ethnic religions at the Bible Teachers' Training School in New York City. The Bible Teachers' College had been founded in 1900 by Wilbert Webster White who had been deeply influenced by William Rainey Harper, a specialist in Hebrew at Yale and later president of the University of Chicago. The school exuded Harper's enthusiasm for reform in theological education and Scott felt at home in this liberal atmosphere. He died on May 9, 1917. In 1909, the trustees of the Ohio State University made him president emeritus. The volatile and innovative Dr. Scott had had but a short tenure as president of Ohio State University, but in his two year administration he gave dramatic focus to the major educational trends in Ohio and those emerging in the nation. Neither Ohio, nor its university, however, could take Scott or the emerging trends in full dosage and his tenure was in fact a traumatic experience from which the institution never recovered. Throughout his life, Walter Quincy Scott was inclined to bring conflicting viewpoints to a head; he saw educational value in the very conflict of accepted versus innovative views. Uncompromising and perhaps overly rash, Scott brought the crucial issues facing the institution into the open. In the aftermath of his ouster at Ohio State University, Albert Allen, the secretary of the board of trustees, whom Chamberlain had accused of stirring up the controversy, resigned. He was replaced by Alexis Cope, a man who was to hold the position until 1905. The power that continued to accrue to that office, however, was of central importance in the university's development.[44]

43. Laurence M. Crosbie, *The Phillips Exeter Academy: A History* (Norwood, Mass.: Phillips Exeter Academy, 1924), pp. 134–39.

44. Ibid., pp. 141–42.

CHAPTER 6

Students and the Emergence of the University

Although enrolled in a unique institution, the students at the Ohio State University were, in many respects, similar to their counterparts on other campuses. This was not entirely so, however, because they attended an institution struggling into existence under different conditions than those surrounding the beginnings of any other institution in Ohio. They studied under a faculty fully conscious of the new and different enterprise in which they were engaged. It was a faculty not at all the hapless victims of a hostile or indifferent state in an institution that was ignored or opposed by farmers, industrialists, and other institutions. While this may later have characterized their self-perception, in the beginning, the faculty was conscious of a mission to do something new in Ohio, even in the face of hostility and indifference. The students shared that spirit. If they differed from students elsewhere it was their direct participation in the debates about the nature of the new school and their opportunity to speak out and express their views.

What kind of students attended the new Ohio college? In large measure, they were residents of Columbus and Franklin County, who, like students elsewhere, attended the institution at hand seeking to serve their own needs and the ambitions of their parents within the program designed by the institution to serve its own needs and ambitions. Within the group, however, were the sons and daughters of faculty members who shared their fathers' views of the worthwhileness of the new experiment. From out of town came a smattering of students attracted by the newness, the uniqueness, the promise of something other than the denominational college atmosphere which the new institution offered.[1]

By 1883, however, a change in student spirit was evident. A poem, "Let Us Unite in Prayer," appeared in the student yearbook, *The Makio*, before Walter Quincy Scott's ouster, and reflected student objections not only to the Board of Trustees' insistence upon compulsory chapel but also to the evident inclination of many faculty members, after a ten-year struggle, to comply:

> As twelve o'clock through all the halls
> The little bell to prayer calls;
> And with its ring it seems to say,
> As it peals forth from day to day
> The Trustees having bribed the bell,
> To speak what it deems false to tell.
>
> .   .   .   .   .   .
>
> We all are here to bow our head.
> And pray to live when we are dead;
> And march like cattle to our stalls,
> While mourning drapes the college walls
> From senior down to lowest prep
> Who looks with awe at every step.
>
> .   .   .   .   .   .
>
> Our teachers too, before us all
> Their bodies big, example small,
> Come slyly in and take their place
> That they may get their share of grace.
> These men are wise and so keep still
> And don't reveal their thoughts at will.

1. For an analysis of the students and their hometowns see the University Catalogs and student directories in the *Annual Reports of the Board of Trustees, 1870–80; The Makio* for the early years includes additional data about students, their home towns, anticipated future occupations, political preferences, and religious backgrounds; see for instance, *The Makio*, vol. I (Columbus, Ohio, 1880), pp. 38–39.

The Trustees do as we all know
That we may thus to heaven go
May they go there before we do
And tell them we are coming too.

.   .   .   .   .   .

And thus their whim becomes a law,
One more august you never saw
Which to repeal we strive in vain
For we must pray though it does pain
But this we write to send above
To show how well we freedom love.[2]

The following year, the editors of *The Makio* implied in their opening editorial that they were under instructions, presumably from the new president, to prevent the "return of former dangerous poetry" and assured their readers that their poets for 1884 were using pens "as pure and wholesome as heaven's air."[3]

Nevertheless, the editors voiced student objections to "that frequently fatal course—a change of superintendency" which resulted from what they called the institution's peculiar form of management. "In view of our knowledge of affairs then and since," said the editors, "we are compelled to voice the unanimous sentiment of the students." The removal of Walter Quincy Scott, they said, from the chair of logic and political economy, was a serious injury to the institution. He was an intelligent teacher, a student of advanced ideas, and a man eminently fitted for developing firm ideas of true manhood, and the students recognized him as their worthy mentor. The student editorial did not so much dispute the right of the trustees to change the institution's presiding officer, as it questioned the wisdom of their denying so effective a teacher his place on the faculty. In a subtle jab at the new Dr. Scott, the editors observed that W. Q. Scott's position would be filled only with "great and almost insurmountable difficulty."[4]

From the beginning, the students at the Ohio Agricultural and Mechanical College had reserved the right to speak out about

2. Ibid., III (1883), 96–101.
3. Ibid., IV (1884), 7.
4. Ibid., IV (1884), 9.

their institution. They directed their attention from time to time to governors, legislators, and the general public, castigating them for inadequate support or, on occasion, praising them for sympathetic assistance. Ohio refused to support a state university, students often lamented, and they mused: "Oh, that we were a worn out canal, or a mismanaged prison." On at least one occasion, the faculty specifically prohibited student lobbying with the legislature as unwarranted student interference with the university's relations with the state government. The students, having reviewed pending legislation in the General Assembly, appeared to present their own views about which bills should pass and which should not.[5]

When it came, students criticized compulsory chapel, and, on at least one occasion, set off a loud demonstration in the basement below the chapel, disrupting the services. They resented compulsory military drill, which the trustees felt was required by the conditions of the Morrill Act, and sympathized with faculty members who as a protest sought to make agricultural and mechanical courses mandatory too since they were also stipulated in the same part of the act. Students long agitated for coeducational boarding clubs and chafed at the prohibitions against such socializing. Even liberal faculty members, however, were disconcerted by this outgrowth of coeducation, and a regular series of "hygiene lectures" for men and "fatherly chats" for the ladies was authorized.[6]

Students also deplored the demerit system whereby they were given demerits for absence, tardiness, coming to class unprepared, and similar offenses with expulsion from school a definite probability for regular offenders. They considered the system old fashioned and not in keeping with the modern and progressive spirit which they envisioned for their college.[7] With the advent of William Henry Scott as president, students were merciless in their criticisms of what they perceived as administrative cowardice and trustee domination. The board degraded the faculty, said students, and made them mere menials by the process of annual election. Between

5. Ibid., V (1885); Minutes of the Faculty, I, 234.
6. Minutes of the Faculty, I, 36, 37, 101, 175–76, 198–99, 203, 276; II, 175–76.
7. *Makio*, VI (1886), 86.

the insolent practice and a policy of low salaries, the students were wont to complain, the best men of the faculty were driven away while the staff filled up with second rate instructors.[8]

Student opinion, as reflected in *The Makio,* placed the blame for much of their displeasure on President W. H. Scott. They characterized him as a prima donna, as behind the times, and as unoriginal, and perfunctory in the classroom. Student behavior toward the new president was so bad during his first year that his colleagues on the faculty sent a special report to the trustees in which they regretted the condition of student morale but absolved the new president of responsibility for it. He had done well in his first year, they all agreed, and it was unfortunate that the students should remain so unreconciled to the new situation.[9]

The second Scott lacked the ability to establish easy and relaxed communication with students which his predecessor possessed and they never identified with him. Washington Gladden said that Walter Quincy Scott inspired students and their feeling for him had been amply demonstrated both at Wooster and at Ohio State University. William Henry Scott, on the other hand, was timid and, as he described it to Rutherford B. Hayes, had an exaggerated aversion to appearing before crowds. Try as he might, he confessed, he had never overcome the weakness, and no matter how well he prepared to address a student gathering, his thoughts would "disastrously leave me when the occasion comes to express them from the platform." Such timidity in a person viewed as an interloper and strict authoritarian was easily misunderstood by the students and given an uncharitable interpretation.[10]

The students almost made a tradition of baiting their president. Three years after his election, student displeasure was unabated, and they accused Scott of sending his son to Johns Hopkins so that he could copy the lectures given there in psychology for his father's use at the Ohio State University. In an imaginary letter from the son, "Chawly," to his father, Dr. Scott, which appeared in *The*

8. Ibid., V (1885), 3, 28.
9. Ibid., V (1885), 4, 88; VI (1886), 86; VIII (1888), 139, 147; Minutes of the Faculty, I, 102 ff.
10. William Henry Scott to R. B. Hayes, June 14, 1888, Hayes Papers.

Makio Ohio State University's president was advised that at Hopkins there was no red tape, no demerit system, no compulsory chapel, and no fighting and bickering among the faculty, all of which, by implication, were characteristic of the Ohio State University. "Chawly" concluded his epistle by saying, "But really, Pa, since my short stay here, I can't help but realize that your plans for running The Ohio State University are as sadly out of date as was your style of cutting hair."[11]

Student complaints about the demerit system and compulsory chapel blamed W. H. Scott, although both changes occurred before W. Q. Scott was ousted. Professor Mendenhall and the earlier Scott had persuaded the faculty to abolish the demerit system in 1881–82. Under the old system, a student was dismissed for accumulating twenty demerits in one term or a total of forty in a three term year. The student could receive four demerits merely for missing a class, two for inability to recite when called upon in any class, and one for arriving late. Others could be assigned as the faculty felt necessary. The reform which Scott and Mendenhall designed eliminated the system entirely, and required that the faculty monitor student behavior and take action only in exceptional, individual cases. Enforcement of standards became a matter for professorial and presidential discretion. Though popular with students, within a year the experiment was considered a failure by the faculty. President Walter Quincy Scott had been dilatory in reporting the compilation of student offenses for faculty perusal, and the faculty had to nudge him twice to take action against those whom the faculty had not excused. Under these circumstances, the faculty favored a reversion to the earlier system.[12]

So also compulsory chapel had been instituted before the new president arrived. The real basis of complaint, however, seemed to reside in the fact that the new president enforced both unpopular sets of regulations in full sympathy with their intent and purpose. He favored both compulsory chapel and the Sunday afternoon alternative which had been suggested in lieu of the daily services. He

11. *Makio*, VI (1886), 86.
12. Minutes of the Faculty, I, 246–47, 317, 323–25, 328–29, 339–40; II, 17–18.

also favored a stricter decorum in general than had his predecessor. In the absence of their champion, the students vented their ire on his successor.

Student complaints about "red tape" were aimed at the growing procedures for scheduling and record keeping which had actually been established before Edward Orton had retired but which became more visible as enrollment mounted. The faculty, under Dr. W. H. Scott, codified procedures for registration, examinations, admission, matriculation, student classification, the provision of credentials, and the maintenance of records. Procedures for organizing the work of the school were developing in almost model fashion from a modern standpoint, but the growing procedures for securing "class cards," determining a "normal load," obtaining permission to carry less than a "normal load," checking records to see whether one was meeting requirements, and the like, became increasingly burdensome to students. Here again, however, it was the second Dr. Scott's attitude that seemed to irritate students most. He was an experienced college teacher and an experienced college president. He welcomed clear cut procedures, unambiguous regulations, and the mental and moral neatness of good order. He was not as popular as his predecessor, but he brought to a fruitful culmination the process of establishing and organizing the university. His methods of operation were pleasing to trustees and the general public.[13]

The organizing of student and faculty behaviors, however, had begun in earnest under the first Dr. Scott. A four level grading system—"Passed with Merit," "Passed," "Conditioned," and "Failed" —with standing to be determined by written examination whenever possible, was formalized within six weeks of Walter Quincy Scott's arrival. The same code for determining student standing specified that a "condition" in a course had to be removed by examination not later than the middle of the following term. It set a minimum load of fifteen actual classroom hours per week in compliance with the standard set by the Association of Ohio Colleges and required that a student be passing in ten of the fifteen in order to remain in school. No special exceptions were to be made for part-time students from the city. The presumption was that the fifteen hour

13. Ibid., II, 32, 178–79, 205, 212, 236–45.

minimum was special consideration enough. The code also required a student to repeat any failed course, and stipulated that if a student failed part of a continuing course he had to repeat the entire sequence or obtain special permission not to do so. At the same time that these standards were established, the faculty also adopted the one year experiment abolishing the demerit system.[14]

During the first Scott's administration, the faculty also adopted an organizational plan for the college requiring that all students, except resident graduate students, enroll in one of four schools and pursue a stipulated course program. The four schools were the School of Agriculture, the School of Arts and Philosophy, the School of Engineering, and the School of Science. The four schools emphasized the philosophical breadth of the school envisioned as the Ohio State University, and in part represented the compromise among conflicting philosophical viewpoints. In the School of Agriculture, the practical and utilitarian program of agricultural education was acknowledged. The School of Arts and Philosophy provided the traditional classical program which was, for many, the very essence of higher education. The School of Engineering embodied the practical mechanical program to which the school was obligated. The School of Science provided permanent status for the new spirit of scientism both as an independent pursuit and as the foundation for agriculture and engineering.[15]

Each of the four schools was governed by a standing committee composed of four members of the respective school faculties and the president of the university. The committees, which were actually subunits of the larger university faculty, had jurisdiction over the studies and the discipline of students within each area. The total faculty became involved in those areas in which the requirements of one school effected students in the others. The faculty then proceeded with an exhaustive rearrangement of courses and a redefinition of degree requirements which transcended the ouster of Dr. W. Q. Scott. All of these changes, and some others, culminated in the second Dr. Scott's administration, and he reaped the student displeasure which many of them occasioned.[16]

14. Ibid., I, 315–17.
15. Ibid., I, 342–43.

During this same period of time, the faculty considered one matter which had little immediate concern for the great majority of students. They sought to delineate and systematize the school's policies and procedures relative to graduate degrees. In June of 1882, in assigning all undergraduates to the four newly designated schools of the university, the faculty exempted graduate students from those divisions. They did not create a graduate school, but their action did indicate that the graduate program was one of total university concern and not the concern of specified curricular areas. There were, as yet, no codified regulations concerning graduate work, but the faculty was opposed to the awarding of doctoral degrees on a purely honorary basis and so informed the board of trustees. The faculty was also insistent that degrees ought not to be awarded without resident advanced study.[17]

In March of 1883, an alumnus of the class of 1879 submitted a thesis entitled, "A Contribution to the Histology of the Mucous Lining of the Upper Eyelid," and asked that he be considered for the doctorate even though he had not been in residence. The faculty referred the thesis to a committee composed of two members of the Ohio State University faculty and Dr. Newell Martin of Johns Hopkins University. Two weeks later, the faculty voted to deny the degree because the committee had reported that the work was not of sufficient merit to justify the awarding of the degree. The faculty also turned down the request of another member of the class of 1879 because the applicant had not specified which doctoral degree he wanted or the field of competency in which he felt qualified. Throughout the decade, the annual reports of the university indicated anywhere from three to seven resident graduate students, predominantly in the science fields, many of whom served as tutors and assistant instructors while pursuing advanced studies.[18]

Finally, in October of 1885, the faculty established a committee to codify policies governing graduate students. By the end of the

16. Ibid., I, 343–46, 348–49.
17. Ibid., I, 332–34.
18. Ibid., II, 32, 33; *Annual Reports of the Board of Trustees to the Governor*, 1875–1885.

year, the faculty adopted regulations which specified that the master's degree should be awarded to students who had: (1) completed a year of residence, (2) passed a suitable examination, and (3) submitted an acceptable thesis. For students who did not meet the year's residence requirement, the degree could not be awarded until after three years had elapsed from the time the student received the baccalaureate degree and then only if, in the opinion of the faculty, the three years had been spent in a suitably educational endeavor. The requirements for the doctor of philosophy degree were: (1) three years residence, (2) study in at least two departments of the university culminated by a successful examinations in both departments, and (3) the submission of an acceptable thesis. The time requirement for nonresident candidates was like that for the master's degree except that the period was to be five years instead of three.[19]

Of more immediate concern to most students, however, the faculty discussed for more than a year the advantages and disadvantages of adopting an elective system. In February of 1886, a committee of the faculty reported that the "university has fallen behind many of its sister colleges in the state" in that it failed to offer its students a reasonable amount of election in their programs. The committee felt "that the people and the students are entitled to demand that we shall keep abreast of the advancing spirit of educational method." The committee's certainty that some system of election should be provided was not matched by an equal certainty in its recommendations. It submitted two schemes and invited the total faculty to resolve their differences. The shift from specified and required programs to freer election was a difficult change for faculties everywhere, and the committee recognized the need for caution and full faculty discussion. The committee was aware, it reported, that it was objectionable to some to depart from the older system, but it assured the faculty that "no one shall be assigned on the one hand to obscurity or on the other to undue prominence" if the faculty established a limited system of electives. After months of debate, the faculty ventured into the ground, establishing a limited

19. Minutes of the Faculty, II, 153, 166–67.

system of elective courses coupled with a series of seminars for upper level students. The changes were to be effective in the 1886–87 academic year.[20]

While all these actions were being taken to codify the procedures and policies governing students in their academic endeavors, the faculty also organized itself for better efficiency. The system of four schools relegated many questions to smaller faculty bodies and freed the university faculty of a great deal of work. Beyond this, the faculty created a Committee on Admissions to handle the examining of students and the determination of the myriad appeals which that process evoked. They also established procedures for certifying high schools by visitations of small teams of faculty. Once a high school had passed such an inspection, its students were admissible without examination or penalty except for specific course deficiencies which they were required to make up. Students from unlisted schools were required to meet the conditions set by the Committee on Admissions.[21]

Finally, by 1887, the faculty had adopted a full statement of rules and regulations governing the college and its four schools, its graduate program, the military battalion, and the preparatory department. Dr. William Henry Scott had effectively harnessed the energies and the interests of the faculty and had resolved some crucial and difficult problems in the school's organization.

The students, however, had been much more concerned about other issues that seemed to them to be of greater or at least of equal importance, but neither students nor faculty seemed to be aware of the widening chasm between their respective interests. The chasm between students and teachers in the old, traditional colleges devoted to mental and moral discipline had been just as wide. In the establishment of most new institutions, however, there was an initial period during which the close relationship of faculty and student grew from shared hopes and mutual hardships. Johns Hopkins and Stanford had enjoyed such a brief interlude in student-faculty relations, but at neither place did it last for more than a decade.[22]

20. Ibid., II, 157, 163, 178–79, 181, 189–91.
21. Ibid., I, 343–44; II, 48–49, 197.
22. Veysey, op. cit., p. 295.

Throughout Edward Orton's administration, the relations of faculty with students were remarkably good. On one occasion Orton observed, "We have been happily free during our short history from the relics of that barbarism that still survive in so many colleges in the shape of hazing and the reckless destruction of property." He estimated that in the first six years of occupancy in the college building that wanton destruction had amounted to no more than a dollar's worth of damage per year. On another occasion he told the board of trustees that the institution had been happily spared of those unfortunate collisions between faculty and students which occurred at other places, interrupting and embittering college life. This era of good feeling might well have ended soon anyway, but student reaction to the ouster of the charismatic Walter Q. Scott hastened that development. The faculty could not have condoned student treatment of Scott's successor nor their sharp jabs at the board of trustees and as a result the interlude came to an end.[23]

New student interests were emerging anyway. To their interest in coeducational boarding clubs, students had added an enthusiasm for dancing parties and other kinds of social gatherings in the literary society rooms which were opposed by the faculty. William Henry Scott was very specifically opposed to dancing parties and, though the faculty as a whole seemed willing to permit such diversions, they reversed their stand in order not to embarrass the President. They suggested that such affairs might be held, but that they ought not to be presented as official student or university functions. Students had also wandered far afield from the campus in the search of living quarters that appealed to them. The faculty then required that they register their domiciles and be subject to faculty visitation. In the face of such faculty opposition, students had become increasingly interested in Greek-letter fraternities. Here again, however, they met with the disapprobation of the faculty. Their teachers had reached a consensus that such organizations should be discouraged at the Ohio State University, but they stopped short of proscribing them. Student relations with students at other campuses as a result of speech and oratorical contests, fraternity chapter exchange visits, and inter-collegiate athletics prompted the faculty

23. Pollard, *History of the Ohio State University*, p. 62.

to establish restrictions on absence from the campus and conditions governing travel as representatives of the university.[24]

The lengthening list of rules and regulations resulted in a growing estrangement between students and faculty and the close identification between the two which had characterized the institution during the formative decade began to disappear. Professors became particularly annoyed at the students' careless use of chewing tobacco which, they said, made floors and walls a deplorable sight. With the installation of a telephone in University Hall, the faculty became even more disturbed by the "indiscriminant use of the telephone made by the college students."[25]

The first of these two problems they solved by firm instructions to the janitors to keep the walls and floors scrubbed as well as possible and by rules prohibiting the use of university facilities after an "unreasonable hour." The second, the faculty debated in vain throughout the decade and the final solution came only with the expansion of the telephone system itself. At one point the problem was so serious that the faculty appealed to the board of trustees to devise a system for resolving it, but they were no more successful. Finally, students were hired to attend the telephone, and students were charged five cents per call to pay for the monitoring.[26]

The most serious conflict between students and the university administration, however, involved the students' penchant for discussing freely whatever university business they cared to discuss. Such freedom occasionally embarrassed the administration in its efforts to win support from the legislature and the public at large. Student fulminations about the university and its affairs raised questions about what might be going on at the school, and the students' delight in shock raised community eyebrows. The *Lantern* and the *Makio* and even student orations at state oratorical contests dealt with the university and its affairs as the rightful province of student concern. Immediately following the ouster of Walter Quincy Scott, the faculty enacted regulations specifying that all stu-

24. Minutes of the Faculty, I, 26, 81, 203, 324, 328–29; II, 80, 84, 134, 162, 264.
25. Ibid., II, 31; I, 302, 310.
26. Ibid., I, 302, 310, II, 30, 31, 64.

dent essays and orations that were to be given publicly had to be approved in advance. This was an effort to tone down the student attack on the trustees and the incoming president. For a time, the faculty even considered prohibiting Ohio State University students from attending the Ohio State Oratorical Contest for 1884 which was to be held at Wooster, Scott's former institution. Walter Quincy Scott's champions in his two former schools, it was feared, would have given the contest a decidedly different complexion from that intended by the professors of literature and elocution who encouraged such gatherings.[27]

In 1885, further restrictions on the students' rights of assembly were enacted. The faculty specified that no arrangements were to be made by students for any public gathering or exercise in a college building without the prior consent of the faculty. Furthermore, since literary society rooms were being used for a variety of student gatherings, the faculty specified that these rooms were not to be used for any other purpose than the usual weekly literary exercises of the groups unless prior approval was obtained. This effectively ruled out their use for social gatherings, secret fraternity meetings, and similar purposes.[28]

The following year, after a steady effort over a period of several years to tone down the content of student publications and their ill effect upon the general public, the faculty prohibited the sale or distribution of any student publications on the university premises on commencement day. The students had come to regard the day as a golden opportunity to present their views to visiting alumni, legislators, state officials, and university friends and parents who attended the ceremonies.[29] On the basis of this ruling, the faculty then constructed procedures whereby students might qualify their publications for campus sale. At first, they asked that the finished publication be submitted to a faculty committee for review and the committee had power to grant or deny the privilege of public sale. A short while later, the faculty required that the galley proofs as well as the final publication be submitted, the first for censorship,

27. Ibid., II, 84, 135, 136, 199; *Makio*, IV (1884), 7; V (1885), 3.
28. Minutes of the Faculty, II, 135, 136.
29. Ibid., II, 199.

the second for review as before. Finally, the procedure required that the manuscript be cleared before the type was set, that the proofs be cleared before the publication was printed, and that the finished product be reviewed before it was placed on sale.[30]

The restrictive policies of the faculty derived from several causes. First and primary was the undimished student criticism of the president and the condemnation of the trustees for firing Walter Quincy Scott. The students refused to forget Walter Quincy Scott for a great number of years, and by the time they had, their anti-administration stance was second nature. In addition, the students at The Ohio State Univesity, like students elsewhere, were attracted to new and innovative concepts of student life that were not in keeping with other traditions nor with popular views of what life among students should be.

Student life was indisputably changing. "Student life is not as might be supposed by the outside looker-on," advised the editors of the *Makio*, and they wrote of student reaction to reading, recitation, and investigation that manifested itself in sports, joviality, and general good times. By 1888, 200 university students and 150 preparatory students belonged to six fraternities and three literary societies, and in addition supported an oratorical association, a Young Men's Christian Association, a Young Women's Christian Association, and a missionary society. The beginnings of sororities for the women were obvious among the less formal women's groups. Students published the *Fortnightly Lantern*, the *Engineer and Critic*, and the *Makio*. They also participated in the university band, the Engineers Association, the Thurman Club, the College Choir, and the military battalion. In addition, there were several baseball clubs, a football team, a coeducational lawn tennis club, a bicycle club, a fencing club.[31]

By 1890, William Henry Scott was generally pleased with student character and conduct, but he considered the plethora of student activities a growing evil. The students gave too much attention to extraneous things, he said. While baseball, tennis, class and fraternity meetings, parties and banquets, and political clubs

30. Minutes of the Faculty, II, 199, 305, 333.
31. *Makio*, I (1880). 3; VIII (1888), passim.

might in themselves be allowable and commendable, he conjectured, they were distractions which together made disastrous inroads on student time. The evil resulted from the immaturity of students and their weak powers of self-restraint, he decided, and he saw it as the responsibility of the school to superimpose the maturity and restraint of the faculty for the shortcomings of the students.[32]

The trends of student life were also viewed with alarm by some outside observers. James M. Comly, a key Ohio newspaper publisher and long-time booster of the state university idea, had once described eastern colleges as being given to "extravagant follies," and, he claimed, that by being so they degraded manhood in a rich man's environment of boat racing, baseball pitching, batting and fielding, and the acting of dramas. The faculties at eastern institutions, the editor had charged, encouraged young men to waste their time in such pursuits, and yet led them to believe that they were the future magnates and rulers of the land. He viewed with alarm the rising hedonism on American campuses and advised Ohio college leaders to prevent similar developments among their charges.[33]

The large number of struggling little colleges in Ohio, Comly observed, were not so bad after all. The growing sentiment to combine them and to abolish the weaker ones in order to build a Cornell, a Princeton, a Harvard, a Williams, or a Yale was not necessarily desirable in view of the trends in student life at these so-called model institutions. Even if "the people of the Atlantic slope," he said, "look down upon the universities and colleges of Ohio . . . with a contempt bordering on the superlative" it was time to consider whether the inferiority did not really exist at the rich men's schools in the East. He took Ohio college presidents and professors to task for being "bulldozed" into adopting the Eastern notion that Ohio's schools were too numerous, too inferior, and too inefficient. The editor reflected the growing self-consciousness of the western universities and a growing sectionalism in higher education which denoted a typical eastern as opposed to a typical western

32. "Report of the President," in *Report of the Board of Trustees of The Ohio State University to the Governor of Ohio, 1890–91* (Columbus, 1891).
33. *Ohio State Journal* (Columbus, Ohio), May 31, 1881.

institution. He also reflected the growing reaction to student hedonism reflected in fraternities, athletics, bands, and the growing social life of the college campus.[34]

John E. Bradley of Jacksonville, Illinois, described the "Higher Life of the College" at the fifteenth annual meeting of the National Council of Education in 1896, denoting the changes that were occurring and confessing that he was somewhat uncomfortable about them. Between 1870 and 1890, he said, the colleges were transformed. Their standards of admission were raised, their courses of study were extended, greater freedom in choice of studies and in personal conduct was extended to students, and fraternities as well as athletic and musical organizations had appeared. The speaker was even more uncomfortable, however, in the discussion which followed his remarks. "A boy in college ought to spend a thousand dollars a year if he can have it," said one commentator. "There should be careful avoidance of all that would interfere with the independent initiative and self-direction of students," said another.[35]

The purpose of college was to provide experiences that developed self-reliance and self-guidance, concluded a professor from Cornell. But it was a different purpose which the speaker from Illinois had denoted: it was the responsibility of the college to substitute its molding influences for the love and watchfulness of the student's home, he had said. It was this purpose, *in loco parentis,* which James M. Comly had had in mind when he talked about the superiority of Ohio's colleges over schools in the East.[36]

The fraternity system, which typified the new spirit in student life, appealed to students in Ohio as well as in the East, and was particularly popular at Ohio State University. In 1871, students at Ohio Wesleyan had observed that the better colleges were the ones with Greek-letter societies. "Old Yale is teeming with them. Young Cornell has grown with their strength," said the editors of the Ohio

34. Ibid., May 31, 1881.
35. John E. Bradley, "The Higher Life of the College," Report of the Committee on Higher Education in N.E.A., *Proceedings of the Fifteenth Annual Meeting of the National Council of Education, Buffalo, N. Y., 1896* (Chicago: University of Chicago Press, 1896), pp. 428–29.
36. Ibid., pp. 429–31; *Ohio State Journal* (Columbus, Ohio), May 31, 1881.

Wesleyan *Collegian.* In fact, said the editors, where fraternities did not exist the school was either too insignificant to attract their attention or else it was controlled by a spirit of fanatical intolerance.[37]

In spite of efforts at some schools to discourage fraternities, they had prospered in Ohio at Miami, Western Reserve, Kenyon, Mount Union, Wittenberg, Ohio Wesleyan, Wooster, and in lesser numbers at other places. There were more chapters at Ohio State University, however, by the 1890's, than on any other campus in the state. The groups had grown informally from campus to campus, and Ohio State University became an important link in that chain of growth. Students from Miami established a chapter at Ohio Wesleyan, and students from the second school initiated a group at Ohio State University. Students from Wittenberg with friends at Ohio State University would persuade them to induct them into the secrets of the order, and they would return to their own campus "pinned out." In this fashion, the secret societies leaped from place to place among an elite twenty institutions while avoiding another twenty that were either too weak, too lacking in social prominence, or militantly opposed to the secret orders.[38]

At the Ohio State University, by 1888, half of the men in the college classes were in fraternities, and yet not one pharmacy or agricultural student belonged to the groups. Over sixty per cent of the seniors and nearly sixty-five per cent of the juniors belonged to the Greek-letter societies, but only four of the members were students in the professional schools. There appeared to be a decided prejudice against the students in utilitarian fields, and the "aggies"

37. Ohio Wesleyan *Collegian* June 7, 1871.
38. The chapter lists of the sixteen fraternities with chapters in Ohio prior to 1900 in *Baird's Manual of American College Fraternities* indicate that between 1830 and 1899, seventy-three chapters of national fraternities were established on sixteen different campuses: Miami, Western Reserve, Kenyon, Mount Union, Wittenberg, Ohio Wesleyan, Wooster, Marietta, Ohio State University, Ohio University, Buchtel, Ohio Northern, University of Cincinnati, Denison, Case Institute, and Cincinnati College. Only one of the fraternity schools ceased to exist and that was Cincinnati College which was later incorporated in the University of Cincinnati. The schools with the largest number of chapters were Ohio State University (11), Ohio Wesleyan (9), Kenyon (7), Wooster (7). See *Baird's Manual of American College Fraternities, Twelfth and Semi-Centenial Edition* (Menasha, Wisconsin: Collegiate Press, 1930).

in particular were made the butt of student humor. The growing
social emphasis and the antiaggie attitude of students did little to
help the university's relations with the agricultural community of
Ohio.[39]

Once again, it was through poetry in the student publications
that the students revealed their attitudes. Increasingly, they turned
their cutting wit on other students rather than on college presidents,
trustees, and governors. One example of their antiaggie literature:

To dig out Greek and Latin roots
We did not come to college;
But of the earth and all her fruits
To get a store of knowledge.

Our thoughts to beef do mostly turn,
To cabbage and tomatoes;
We want the cheapest way to learn
Of raising big potatoes.

And when we've found out how to grow
The rich and luscious pumpkins
Then home to father's farm we'll go
And shine among the bumpkins.[40]

By 1895, student life was thoroughly preoccupied with the activities of the in-groups as opposed to the nonfraternity men and the
relative strength of the two in various campus competitions. This
dichotomy illustrated another developing difference between eastern
and western college campuses. At eastern institutions, fraternities
embraced a good majority of students where they existed while in
the west, student bodies on state university campuses and on many
private college campuses, were much more evenly and more sharply
divided.[41]

39. *Makio*, VIII (1888), 45–59.
40. Ibid., VII (1887), 60.
41. Veysey, op. cit., p. 270.

At Ohio State University, the non-Greeks worked to organize a Student Senate in order to contend with the powerful interfraternity organization. Among the fraternities, however, the groups which were established earliest on the campus disputed with those which came later about their qualifications to join the Interfraternity Association and to sit on the editorial board of the *Makio*, which was published by the fraternity association. The student newspaper, the *Fortnightly Lantern*, advocated the cause of the newer, unrecognized fraternities, and a rival paper, the *Indicator*, was established to defend the four old-line fraternities. The "fraternity war" became the major issue in the lives of most students at the time, and the students became more divided. Independents, through the Student Senate, sought to gain ascendancy over the split Greeks and the embattled Interfraternity Association, and to wrest control of the *Makio* from them.[42]

Similar developments in student life on other campuses aroused increased interest in the nature of the college experience. G. Stanley Hall, one of the earliest psychologists to give extensive time and effort to the study of the adolescent, saw the American college student at the turn of the centrury as living in a play world and displaying "psychic infantilism." The mock baby-talk of student theatricals, the phenomenon of pig Latin and the nonsense syllables in college slang, cheers, yells, and songs helped to persuade Hall of a rampant student "babyism."[43]

Students, however, reflected the social and economic ambitions of their parents in post–Civil War America and their own desires to have a good time. College was increasingly a period of happy times and joyous friendships for a select four per cent of the college-aged population who were preparing themselves for life in an urban, industrial society which placed a premium on the personal and social qualities which the new student culture emphasized. It was all related to the more general reform of higher education which dealt with curriculum and teaching methods. The public pressure for a more practical and more utilitarian college program was

42. *Makio*, XV (1895), 33–34, 71, 89.
43. G. Stanley Hall, "Student Customs," in *American Antiquarian Society Proceedings*, 1900–1901 (Worcester, Mass.: American Antiquarian Society, 1901), pp. 85–88, 91; Veysey, op. cit., pp. 277–78.

matched by student pressure for a more relevant experience for students in their daily lives.[44]

Developments in student life at the Ohio State University, in spite of the alarm sounded by James M. Comly, were quite in keeping with this national trend. As the university grew, the students became more and more segregated into small groups, student life became increasingly organized and ritualized, and student-faculty relations became less intimate. Under the eyes of their preoccupied teachers, they evolved a student culture which provided them with a miniature world that would effectively test the fledgling self-made men of America. Unsympathetic academicians were convinced that most of the students would not attend classes at all if they could get the degree without doing so. A great many students were convinced, as their later behavior in a growing number of alumni associations indicated, that they learned their most valuable lessons outside of class.[45]

44. Frederick Rudolph, "Neglect of Students as a Historical Tradition," *The College and the Student*, ed. Lawrence E. Dennis and Joseph F. Kauffman, American Council on Education (Washington, D. C. 1966), pp. 51–53; Veysey, op. cit., pp. 269–72, 282.

45. Rudolph, "Neglect of Students as a Historical Tradition," pp. 51–53; Veysey, op. cit., p. 273.

CHAPTER 7

The Farmers' Victory

The farmers of Ohio had never been happy about the Agricultural and Mechanical College. When its name was changed to "The Ohio State University," the farmers charged that the men running the school were ashamed of its lowly mission to provide higher education for the industrial classes, and that they were ambitious for different things. Their perennial complaint was that farm boys could not gain admission; that if they did, they were not received hospitably; that if they remained, they generally could not meet the requirements for the degrees because of preparatory deficiencies, or else they took a degree in engineering or some other nonagricultural field. "No college or university of general education in the United States will show a smaller proportion of its graduates engaged in agricultural pursuits than this agricultural college of Ohio," charged the editors of *Farm and Fireside* magazine, and they initiated a major campaign to bring several mounting pressures for change to fruition.[1]

The *Farm and Fireside* magazine was an outgrowth of a house organ for the farm machinery industry of Springfield, Ohio, published by Mast, Crowell, and Kirkpatrick. The publishers represented that group in Springfield which, in 1870, had most ardently sought to have the Ohio land grant college located in their city. Since that time, they had made Springfield one of the world's

1. *Farm and Fireside*, X, no. 11 (March 1, 1887), 181.

largest producers of farm machinery. They had not become reconciled to the program of the Columbus institution, however, and they used their influential journal to focus farmer discontents.[2]

Charles E. Thorne, the editor of *Farm and Fireside,* was not a stranger to the affairs of the Ohio State University and its relations with the farmer, nor was he a stranger to the farmers. Thorne, who grew up on a farm in Greene County, Ohio, after a brief start on agricultural education at Michigan Agricultural College, had studied geology under Edward Orton at Antioch College in Yellow Springs. After several terms he returned to farming, but was crushed by crop failures in 1875 and 1876. At that point he visited Norton Townshend for advice. Upon the recommendation of Edward Orton, his former teacher and by then the president of the Ohio State University and a friend of his father's on the board of trustees, Thorne was appointed foreman of the experimental farm. Beginning his duties in March of 1877, Charles E. Thorne performed well and by November was named farm manager, reporting directly to the board of trustees. The Board was pleased with Thorne, but Thorne was not very happy about the meager resources allocated to the experimental farm, and he became increasingly disenchanted with agricultural education via the Ohio State University. In 1880, he resigned but was persuaded to stay. A year later, however, he left and shortly thereafter began the development of *Farm and Fireside* magazine for the Springfield implement manufacturers.[3]

The new house organ prospered and grew rapidly. Soon the *Farm and Fireside,* claimed its publishers, reached more farmers than any other farm paper in the rich heartland of America. By 1886, copies were mailed twice monthly to 210,000 different addresses, and the editors claimed a million readers. Within the decade, circulation rose another 20 percent.

In 1886, as the possibility of increased federal support for the land grant colleges appeared, Thorne decided that it was time to press the issue of agricultural education at Ohio State. The sixteenth annual report of the university provided statistics which

2. Ibid., X, no. 2 (October 15, 1886), 1.
3. Mendenhall, op. cit., pp. 474, 513, 1153.

enabled Thorne to document his and the farmers protests. Of ninety-three persons who had graduated from the institution between 1870 and 1886, he pointed out, thirty-seven received the degrees of bachelor of arts and bachelor of philosophy; twenty-seven received the bachelor of science degree; another twenty-seven had received degrees in mining, mechanical or civil engineering, but only two had received the bachelor of agriculture degree. Furthermore, of the sixty-seven men who graduated prior to 1886, twenty-three were working in engineering fields, twelve were in law, eleven were school teachers, seven were merchants or bookkeepers, four were journalists, four were in medicine, two were clergymen, one was a graduate student, and one was a soldier. The two remaining graduates were a farmer and a fruit grower. For an institution which sought to serve an emerging urban-industrial society the produce of its early years was commendable.[4]

The editor of *Farm and Fireside*, however, cited this conclusive evidence that the leading object of the Ohio State University was not the teaching of those branches of learning which related to agriculture. By way of contrast, the editor referred his readers to the example of the State Agricultural College of Michigan where more than 50 percent of the graduates were farmers or in kindred pursuits. Sixteen of these had become professors of agriculture elsewhere in the nation. L. N. Bonham, secretary of the Ohio State Board of Agriculture and publisher of the *Ohio Cultivator*, showed his enthusiasm for good practical education, said the *Farm and Fireside* editor, by sending his only son to the Michigan institution.[5]

The differences between the agricultural colleges of Ohio and Michigan were attributed to several causes by Ohio State University's critics. The background, experience, and sympathies of the trustees of Ohio State University were characterized as only incidentally related to the agricultural community, if they were related at all. The curriculum, said critics, was predominantly classical or oriented toward the city and industry; entrance requirements

4. *Farm and Fireside*, X, no. 11 (March 1, 1887), 181; *Sixteenth Annual Report of the Board of Trustees to the Governor of Ohio* (Columbus, Ohio, 1887).

5. *Farm and Fireside*, X, no. 11 (March 1, 1887), 181; no. 17 (June 1, 1887), 279.

were geared to city high schools and classical academies; the research emphasis was inappropriately focused, and the school failed entirely to disseminate practical knowledge to farmers in the field. Furthermore, said the university's critics, the agricultural program was hidden in the general university structure, and the amount of financial support which found its way through that structure to the agricultural program was minimal. By its very structure, they claimed, the university diverted the funds intended for practical education for the industrial classes to support the dream of a great state university which the state was otherwise unwilling to support. Beyond these criticisms and related to all of them, there was the general feeling that the university failed to comprehend or understand the farmer, his personality, his prejudices, his needs, or his environment. There was the implication that the institution would really not be interested in the farmer at all except for the need to meet the conditions of the Morrill Act in order to have access to the land grant fund.[6]

Three recommendations emerged in an effort to correct the situation. First, it was suggested that the university meet the farm boy where the rural school system left him and provide a transition to the higher learning program of the agricultural college. Second, it was suggested that funds for the support of agricultural studies, agricultural experimentation, and the dissemination of practical knowledge should be specifically channeled to appropriate program areas in order that they not be diverted to support the full university program. And third, it was advised that the university have a president whose general orientation and sympathies were with the farm community.[7]

Successful agricultural colleges, said the editor of *Farm and Fireside,* those which had gained the confidence and the support of the agricultural population, and thereby also gained the support of their state legislatures, had two things in common. They had a president and a professor of agriculture "whose education, tastes, and sympathies are in full accord with the life of the farm." Most

6. Ibid., X, no. 10 (February 15, 1887), 161; no. 12 (March 15, 1887), 197; no. 13 (April 1, 1887), 213; no. 21 (August 1, 1887), 343.

7. Ibid., X, no. 6 (December 15, 1886), 97; no. 13 (April 1, 1887), 213; no. 22 (August 15, 1887), 359.

land grant colleges were failures, the editor said. "The university system as applied to the problem of industrial education," he concluded, "is a complete failure." The reason given was that, in the ambition to found great state universities, presiding officers had been selected for the wrong reason.[8]

With the selection of a proper president, however, advised the editor, the attitude of a college would change. It would treat the farm boy more sympathetically in the admissions procedure, and a fairer distribution of financial resources within the school's program would be forthcoming. Texas Agricultural and Mechanical College was given as a good example of a Morrill Act failure that later found its way to success and tax support. It opened in 1876, said the editor of *Farm and Fireside,* but like most Morrill Act colleges it began in "the traditional ruts of drill in the so-called classics—mementos of dead and buried centuries—to the neglect of the very lively issues of the living present." As a result, students avoided the school, and criticism from without and dissension from within brought the school to the verge of ruin. But then it was reorganized, said the editor, with a vigorous and sympathetic staff, and courses that began "low down, so low that any farmer's boy . . . might enter. . . ."[9]

A report by James H. Canfield, Chancellor of the University of Nebraska, and later president of the Ohio State University, on "The Opportunities of the Rural Population for Higher Education" later verified Thorne's assertions about educational opportunity in rural Ohio. His report supported farm critics of land grant colleges in every detail. Canfield had sent questionnaires to state school superintendents, responsible officers in state colleges and universities, city and county superintendents and principals, and to other known educators. Of nearly four hundred institutions of higher education studied, the committee reported that only sixty-five "have freed themselves from the embarrassment of a preparatory department," and yet only half of the state universities offered such work. Furthermore, the unanimous voice of the state colleges and universities surveyed, according to the report, was that there were

8. Ibid., X, no. 22 (August 15, 1887), 359; no. 3 (April 1, 1887), 213.
9. Ibid., X, no. 4 (November 15, 1886), 65.

virtually no opportunities offered to the people of the rural districts to prepare themselves for college. The Superintendent of Public Instruction in Ohio had responded to the committee's questionnaire by observing that "high schools have destroyed most of the old academies . . . and yet they do not take the place of the academy so far as the educational interests of country youth are concerned." In their place were city high schools and the academies attached to the denominational colleges. Canfield's committee concluded that state educational systems were very generally partial and chaotic, and that the mass of the rural population was dependent upon chance or the favor of some city for the educational link between the common school and the college. Canfield himself became convinced that the mission of state universities included the fostering of rural secondary education, and he brought that conviction with him when he became president of the Ohio State University. This had also become one of the major complaints of Ohio farmers about their state university and a primary objective of their efforts to reform the institution.[10] For Thorne, the only possible way to save the Ohio State University was for the University to save rural secondary education.

It became increasingly apparent, however, that financial support was the key to any kind of reform of Ohio's agricultural college. The legislature had never been generous, and farmers endorsed that neglect. As costs increased and the public attitude toward higher education in general changed, the pressures for additional support became greater. The implementation of the state university idea in Ohio had been originally predicated upon the availability of three sources of revenue: the Morrill Land Grant fund, the Ohio University and Miami University foundations, and legislative appropriation. For a decade and a half, however, the land grant fund and student fees had had to carry the burden. The introduction, in 1886, of the Hatch Bill in the United States Congress, providing additional funds for the support of agricultural experimentation seemed to the university officials to be a means for strength-

10. James H. Canfield, "The Opportunities of the Rural Population for Higher Education," Report of the Committe on Secondary Education, *The National Council of Education Proceedings of the Ninth Annual Meeting, Nashville, Tenn., July, 1889* (Topeka, Kansas: National Council of Education, 1889), pp. 28–51.

ening the agricultural program of the school, and a way of allaying criticisms that the program was inadequately supported. To the farm press and the State Board of Agriculture, however, it was the signal to marshal forces against what they called the further misuse of federal appropriations.

The bill as originally drawn would allocate $15,000 annually for agricultural experimentation to the nation's land grant colleges. This was the most glaring weakness in the bill, said the *Farm and Fireside* editor. Amendments were suggested that would allocate the funds to independent agricultural experiment stations in states where such stations existed, but the *Farm and Fireside* advocated an amendment which would give states discretionary power to decide whether the funds went to an agricultural college or to an experiment station. There were many who opposed the original bill because they feared that the money would "be swallowed up in impractical work" as the Morrill grants had been in some places with no real benefit to the farmers. If the state legislatures had discretion in the allocation, however, said Thorne, those agricultural colleges which had fulfilled their obligations and their mission would be rewarded and those which had not could be denied the new assistance. There was no danger, the editor was convinced, that any legislature would make the same mistake twice.[11]

Farm leaders from many states lobbied in Washington to so amend the Hatch Bill, and they succeeded. *Farm and Fireside* campaigned vigorously for the amendment and, after the amendment and the Hatch Act were passed, pressured the Ohio legislature to take advantage of the discretionary provision by awarding the grant to the separate experiment station. The magazine launched its campaign concerning the Hatch Bill in its Christmas issue. It described the bill in detail for its readers and advocated the amendment authorizing discretion. The editors then discussed the bill in every subsequent issue, and whipped up enthusiasm among farmers and pressure on the legislature for its point of view.

In early February, the bill was considered by the annual convention of the State Board of Agriculture. President Scott and other officers from the university presented the school's appeal that the

11. *Farm and Fireside*, X, no. 6 (December 15, 1886), 97; no. 7 (January 1, 1887), 113; no. 8 (January 15, 1887), 129.

grant be awarded to them. The master of the State Grange and president of the State Board of Agriculture, however, defended a resolution endorsing the amendment that would give the legislature the discretion. After the debate, the convention voted 37 to 7 to support legislative discretion.[12]

The publishers of *Farm and Fireside* maintained that Ohio more than any other state in the Union illustrated the necessity for the amendment. Ohio's land grant college, they said, was run by a board on which no farmer held a seat, and it put 98 percent of its graduates into nonagricultural fields. It would be no more absurd to entrust the running of a medical school to a board of farmers, they said, than to put agricultural experimentation under businessmen and lawyers. They implied that the Ohio State University's interest in the Hatch Act was based solely upon its need for funds and not upon an interest in agricultural education. This time, however, said the editors, the farmers were united in their demand that this fund remain under the control of farmers and, they added, the legislature was thoroughly in sympathy with that demand.[13]

In early March, the Ohio Assembly voted 70 to 7 in the House and unanimously in the Senate to award the $15,000 appropriation to the Ohio Agricultural Experiment Station. It was a major defeat for the Ohio State University and a strong factor in strengthening the agricultural program at the expense of the general and scientific program. *Farm and Fireside* claimed major credit for the overwhelming vote, and President W. H. Scott and Professor Norton Townshend seemed to agree that the journal's role had been crucial. The vote was a striking illustration of the value of a well-supported agricultural journal, claimed the editor. *Farm and Fireside* unquestionably, he said, was the voice of an immense constituency. His was the only journal in Ohio, he observed, that took the farmers' position early enough to enable them to make known their views before it was too late. In addition, the magazine had issued a special bulletin to legislators, and to 1,200 farm leaders throughout the state, securing the endorsement of influential farm-

12. Ibid., X, no. 12 (March 15, 1887), 197; no. 10 (February 15, 1887), 161.

13. Ibid., X, no. 12 (March 15, 1887), 197.

ers in every representative's district. Norton S. Townshend wrote to every legislator to counter the *Farm and Fireside's* campaign. The magazine published his letter and attempted to refute it point by point. They also observed that no agricultural college could hope to succeed unless the professor of agriculture was in sympathy with the aspirations of the farmers of his state, and eventually the editor replaced the professor as director of the experimental farm. All the newspapers of Columbus threw their influence to the side of the university to counter the organized campaign in the legislature, but all to no avail.[14]

Following the victory over disposition of the Hatch Act funds, *Farm and Fireside* launched a severe attack upon the Ohio State University. Thorne admitted that the institution's facilities were excellent for anyone "of mature judgment and independence of character" who wanted a general education. The phrasing, however, implied a questioning of the moral environment for youths of more tender years and more conservative backgrounds. "Of schools for intellectual training purely," Thorne further observed, "we already have a super abundance." What the state really needed was a school like the land grant schools of Michigan or Kansas, he said, and that was what it obviously did not have.[15]

President W. H. Scott noted with regret the attitude toward the university expressed in the journal's columns. The criticism, he said, was unjust because undeserved, and impolitic because it tore down what in the long run the journal obviously hoped to build up. "Let *Farm and Fireside* make known throughout its wide circulation," the President pleaded, "the advantages here open to the farmer's son . . . urge him to come. . . . " The industrial side of the university had been rapidly developing for several years, he said, and he outlined that development. In 1881, the school created a department of botany and horticulture. In 1884, the department of agricultural chemistry was established. A year later, 1885, the department of veterinary medicine had been initiated. He listed, by year, the funds spent for buildings, laboratories, and livestock for

14. Ibid., X, no. 13 (April 1, 1887), 213; no. 14 (April 15, 1887), 231.
15. Ibid., X, no. 14 (April 15, 1887), 231, 235; no. 15 (May 1, 1887), 247, 248–49.

the agricultural program, and he outlined curricular modifications which, since 1883, had moved in the direction of a popular agricultural program. The program and the facilities were available, he insisted, but farm organizations and the agricultural press, rather than encouraging farm boys to take advantage of the opportunities discouraged them from coming. "We want them to come," he said, "lend us your aid."[16]

The editor replied that he did not intend to misrepresent the university, and that in his opinion, he had not done so. The problem was one of attitude, he said. For President Scott, industrial education was a "side issue" to be "built up," he observed, and not the major reason for the existence of the university. Without at the time being specific, the editor implied that, as part of the price of peace with the farmers, the university had to have a president with something more than earnestness, honesty, and intellectual ability. Later, he said he had to have something as subtle and as intangible "as the mysterious force which gave the Preacher of Nazareth such power over the poor and illiterate, while his name remained an offense to the rich and learned." On still another occasion, Thorne observed that most agricultural college presidents seemed to be men who remembered the farm "only as a place of toil and grime, a treadmill of endless drudgery," whereas they should be men who believed with farmers that theirs was the most honorable vocation of men.[17]

Alexis Cope, secretary of the board of trustees, and Charles E. Thorne, corresponded at some length about the clash between the farmer and the university. Cope implied that *Farm and Fireside* was unfairly critical and offered no constructive solutions. Thorne, by letter, was very much more specific about "constructive" solutions than he was in his magazine. The university should eliminate the arts and philosophy departments altogether, he said in a reply to Cope. It should then cut off the junior and senior years of the remaining courses. What was left should then be reorganized as

16. William Henry Scott to the Editor, *Farm and Fireside*, X, no. 15 (May 1, 1887), 248–49.
17. Ibid., X, no. 15 (May 1, 1887), 247; no. 12 (March 15, 1887), 197; no 13 (April 1, 1887), 213; no. 21 (August 1, 1887), 343; no. 22 (August 15, 1887), 359.

courses in agriculture and mechanical arts in which manual work
and mental training were evenly balanced. When these things were
done, said Thorne, he was sure that the university would have the
cordial support of granges, agricultural conventions and legislatures.[18]

It was idle to talk of making the Ohio State University a success
under any different plan, Thorne continued, because the entire
progress of the university from 1870 to 1887 had been in the wrong
direction. "There is room in the nation for one Cornell for the
higher education of teachers of agriculture," said Thorne, but for
people who go back to the farm and not into the classroom a Cornell was not what Ohio needed. If the Ohio State University was
to be in fact a state university and not a school, "the leading object
of which" was agriculture and mechanical education, then the state
had to provide rural and agricultural high schools while reducing
the classical program and strengthening the industrial. But that, to
Thorne, seemed superfluous since there was already an abundance
of schools in the state devoted to classical and polite education. In
essence then, Thorne was reasserting the practical farmer's view of
the agricultural reform movement eclipsed earlier after the Morrill
Act victory in 1862. The muddy shoe farmer wanted practical,
everyday, experiment station kinds of help and not the kind of help
that came from professors of agriculture. Cope pointed out to
Thorne that the Ohio State University program had been designed
by Norton Townshend and Judge T. C. Jones of Delaware, two
staunch friends of the farmer and early leaders for agriculture reform, but Thorne countered that they had been mistaken and that
Jones for one had later admitted as much. The early agricultural
reformers had not really been in touch with the plain dirt farmers
who, in intervening decades, had been aroused from lethargy and
organized to seek practical redress for their grievances.[19]

In an ongoing effort to diminish the *Farm and Fireside* magazine's attacks on the university, however, Alexis Cope, secretary of
the board of trustees, sent a catalog for the 1886–87 academic year

18. Cope to Thorne, March 10, 1887, in Mendenhall, op. cit., pp. 501–9.
19. Thorne to Cope, March 12, 1887; March 15, 1887, in Mendenhall, op.
cit., pp. 501–9.

to the editors and called it to their attention. "We learn that some very imporant changes have been made," Thorne observed. First, he noted that the School of Agriculture was listed first and not fourth as previously. Second, he reported a rearranged agricultural course and heralded it as a major change. The new course began with a single preparatory year instead of the two-year preparatory program previously required of common-school graduates. The courses required in that year, he observed, were such as no farmer could afford to neglect: agricultural chemistry, physical geography, physics, practical mechanics, field measurements, and botany. It was an eminently practical course outline.[20]

The freshman year of the new program included: the management of domestic animals in health and disease; principles of feeding, breeding, and veterinary medicine; anatomy, physiology, and materia medica; and algebra. The preparatory and freshman years, then, constituted the new short course and could be taken as a terminal program. Of greatest importance, however, observed Thorne, was the fact that while the short course was previously independent of other courses, it was now introductory to the degree program in agriculture. The student could move from the common school to the short course and, if he desired, from the short course to the degree program. Finally, said the editors of *Farm and Fireside*, after ten years of denial, the university had admitted that its work was not complete until it had provided a channel from the common school to the college for rural youth. Now the gateway had been provided and, while much remained to be done before the Ohio State University completely fulfilled its obligation, the way toward reconciliation had been provided. The publishers then urged that local granges and farmers' clubs study the new catalog and then urged that farmers consider the school as a place for their sons. "Peace is always pleasanter than war," continued Thorne, "and if the time has come that we can accomplish our purpose by peaceful methods, let us not neglect our opportunity."[21]

The strategy of the farm critics must have been disturbing to university officials. The new agricultural program which elicited

20. *Farm and Fireside*, X, no. 19 (July 1, 1887), 310.
21. Ibid.

such a rapid change of attitude had been under faculty consideration before the Hatch Act embroglio and Alexis Cope had so informed Charles E. Thorne. The series of developments which
President Scott had outlined had not passed unnoticed in the agricultural community. It was apparent, however, that in addition to
program reforms and a link between common schools and college,
a greater security of financial resources for agricultural experimentation, and a position of strength in a separate experiment station
board of trustees were essential to securing farm support for the
university. The need for these two safeguards Thorne had learned
first hand during the four years he had managed the college farm.[22]

With independent financial resources for the agricultural experiment station, the conflict between the two sets of trustees, those for
the college and those for the adjoining experiment station, formalized the conflict between the farmers and the college. Support for
the existence of a separate experiment station had arisen in 1882 in
complaints that the only funds available to finance agricultural research were the profits, if any, from the experimental farm. It was
Charles E. Thorne's original complaint when he was manager of
the farm. University funds which he felt should have been available for agricultural research quite as readily as for any other kind
were used for other purposes, including research in engineering
and mechanical fields. With a separate station and its independent
budget, and with the university committed by legislation to provide
space for the work, increased agricultural experimentation was
assured. The acquisition of the Hatch Act subsidy, then, enhanced
the work further and put it totally beyond the control of the university trustees. It further demonstrated that the advocates of
practical agricultural education had secured a permanent and equal
status with advocates of the state university. For proponents of a
great state university it represented a serious if not fatal hindrance
of their work. In the final analysis it meant that while one generation of state leadership had used the Morrill grant to establish a
state university, another generation negated that decision in fact,
if not in law.

22. *Minutes of the Faculty*, I, 342–46, 348–49; *Farm and Fireside*, X, no. 12
(March 15, 1887), 197.

CHAPTER 8

Peace with the Farmers:
A New Departure

The confrontation of the two sets of trustees—one set for the university, another for the experiment station—provided for a show-down between the conflicting parties within the state. Immediately there were efforts to reconcile the two groups, but it appeared that finally the farmers were in a position to win their case with the advocates of a new state university. In a move to bring about reconciliation with the least loss to the broader program, Edward Orton suggested that Rutherford B. Hayes, the former president of the United States and a three-term governor of Ohio, be appointed to the university board. Edward Orton, who knew something of the broad and balanced program which Hayes had envisioned for the university when he appointed its first board of trustees saw in Hayes a viable course toward resolution of the mounting conflict. He was particularly concerned about the weakening defenses of the supporters of a broad program and felt that Hayes would provide strength and even enthusiasm.

First, however, Orton wanted to determine if Hayes would be willing to serve. On a trip to Fremont to deliver a lecture, Orton visited Hayes at Spiegel Grove. He helped the former president plan the tapping of natural gas deposits at the Grove to provide heat for the homestead, and while there indicated the interest of some that Hayes assume a role in university affairs. Upon his return to Columbus, Orton indicated publicly that Hayes was interested in the university, but that he did not know whether Hayes would in fact accept an appointment. "I kept entirely within the limits indicated," he wrote Hayes, but he pushed for Hayes's nomination and viewed the possibility with great satisfaction. Orton brought back word to Alexis Cope that Hayes would indeed accept an appointment, and Cope broached the matter to Governor Foraker. He was disappointed at Foraker's response. He did not see why he should appoint President Hayes to the university board, reported Cope, because the president had never done anything for him. He agreed to speak to Hayes about the matter, however, and did so while Hayes was in Columbus for a wedding some weeks later.

Although Hayes behaved as though he was only casually interested, the opportunity to serve as a trustee of the Ohio State University was a god-send for him and he accepted eagerly. After his term in the White House had ended in 1881, and he returned to Fremont, Ohio, Hayes had pondered the question of what happens to a chief magistrate of the republic who retires to private life. He felt that he should immediately take part as a private citizen in the work of his family, his community, his state and his nation. This he did and yet a void remained.

He rejoined the Odd Fellows, joined a local post of the Grand Army of the Republic, became a director of a bank and focused his energies on its $50,000 capital as though it were the national treasury. He also managed a library, helped to establish a board of trade in Fremont, dabbled in real estate, served the county fair association, and, though he refrained from joining a church, he served as a trustee of his wife's Methodist church and led the fight to have its pastor, who had been removed, reinstated. He worked endless hours for the Peabody Education Fund and the Slater Fund to strengthen education in the South. He also served as a trustee for Western Reserve University and the Ohio Wesleyan University. He confessed in his diary that he thought it a good thing for him to promote general education for the public. He was not interested in writing, he said, so he focused his attention increasingly on active service to education. He may secretly have desired a university presidency, but in any event to his role as trustee at the Ohio State University he brought enthusiasm, skill and commitment.

President Scott told Hayes that his appointment represented the best possible choice, the ideal of what a trustee appointment should be. "I rejoice, in common with all the friends of the university," he said, "that the Governor has acted so wisely." The appointment, he indicated, meant that the university might more rapidly advance to the rank that it ought to occupy. The students greeted Hayes' appointment with characteristic novelty. They represented him in a cartoon in the *Makio* with angel wings, standing ankle deep in mud and attempting to lift the Ohio State University from the mud of mediocrity. They pictured him as gazing across the river, beyond Otterbein College, Ohio University, and Buchtel College, resting on firm foundations on the opposite bank, to the University Heights overlooking the river. On the heights, where by the direction of his gaze he was obviously planning to put the Ohio State University, were Cornell, Harvard, Princeton, Columbia, and the University of Michigan.[1] The farmers, however, if the editor of *Farm and Fireside* correctly reflected their view, were not enthusiastic about the new appointment. Hayes, said the editors, replaced the last working farmer on the board of trustees. But the Hayes' appointment should have impressed them and later did. Hayes confessed in his diary at the time of his appointment: "My impression is in favor of a policy which will restore harmony between the university and the farming interest."[2]

In another place, Hayes indicated that the price of financial support for the university through the legislature was quite obviously peace with the farmers and his appointment was crucial in such a rapprochement. Nevertheless, Hayes brought to the board a special interest in education. He had been very much interested in Negro education and had served on the board of trustees for the Slater

1. Edward Orton to Rutherford B. Hayes, January 27, 1887, Hayes Papers, Rutherford B. Hayes Library, Fremont, Ohio; W. H. Scott to Rutherford B. Hayes, February 1, 1887, Hayes Papers; *Makio*, VII (1887), 92; Harry Barnard, *Rutherford B. Hayes and His America*, (Indianapolis, Ind.: Bobbs-Merrill Co., 1954) pp. 503–7.

2. *Farm and Fireside*, X, no. 11 (March 1, 1887), 181; Charles R. Williams (ed.), *Diary and Letters of Rutherford B. Hayes*, entry for November 25, 1887.

Fund which aided Negro schools in the South. He supported the fund's director in his conflict with Daniel Coit Gilman, another trustee and president of Johns Hopkins University, and upheld the director's policy of denying aid to schools which sought to duplicate the white man's classical college. The director favored those institutions which gave the Negro in the South an opportunity to learn a vocation, thus giving him a place to start in economic society. One of those to whom he extended a special consideration as a Slater fund trustee was William E. B. Dubois, who later helped establish the National Association for the Advancement of Colored People.

Hayes was also deeply interested in the manual training movement and thought that all children, black or white, rich or poor, should be taught to handle tools skillfully. He sent his own son to the manual-training school in Toledo for a year before he went east to Cornell. In fact, central to Hayes's notion of what a people's college should be was a broad program of industrial education. "I would aid no institution," he told Alexis Cope, secretary of the board of trustees, "which does not provide industrial education." On the subject, he described himself as a radical and added, "My plan is essential. It is the cornerstone. With it an institution must succeed. Without it, it must fail." While Hayes generally proposed to move slowly and to avoid antagonizing anyone, he was aggressive on this point and his views were somewhat disconcerting to Cope and others who feared for the life of the broad university program. Hayes, however, felt that the future of the Ohio State University depended upon strengthening its program for industrial education, and that only aggressive action in that direction could save the broader program in the final analysis. Under the circumstances, he said, "our university is our first and chief care," and duty in the performance of that charge required that they push insistently for industrial education regardless of opposition. Pushers always win, he told Cope, if their timing was correct. He said that he believed in making the Ohio State University a people's college, a college for farmers and mechanics in the best sense, "something different from the common old-fashioned classical college." He thus reflected the farmers viewpoint very well and he was prepared to move ahead immediately in that direction. Within a year, Alexis Cope credited the "change of front" which Hayes's views had brought about with allaying antagonism and turning public sentiment in favor of the university.

Rutherford B. Hayes also brought to his new post a breadth of interest in higher education which was reflected in his trusteeships at Western Reserve and Ohio Wesleyan Universities as well as the Ohio State University. This breadth of interest, commitment to popular education, and conviction that harmony was needed for Ohio State University were focused by his administrative acumen and his skills at conciliation. As congressman, governor, and president, he had grown as an administrator, and this growth had culminated in an attack upon the spoils system of national administration. As a legislator and an attorney, he had learned the art of compromising valid, though conflicting, interests and as president had applied the art to the reconciliation of North and South and the termination of military reconstruction of the former Confederate states. As governor of Ohio, moreover, he had been instrumental in getting the Ohio State University started and had appointed its first board of trustees. "If anybody was its founder," he told William Henry Smith, "in the words of Governor Corwin, 'a great part of it I am which.'" Hayes worked hard to get his way with the Morrill Act fund and, as was said later, he "shaped the necessary legislation, procured its passage, and appointed the board of trustees which located the university, prescribed its general courses of study and elected its faculty." He, therefore, felt an on-going responsibility for the institution.[3]

The new trustee's qualifications were excellent and he tackled immediately the problem of antagonism between the two sets of state trustees. Joseph H. Brigham, who, as president of the Ohio State Board of Agriculture and one of the university's severest critics had led the effort to get Senator Sherman of Ohio to work for the Hatch Act amendment, had just been appointed to the Agricultural Experiment Station Board of Control. He was considered

3. Harry Barnard, op. cit., pp. 506, 508; Hayes, *Diary*, entry for December 10, 1890; R. B. Hayes to Alexis Cope, February 8, 1888, R. B. Hayes correspondence, manuscript collection, Ohio State University Library; Alexis Cope to R. B. Hayes, February 10, 1888, Hayes Papers; R. B. Hayes to William Henry Smith, November 27, 1887, Hayes Papers.

to be a bold and aggressive leader of the farmers of the state, one who gave focus to the power of the Grange and other militant farmer organizations. His recent activities in Washington undercut the delegation sent by the university and embarrassed some of the university trustees. They considered him personally offensive and preferred an open break with the Board of Control rather than working with Brigham. If they could, they would order the experiment station off the campus grounds. "We are on the eve of a bitter quarrel," said Alexis Cope in providing Hayes with a detailed summary of the dispute, one that would be "hurtful to both institutions, and especially so, I fear, to the university."[4]

Rutherford B. Hayes, cognizant that such a break would have far reaching repercussions, introduced resolutions stressing the importance of friendly and cordial relations, and emphasing that the two institutions should mutually assist each other in their common labor. He recommended that both boards meet jointly together to settle their differences. When the two boards did meet, Hayes, in his quiet but forceful manner, took charge of the session and presented his view of matters. He gave none of the other trustees an opportunity to add to or amend his remarks but concluded by asking the Experiment Station Board of Control what the university might do to help them.[5]

The outspoken Brigham, however, was not the respondent for the Board of Control. Instead, Seth H. Ellis, who had served on the university board from 1878 to 1887, and whose place on the board Rutherford B. Hayes had been named to fill, answered for the Experiment Station Board. These two men, Hayes and Ellis, successfully controlling their respective boards, constructed the dimensions of the settlement. In a memorandum of understanding which all signed, the relationships of the two institutions were specified. A division of property was agreed to, acknowledging the station's independent status and increasing the facilities for agricultural experimentation provided by the university. In turn, the experiment station agreed to use university faculty members in its research,

4. Alexis Cope to R. B. Hayes, October 20 and November 11, 1887, Hayes Papers; Mendenhall, op. cit., pp. 121–22.

5. Ibid., pp. 124–26.

and to employ undergraduate and graduate students as often as possible thus blending the educational efforts of the university with the experimental programs of the station.[6]

Hayes' handling of the joint session of the two boards had less official but equally far reaching effects. Alexis Cope had identified Seth Ellis, Hayes' friend; J. H. Brigham, president of the State Board of Agriculture; and Charles E. Thorne, editor of *Farm and Fireside* and Norton Townshend's successor as director of the Experiment Station, as the three moving and controlling spirits behind the station as a focus of power. In the settlement of the dispute, Hayes won the confidence of all three. His relations with Ellis were already good, and the two men worked effectively together. The blunt Brigham, after the settlement, told Hayes, "I agree that no hasty action is advisable," and he indicated that he would not press for an immediate change of presidents. He indicated a willingness to work amicably with the university and said he held no ill will for any of its trustees.[7]

Nevertheless, Secretary Brigham of the State Board of Agriculture and, by 1891, master of the National Grange of the Patrons of Husbandry, told Hayes that the growing disposition to make the Ohio State University a famous university raised some important questions. If it became famous for "turning out students who can do something besides the professions," he said, that would indeed be fame worth pursuing. He was inclined, however, to deprecate the fame that accrued from adding things like medical colleges which tended to overshadow the essential purpose of the institution. He thus indicated a further concern of the farm element that the trend to add law and medical programs would further eclipse the agricultural program and stretch scarce budget dollars even further. After the meetings of the two boards, however, Brigham's confidence in Hayes was sufficient to enable him to trust that settlements of these and other perplexing issues were possible.

Charles E. Thorne, the vociferous and highly critical editor of *Farm and Fireside*, was even more captivated by Hayes in action.

6. Ibid., pp. 126–27.
7. Alexis Cope to R. B. Hayes, October 20, October 27, 1887, Hayes Papers; J. H. Brigham to R. B. Hayes, December, 1887, and December 17, 1887, Hayes Papers.

"I came away from that meeting," he told Hayes, "feeling that now, at last, we are to have recompense for the years of anxiety and sore disappointment." He apologized for the very brief allusion to Hayes' appointment as a trustee in his magazine and added, "I did not know at that time how deeply interested you were in the cause of industrial education." He offered Hayes the columns of his publication to give broader circulation to his views. A week later, after reviewing Hayes' further comments on industrial education, Thorne expressed surprise that Hayes went even farther than he had suspected in his advocacy of the people's college. Hayes' views, and his influence, said the editor, would remake the university without the "friction and upturning" of the previously demanded reorganization.[8]

Hayes' settlement of the dispute accomplished one other thing as well. Alexis Cope, prior to this series of events, had not expressed the confidence that others had in the ability of the new trustee from Spiegel Grove to solve the university's problems. Nevertheless, beginning at this time he indicated a growing admiration for Hayes and his ability and skill. Out of the series of events Hayes likewise grew in his respect for the board's Secretary, and the two became an important and effective team. "I feel that we owe you a great debt," Cope told Hayes shortly after the settlement. Three months later, the Secretary confessed that he saw the university's future lay in the direction which Hayes would take it. "Write me frankly about any subject," Hayes later told Cope. "I trust you. I have no other correspondent at Columbus," he said.[9]

The settlement was furthered a little later on when Governor Foraker appointed Brigham to the university board of trustees. Members of that body resisted such a development; they said it was like inviting the enemy within the gates. The board would have preferred that Seth H. Ellis be reappointed as the best man to sit on both boards and provide needed liaison. Hayes, however, indicated that nothing less than Brigham's appointment would convince the

8. J. H. Brigham to R. B. Hayes, December 17, 1887, Hayes Papers; Charles E. Thorne to Hayes, December 10, December 16, 1887, Hayes Papers.

9. Alexis Cope to R. B. Hayes, November 24, 1887 and February 8, 1888, Hayes Papers; Rutherford B. Hayes to Alexis Cope, January 17, 1892, R. B. Hayes Correspondence, Manuscript Collection, Ohio State University Library.

agricultural interests of the university's earnest desire to make peace
with them, and that they would regard Ellis as not fully the representative of the farmer.[10]

Brigham's appointment was the first of a hoped for sequence in
which, ultimately, the two Boards would have become identical.
This was another of Hayes's suggestions for terminating the antagonism, but carrying it out required the cooperation of governors
for the next nine years in appointing trustees to each board who
already held seats on the other one. This was hoping for too much
of a bipartisan spirit, however, and the practice began and ended
with Governor Foraker's appointment of Brigham.

Nevertheless, a way to judge the efficacy of the Hayes-Ellis settlement soon presented itself. In 1890, Justin Smith Morrill introduced a bill in the Congress to supplement the aid given to agricultural and mechanical colleges in 1862. Under the new proposal,
Congress would appropriate for each land grant college, $15,000
for the year ending in June, 1890; $16,000 for the year ending in
June, 1891; $17,000 for the year following, and so on until the
amount reached $25,000 per year. The editors of *Farm and Fireside*
expressed the opinion that this bill would "eventually cause a thorough reorganization of these colleges and bring them back to their
original purpose."[11] This time, however, the editors appealed to
farmers to stir up their representatives in the legislature to see that
the fund was not stolen and to see that it was awarded to the Ohio
State University.

The act was passed, and subsequently the Ohio legislature
awarded the entire fund to the Ohio State University. An effort was
made to divert half of the new fund to Wilberforce University to
support agricultural and mechanical education for Negroes. The
new law specified that no money should be paid out to any state
where a distinction of race or color governed the admission of
students unless a state established a separate agricultural and
mechanical college for the Negroes. The campaign to secure part
of the new grant for Wilberforce was based upon this part of the
legislation. Spokesmen for the Ohio State University, however,

10. Mendenhall, op. cit., pp. 123, 128.
11. *Farm and Fireside*, XIII, no. 20 (July 15, 1890), 333.

pointed out that there were no racial restrictions on admission at the Columbus campus, and that there was, therefore no basis for a division of the fund.[12]

Farm and Fireside carried on a public campaign defending the university position. When the legislature acted as it did, awarding the full grant of the second Morrill Act to the Ohio State University while making a separate appropriation for Wilberforce, the editors lauded the action. "The Ohio legislature finally did the right thing," said the editor, "and provided that the whole appropriation . . . should go where it belongs, to The Ohio State University." The editors then continued in a new vein for *Farm and Fireside.* The success of the university in meeting the needs of the farmer was not entirely the responsibility of the university, they observed. While the university could provide a thorough, practical, and scientific program in agriculture, only the farmers could give it the support and the reputation that would make for ultimate success. "Upon farmers themselves," the editor concluded, "depends whether or not they will send their sons to one of the best educational institutions in the country."[13]

In most respects, the Hayes-Ellis settlement solved the problem of farmer opposition which had confounded the efforts of the university's friends for seventeen years. With the university as the advocate of the scientific basis of agricultural and mechanical education and the Experiment Station as the champion of the practical, the two conflicting views on the nature of education, at least for the farmers among the industrial classes, had positions of power from which to operate. The Experiment Station, with separate financial resources and the support of farmers who wielded controlling influence in the legislature, initially had the upper hand and had forced a modification of the university's position. At the time, Hayes appeared to be willing to pay almost any price for the needed peace, but that was not the case. As an experienced politician, he had known better than to pay more of a price than was required just as well as he knew that the trustees dared not offer less. Farmer protests against the university had also included a demand

12. Ibid., XIV, no. 12 (March 15, 1891); Mendenhall, op. cit., 132–36.
13. *Farm and Fireside,* XIV, no. 16 (May 15, 1891), 271.

for a more acceptable president, one whose sympathies for the farm and the farmer were unmistakable. William Henry Scott offered his resignation in June of 1887, but the board referred it back to him to be considered on another occasion. This was not the time to change presidents to Hayes's way of thinking, for to do so would require that the new man meet the requirements of the agricultural interests at a time when their power seemed most formidable.[14]

Hayes, as he indicated later when a new president was to be chosen, was completely opposed to the selection of any man who would go too far in making the Ohio State University a farmers' college entirely. He used his influence to defeat William Isaac Chamberlain for that post, and personally favored a man of much wider sympathies and a much more liberal outlook, the Reverend Washington Gladden of Columbus. The next president, Hayes said, should be a man of such breadth and depth that he could please the farmers without surrendering the other legitimate interests of a full-fledged state university.[15]

At the time, there was considerable talk of making Hayes himself the president of the institution, and it was actually this possibility which prompted Scott to offer his resignation. He was willing to be succeeded by Hayes because he felt that the full mission of the university would be safe in his hands. Hayes, he said, would bring to the office a rare combination of qualities that would strengthen the university internally and in its relations with the state government and the general public. At first, he said, he took it for granted that Hayes would not be interested, but later urged Hayes to consider the possibility. The office would enable him, Scott advised, to guide educational development in Ohio and the central west by securing for the university ample resources and genuine power to realize its potential. The result would be the elevation and enobling of the choicest minds of the state, he said, and this was a reward sufficient to induce such a man as Hayes to consider the possibility.[16]

14. Ibid., X, no. 21 (August 1, 1887), 343; no. 22 (August 15, 1887), p. 359; *Record of Procedings of the Board of Trustees*, 341.

15. Hayes, *Diary*, entry for December 10, 1890; Mendenhall, op. cit., pp. 153–55.

16. William Henry Scott to Rutherford B. Hayes, May 17, 1887, Hayes Papers.

Hayes, of course, was undoubtedly aware that he was not the kind of man which the agricultural interests saw as the Ohio State University's next president. One former trustee and a long-time critic of the institution wrote Hayes as soon as the presidential rumor reached him. "I see they want you to be president of the state university," he said, and added that he "reckoned" that Hayes would hardly agree to that. He expressed pleasure that Hayes was a trustee, and he hoped that he would use that office to help make the institution what the Morrill Act had intended it to be. He complained that as it was, it was merely an excellent school for the young people of Columbus, where they might conveniently study courses already offered at a host of other, more distant, institutions.[17]

J. H. Brigham advised Hayes that the best policy probably was to retain Scott until "*the man*" could be found. The only valid criticism of Scott that he had heard, he said, was that Scott could not win the respect of the students, and that was not so critical as to require immediate action. In view of the new policies of the board since Hayes' arrival, he implied, he would not urge Scott's removal. The right kind of man for the post would be difficult to find, he concluded, and the change should not be made until such a man was located and secured. Brigham's candidate would be a man like Henry E. Alvord, he said, "who would have been elected president of the Massachusetts Agricultural College had it not been for the pigheaded stupidity of some of the trustees." The letter left no doubt that Brigham's thoughts about the Ohio State Universiy's next president did not encompass a man such as Rutherford B. Hayes.[18]

For the next twelve years, then, the university faced the problem of finding the right man. It faced at least one other crucial problem, too. The board of trustees, having assumed the responsibility for making amends with the farm interests, had in fact also assumed direct responsibility for effecting changes within the university commensurate with that settlement. They had, furthermore, accorded to Rutherford B. Hayes informal and what amounted to extralegal authority. The president of the institution had indicated

17. T. C. Jones to R. B. Hayes, May 19, 1887, Hayes Papers.
18. J. H. Brigham to R. B. Hayes, December [?], 1887, Hayes Papers.

that he would resign in Hayes' favor; the farm interests had indicated that with Hayes' controlling voice on the board they could readily abide the incumbent; the board secretary had indicated that he and the entire board recognized that Hayes had, in fact, indicated the direction in which they should go. All had accorded to Hayes the position of leadership at the Ohio State University. It was a position of power which grew out of his own personal stature and it was accorded to him voluntarily. In some respects, however, the position of "prime minister" which he occupied continued after his death, and it was assumed at that time by William Isaac Chamberlain, the man whom Hayes had passed over in the search for a new president.

CHAPTER 9

Consensus through Structure and Process

The performance of the board of trustees changed when Rutherford B. Hayes joined that body in 1887. In some ways, he merely furthered some trends already underway, but he also changed the board's way of seeing its own function. Just as student life and faculty behavior had become better organized, so also did the board of trustees organize itself for greater efficiency. Hayes had some specific notions about how the board's work should be conducted, and he moved immediately to make some changes.

First, however, he dealt with the problem of compulsory chapel, with which he had little sympathy. He persuaded the board to amend its by-laws to give the "President of the Faculty" discretion in excusing students from compulsory chapel services on reasonable grounds. The board's action requiring chapel had been welcomed by Ohio's conservative Protestants, and Hayes did not wish to disturb the resultant peace. Catholics and Jews, however, highly resented the requirement, which they felt closed the doors of the state university to their children. It was this problem which Hayes wanted to solve, and, with the adoption of his amendment to the by-laws, this was accomplished.[1]

The wording of Hayes' amendment, however, indicated the frame of reference within which his other proposals for change would be

1. *Record of Proceedings of the Board of Trustees*, pp. 345–46.

formulated. He had referred to the "President of the Faculty," not
of the university, and this concept explained the nature of his subsequent actions. He perceived the president as a dean of faculties
and the board as the administrative unit within the university.
Perhaps, as an attorney, this was to him the logical implication of
the Cannon Act which created the university and extended to its
board of trustees full authority to conduct the affairs of the institution. Perhaps, too, the need to bring peace, harmony, and increased
financial support compelled him to view the structure in this way.
Of crucial importance also, however, was Hayes's tremendous capacity for administration and the apparent absence of enough demands to make full use of it in Fremont. In any event, Hayes perceived the board as directly involved in the administrative affairs
of the Ohio State University.[2]

From the beginning, the board had behaved pretty much in this
fashion. They had, from time to time, appointed superintendents
of buildings and grounds, bursars, and men to supervise the construction of new buildings. Department heads had responded directly to the board with requests for equipment. One of Walter
Quincy Scott's problems with the board had been his insistence that
all such matters come to him first for his subsequent transmission
to the trustees. Hayes's concept, therefore, was not radically new,
but he organized and formalized the structure that reduced the
institution's president to the role of dean.[3]

Hayes's view of the trustee function was indeed a broad one. In
November of 1887, shortly after his appointment, the board agreed,
at Hayes's suggestion, to select an approved landscape gardener to
construct a general campus plan to guide the trustees in their
future decisions about buildings and grounds. In the same month,
he was instrumental in action directing professors to submit requests for special legislative appropriations through the "President
of the Faculty." They should indicate what they needed, their pri-
ority for each request, and an estimate of the cost involved. The

2. Ibid., pp. 336 ff.
3. Ibid., pp. 80–81, 174, 176, 218, 231; see also, "Report of the President
for 1882–1883," *Report of the Board of Trustees to the Governor of Ohio*
(Columbus, 1883), pp. 17–33.

board would then combine these with other needs of the university in a request to the state legislature. Annual financial support could be justified by advanced planning which revealed needs, costs, and priorities and which related dollar requests to program plans in a specific fashion.[4]

The following month, Hayes recommended to the board that its secretary open an office at the university and that, in addition to his duties as secretary, he also perform the duties of "Registrar of the institution under direction of the Board of Trustees," not that of the president. The board accepted the recommendation. Hayes then suggested the appointment of President Scott and the secretary, Alexis Cope, as a committee of two to arrange for an office for the trustees and their secretary in the university building. From then on, the board met in the secretary's rooms at the university, and the board's secretary became an on the scene advisor, observer and administrator.[5]

For many years, observed Thomas C. Mendenhall, Cope's greatest joy was in the intimate relations between himself and a few of the older members of the faculty. The "choice spirits," so-called, gathered in Cope's office regularly to discuss the university and the world at large. There students sought him for advice and help. He was a counselor for students, consultant for faculty, and agent for trustees.[6]

Hayes had a broad notion of the role of the board's secretary, and he mixed executive and secretarial assignments for him. As his appreciation of Alexis Cope's abilities grew, his dependency on him likewise grew. He saw the secretary as the full-time executive arm of the board of trustees. Invariably, Hayes moved to include the secretary on all committees appointed by the board, and he referred many matters to the secretary with power to act. In this manner, the secretary was directed to purchase gas fixtures for the university building, to lay gas mains, to build a bridge across Neil Run, to clear woods, to let fuel contracts, to purchase equipment for the

4. *Record of Proceedings of the Board of Trustees*, pp. 345–46.
5. Ibid., p. 349.
6. Mendenhall, op. cit., p. xxi.

military battalion and the university band, to plaster and repair dormitories, and to supervise their rental as a hotel during the Columbus celebration of the national centennial of the establishment of the nation under the Constitution. The secretary, therefore, served as business manager and superintendent of buildings and grounds as well as registrar and secretary, all under the direct supervision of the board without specific obligation to the university president.[7]

Hayes and Alexis Cope carried on an extensive correspondence about university business, and Hayes normally arranged to confer with the secretary before the board met. Cope in turn kept Hayes well informed about every facet of university activity. He reported opening enrollment figures and described the students: "The new students are more mature than usual. We have not drawn as largely from the farms as we hoped." And he reported on attrition. "The mortality through failures and conditions was quite large . . . The boys are too young to be left so largely without restraint." On one occasion he sent Hayes a copy of a final examination in freshman rhetoric which, he said, had seemed unduly difficult. Only thirteen out of a class of sixty had passed it, but, he added, "Professor Welsh was induced to *reduce* the standard so that only thirteen wholly failed."[8]

If Hayes functioned, ex officio, as president of the university in so many respects, it was Alexis Cope who made it possible for him to do so effectively. Cope advised him of what appeared to be crucial or impending problems and thereby helped Hayes to decide whether he could miss a board meeting or come late. On one occasion, he advised that although he knew it would be difficult for Hayes to come to Columbus, he anticipated that the board was going to disagree with the president on a faculty appointment and that he should come to prevent a rupture. On another occasion, Cope wrote, "At Monday's meeting we will clear away the rubbish and be ready for solid work Tuesday morning when you will be

7. *Record of Proceedings of the Board of Trustees*, pp. 345–46.
8. Alexis Cope to R. B. Hayes, October 6, 1887, January 23, 1888, Hayes Papers.

here." Together the two men made an increasingly effective team for administering the affairs of the institution.[9]

Hayes' penchant for expediting board business by referring it to the secretary was also evident in his efforts to refer less routine matters to the board's executive committee with power to act. The executive committee, composed primarily of Franklin County residents, and served by the board's efficient secretary, therefore, became empowered to act for the board at a policy level without awaiting a full board session. The practice further strengthened the role of the board as a direct policy determining unit in the administration of the university.[10]

The work of the university was expanding to the point that a single man as president could not be expected to do it all. Rather than redefining the role of president, however, and providing assistants for him, the board expanded and formalized its own procedures for carrying out the commission of authority granted them in the Cannon Act. Hayes' role in this development was far more definitive than would normally be the case for a man holding a seat on the board. He had the experience, the prestige, and, having retired from politics and public life, the leisure to devote to the Ohio State University and its problems. He was comfortable in the confidences of politics and in the lobbies of legislatures, and the friends of the university showed him great deference. Much of his influence derived from his confident assumption that university needs would eventually be met by legislative appropriation if it but charted an appropriate course.[11]

In 1890, when it became obvious that the university would run a deficit unless it increased student fees, Hayes helped to arrange for state approval for the university to operate at a deficit. This provided a direct pressure on the legislature for on-going financial support which was, in fact, realized the following year with an annual statewide tax to support the university. This had been an objective

9. Alexis Cope to R. B. Hayes, August 18, 1888, June 17, 1892, Hayes Papers.
10. *Record of Proceedings of the Board of Trustees*, pp. 336 ff.
11. Mendenhall, op. cit., p. 158.

of the board since before Hayes' appointment, and his power over the board rested in part on the belief that he could help to bring the hope to realization. He used his influence over the board with little hesitation. One last obstruction in bringing peace, harmony, and money to the state university, for instance, was its interest in the Virginia Military District land cession assigned to the university in 1882, and Hayes induced the Board to settle that controversial matter as well.[12]

In 1871, the federal Congress had ceded to the state all unsold lands in the Virginia Military District which was that portion of Ohio reserved for Revolutionary War veterans by Virginia when that state surrendered its claims in the Northwest Territory in 1784. The district included all of the land between the Scioto and the Little Miami Rivers, and included the cities of Chillicothe and Franklinton. The state legislature in turn gave the unclaimed lands to the university. Within a period of eighteen years, the university collected nearly $65,000 from this source and by 1925 the total fund had reached a quarter of a million dollars. The support was not obtained, however, without alienating a great number of people.[13]

In the early efforts to realize substantial funds from this source, the board of trustees had authorized land agents to search out property belonging to the university under the terms of the cession. In the process, considerable ill will was generated throughout the district, which touched all or part of twenty-two of the state's eighty-eight counties. The board later claimed that it had not approved of taking advantage of technical defects in titles or the negligence or ignorance of those occupying the land. The university's land agents, however, worked for a percentage of the value of the lands which they secured for the college, and were less circumspect. One such agent, for instance, worked for a third of his "find" plus expenses. His alleged discoveries totaled 60,000 acres, worth a million dollars, and the resultant furor brought action from the state legislature.[14]

12. *Record of Proceedings of the Board of Trustees,* pp. 399–405.
13. Mendenhall, op. cit., pp. 57–63.
14. Ibid., pp. 62–63; suits relative to this agent's claim against the University continued in the courts until the turn of the century.

To protect property holders in the Virginia Military District, the federal Congress had passed several acts to clarify its original cession, but the courts of Ohio had ruled in favor of the university's land agents. They had stipulated that any land entry made prior to 1852 but not properly registered with the General Land Office in Washington was, in effect, void, and that the land had passed to Ohio by Act of Congress and to the university by the act of the state legislature. As a result of the court's ruling, the search for "vacant" lands became greatly intensified in 1887 and 1888. Finally, on March 14, 1889, the legislature specified that the university should deed to any applicant with evidence of possession, the disputed property in the Virginia Military District. The person requesting a deed should pay the university a two dollar fee and, if he also paid all court costs in cases where suits had already been brought, the state would reimburse the university at the rate of one dollar per acre.[15]

The bill passed by the legislature had been drawn up by Alexis Cope and Thomas A. Cowgill, a member of the board of trustees, presumably at Hayes' direction. The trustees of the university, however, would have to formally agree to the arrangement before it could go into effect, and some of them were extremely reluctant to do so. Particularly reluctant were two trustees whose homes were within the Virginia Military District and who left the board after its land affairs were settled. On the first vote on whether or not to accept the plan for settlement, the trustees were split evenly. Rutherford B. Hayes voted for the settlement and stressed the importance of resolving the whole problem. In an evening session following an extended dinner at which less formal discussions took place, the board reconsidered the matter, and approved the settlement by a five to one vote.[16]

In this manner, in all areas where the university had become involved in contention, Hayes sought a peaceful adjustment. He had designed a measure giving the president discretion regarding compulsory chapel attendance, paving the way for peace with

15. Ibid., pp. 59–62.
16. *Record of Proceedings of the Board of Trustees*, p. 376; Alexis Cope to R. B. Hayes, February 2, 1888, Hayes Papers.

Catholics and Jews in Ohio if not with theological liberals. He had designed and engineered a memorandum of understanding between the Agricultural Experiment Station and the university which symbolized a broader rapprochement between the school and the state's farmers. He had persuaded the university board to accept "the enemy" within their camp in the person of the secretary of the State Board of Agriculture as a further demonstration that hostilities were at an end. In addition, then, Hayes had also persuaded the trustees to accept peace in the land wars of the Virginia Military District.

In 1890, however, Hayes and Cope perceived what they thought was another attempt to reorganize the board of trustees. James E. Campbell, the successful Democratic candidate for governor, had indicated that he thought that the board would have wider influence if it were enlarged. Though he claimed that it was not his intention to reorganize the board for political reasons, Hayes did not accept his professed good intentions. He took direct and speedy action to forestall the governor's plan and indicated that he was not inclined to compromise everything merely to avoid a fight. Regardless of the governor's intentions, Hayes told Cope, if he reorganized the board so soon after his election it would be regarded as a party move for power and spoils and would establish once again the precedent of changing the board with Ohio's political winds. "To prevent this," he added, "I am ready to give the Democrats the present Board of Trustees." He advised Cope to let the governor know that one of the trustee's terms would soon expire and that on that date Hayes himself would resign. Campbell could then appoint two Democrats and assume control.[17]

Cope showed Hayes' letter to Campbell and reported that the governor said that he did not desire political reorganization, that he really felt that a larger board would extend the university's influence, "that it would never do to accept your resignation," and that he wanted to talk with Hayes about the matter. Campbell later wrote Hayes to tell him he wanted him to remain on the board and that he had "not the slightest intention that the institu-

17. R. B. Hayes to Alexis Cope, February 23, 1890, R. B. Hayes Correspondence, Manuscript Collection, Ohio State University Library.

tion shall be run into politics." Campbell seemed genuinely interested in the welfare of the institution, and, observed Hayes, "seems sincerely right on the whole subject." [18]

In 1891, diminishing pressures to restrict the university coincided with mounting interest in providing it with greater financial assistance. There was something of a "boom" in higher education in America in the 1890's, and Hayes and the other trustees had maneuvered into a position to take advantage of it. Throughout the nation, enrollments were increasing, gifts from philanthropists were becoming almost common, and state appropriations were rising. It was a national phenomenon transcending purely local causes.

Enrollments increased for a variety of reasons. For many people, there was growing affluence in the nation's burgeoning industrial economy, and there was, therefore, more money for expensive ventures like higher education. Furthermore, the institutions had changed their programs and were meeting the prospective student more on his own terms than ever before. The elective system had become almost universally copied, if not in its entirely, at least in principle. In addition, utilitarian criteria for curriculum planning were widely observed and applied. The expansion of public high schools likewise increased the opportunity for students to enter college.

Beyond these factors, an increasing number of parents, particularly among the families of the self-made men of American business and industry, began to view the college degree as a verification of their newly found status, and a mark of their achievement in socially mobile America. This aspect of the increased popularity of higher education also accounted in large measure for the growing hedonism on college campuses and the changing nature of student life.[19]

Philanthropy also contributed to the newly found prosperity of higher education. New institutions like Clark and Stanford drama-

18. Alexis Cope to R. B. Hayes, February 27, 1880, Hayes Papers; Governor James E. Campbell to R. B. Hayes, March 11, 1890, Hayes Papers; R. B. Hayes to Alexis Cope, March 18, 1890, R. B. Hayes Correspondence, Manuscript Collection, Ohio State University.

19. Veysey, op. cit., pp. 258–65.

tized the university in American life. The University of Illinois benefited directly as a result of the establishment of the University of Chicago. Illinois state legislators chafed at the comparisons made between the private university at Chicago and the state university, and the political parties vied to see which would be designated as the friend of higher education.[20] Not all academicians were pleased with the devolopments of the 1890's. Students, legislators, and businessmen had ulterior interests in higher education, some felt, and were not devoted to the search for truth. Criticisms of the gay life of students, the political pressuring of politicians, and the iconoclasm of businessmen as trustees mounted from a minority who opposed the emerging American university idea.

While some academicians may have questioned the trends, however, others willingly accepted the newly offered assistance and with it strengthened graduate programs, university research, and modest sabbatical leave programs. In a few places, the new-found prosperity permitted the establishment of research professorships with resultant freedom from heavy teaching loads.[21]

Direct annual legislative aid to the Ohio State University, however, had one further hurdle. In 1891, Nial R. Hysell, speaker of the House of Representatives, had taken charge of a bill which sought to incorporate the suggestion of governor James E. Campbell, a Democrat from Butler County, that the time had come to supplement the land grant fund by a permanent state appropriation. Immediately, the friends of Ohio and Miami universities insisted that they should also be included in any annual appropriation. It was their intent to block any action that would aid the Ohio State University without aiding the two older institutions. Spokesmen for the Ohio State University, however, were adamant. They did not oppose aid to the other two, they said, but they would not agree to a division of the fund authorized in this particular bill. If the

20. Allan Nevins, *Illinois*, pp. 158–59; for a thorough treatment of the role of philanthropy in higher education see Merle Curti and Roderick Nash, *Philanthropy in the Shaping of American Higher Education* (New Brunswick, N. J.: Rutgers University Press, 1965); for the classic position of the latter group, see Thorstein Veblen, *The Higher Learning in America* (New York: B. W. Hirebock, 1918); Veysey, op. cit., pp. 277–80.

21. Ibid., pp. 175–76.

other institutions were to have aid, it should be by separate legislation. As an indication of the changing climate for higher education and the results of Hayes' program of measured appeasement, friends of the Hysell bill, seeking votes in the legislature, were not inclined to compromise or to bargain. Instead, they told assemblymen that they had the votes to pass the bill as it was, and, in at least one case, told a recalcitrant assemblyman that he did not dare to vote against it. The bill passed, and it was not amended to include the other two institutions. With the passages of the Hysell Act, the state began, in a fiscal sense, to support a state university. Shortly thereafter, measures to benefit Ohio and Miami Universities were also enacted, although the relationships among the three state institutions remained undefined.[22]

Indicating that student journalists could praise as well as blame, the editors of the *Makio* for 1891 dedicated the volume to Governor Campbell and the Hon. N. R. Hysell as friends of education and justice, and included full page portraits of the two men. They heralded the beginning of "The Golden Age at Ohio State University," and called for the addition of law and medical schools. They praised Alexis Cope, secretary of the board of trustees and the board's executive agent on campus, as a leader of the "recent university movement." Coincidental with the passage of the Hysell Act and the growing momentum of the "university movement," the students noted growing and wide-spread support for the university in the newspapers of the state, and the organization of alumni associations throughout Ohio. The idea of a great state university for Ohio seemed to be growing with renewed vigor, and the students were enthusiastic.[23]

The advent of state support in Ohio coincided with similar trends elsewhere in the nation. In fact, universities everywhere seemed to share in a common development that included not just the increased enrollment and enhanced resources already discussed, but also common developments in administrative techniques which sought to strike a balance between the authority of governing

22. Mendenhall, op. cit., pp. 142–45.
23. *Makio*, XI (1891), 10–12.

bodies and the independence of faculties. In a sense, the university in the 1890's, like American business and industry, witnessed the emergence of an administrative structure that, in the field of higher education, superseded and then monitored the several philosophic orientations which had sought to define the university in the years that followed the Civil War. Commensurate with this was the emergence of a self-conscious academic community which sought to preserve its freedom within the developing structure.[24]

In one respect, at least, developments at the Ohio State University did not coincide with the national trend. The increased authority of the university president and the emergence of the office of dean was typical of a national pattern of university administration. In Ohio, however, the board of trustees performed more of the non-academic functions and at the same time retained ultimate authority for academic functions as well. The president was just as often called the president of the faculty as he was the president, and the board was inclined to view its own secretary as its primary administrative arm. The arrangement had derived from the original charter act of the university which subjected the president to annual reelection along with the rest of the faculty. It was strengthened by the legislature's power to limit the salary of the president, and thereby severely restrict the board's efforts to secure men for the position. The condition was further developed by the reorganization of the board in 1874, at which time the secretary of the board of trustees became a salaried officer with expanded duties approved by the governor. As a result, the secretary became beholden to the governor for his post quite as much as he was to the trustees, and he was not at all dependent upon the president of the university.[25]

Later, in the process of eliminating periodic political reorganization of the board, the two board offices, secretary and treasurer, were retained as separate posts in spite of the pleas of Orton, Scott, and the secretaries and treasurers themselves that the posts were complementary and should be combined. As separate posts they were split between the two major parties. When a Republican governor approved a Republican secretary, the board generally

24. Veysey, op. cit., pp. 268, 302.
25. Joseph Sullivant to R. B. Hayes, January 25, 1876, Hayes Papers.

elected a Democrat as treasurer as a hedge on future changes in the political control of the state and as a protection against charges of corruption and politically inspired investigations. When the party of the secretary changed, presumably a new treasurer was appointed as well. The final factor which weakened the post of the president, however, was the effective leadership of the institution by Hayes during a long period of years during which he sought to remove the board from politics, make peace with the institution's enemies, and create the conditions which would induce the right man to take the president's responsibilities. This objective was one goal which Rutherford B. Hayes did not achieve before his death.[26]

26. Henry S. Babbitt to R. B. Hayes, June 4, 1888; Alexis Cope to R. B. Hayes, June 9, 1888, Hayes Papers.

CHAPTER 10

Unfinished Business

Ohio's land grant college, it seemed, had always spent a large proportion of its time in the search for just the right man to be its president. Even in the beginning, in 1870, the trustee's first choice, former Governor Jacob D. Cox, turned them down, later to become president of the University of Cincinnati. Their second choice accepted the appointment but later relinquished it because of political embarrassments. Finally, in 1873, after the institution had been located, its course program outlined, its faculty hired, its buildings designed and contracted for, and its great seal designed—all by the board of trustees—Edward Orton accepted the high office. Within five years, however, he had submitted his resignation. His resignation remained before the board for three years before it was finally accepted. Within another two years, however, his successor had failed of annual reelection. The Reverend William Henry Scott, president of Ohio University, was then inaugurated as the institution's third president.[1]

The second Dr. Scott remained in office until 1895, but as early as 1887, four years after his installation, he offered to resign. Thus, between 1870 and 1890, for scarcely more than nine years had the institution been certain of its president; in eleven of those years,

1. See Chapter V, supra.

the office had either been vacant or held by a man who had already decided to resign. Of the nine more certain years, four were served by Edward Orton, whose broad and liberal views of what a state university should be had met growing opposition, and five by William Henry Scott, whom the board called the "President of the Faculty."

Beginning with the indication by William Henry Scott in 1887 that he would resign, the board was faced with the question of his successor. Not until seven years had passed, however, were they able to agree upon a man for the post whose appointment was feasible and within five more years that man had resigned. The activities of those years and the variety of men considered indicate the extreme lack of agreement about the nature of the position or the purpose of the university with which the board struggled. The advice of some of the men who refused the position emphasized the dichotomy between developing national practices and local developments at the Ohio State University.

In the first place the institution was saddled with an extremely powerful board of trustees and the board itself had developed a tradition of active participation in institutional affairs via a board secretary resident on the campus and beholden to the governor for his job. The board had also evolved the role of unofficial "prime minister", a leading trustee who exercised authority of presidential proportions. This post was first held by Rutherford B. Hayes, who earlier as governor had in fact created the institution. It was held secondly by William I. Chamberlain, a former college president, a disappointed candidate for the presidency of the Ohio State University and chairman of the presidential selection committee at the time of Hayes's death. Add to this twenty year development the heritage of the Walter Quincy Scott ouster, board control over appointments and tenure, and an unbelievably low salary schedule, and the dimensions of the problem become quite clear.

In 1890, William Isaac Chamberlain, formerly of the Ohio Board of Agriculture and Walter Quincy Scott's outspoken defender, resigned as president of the State Agricultural College of Iowa. He confided to friends there that he was certain that he would be

the next president of the Ohio State University. Such a development would have pleased the farm bloc. Chamberlain had been an
energetic and popular member of the State Board of Agriculture,
and had expanded the functions and services of that group. In
1886, he had been chosen president at Iowa. The following year,
Rutgers recognized his work for the farmer by awarding him an
honorary degree. At Iowa, he had retained his views concerning
academic freedom, and he protected the concept of permanent
tenure for faculty members.

But Chamberlain at Iowa was too meticulous as an administrator,
and his religious views were considered to be too narrow. His
strict Sabbatarianism embarrassed the more free-thinking scientists
on his faculty. The faculty was not enthusiastic about Chamberlain,
agricultural interests were split over him and other issues, and the
students viewed him, evidently, like the Ohio State University
students viewed William Henry Scott. In 1890, the graduating
class absented itself from the baccalaureate service as an affront
to the president, and it was obvious that he had lost control of student behavior. In full confidence that the sequence of events
in Ohio fomented by his friends in the state agricultural movement would make him president at the Ohio State University,
Chamberlain submitted his resignation at Iowa, and it was promptly
accepted.[2]

Hayes, however, did not have as much confidence in Chamberlain as Chamberlain had in Hayes. Hayes recorded in his diary
that certain members of the board wanted Chamberlain, and that
he had agreed to consider the case impartially. He insisted, however, that he had made no promises. It became increasingly evident in light of Hayes's other successes that the board would defer
to Hayes on the matter, and they awaited his decision. "It will
strengthen us with the farmers," he confided to his diary. "Make
it in fact, a mechanics' and farmers' college and gain thus in the

2. Earle D. Ross, *The History of the Iowa State College,* pp. 140–15;
*Addresses Delivered at the Inauguration of W. I. Chamberlain to the Presi-
dency of the Iowa State Agricultural College, November 9, 1886* (Ames, Iowa,
1886); Mendenhall, op. cit., p. 166.

legislature the needed votes for its liberal support." Here, Hayes was thinking of the tax levy for the university's support, which the university had sought for several years and which would be approved in 1891. "The truth is," Hayes continued, "I fear Chamberlain is not large enough in head and character for the place. But —?" Hayes did not finish the sentence, but he did not ultimately agree to the selection of Chamberlain. As a result, it was not possible to choose anyone else for a while, and there the matter rested.[3]

The university awarded Chamberlain an honorary degree, and he returned to his work with the State Board of Agriculture. Within a few months, however, he was appointed to the University board of trustees by Governor William McKinley. With his ten years' background as a college teacher, and his four years as a college president in addition to his long career as a trusted leader among agricultural interests, he was a formidable trustee. Thomas C. Mendenhall, former professor of physics at the university, observed that Chamberlain frequently appealed to his experience as justification for the board's following his advice. From 1893 to 1895, Chamberlain served on the committee which searched for Scott's successor, and he assumed the role of "prime minister" when it was vacated by Hayes in 1893.[4]

The failure to find a new president was not because the board did not try. The list of men whom it considered represented as diverse a group as any college might possibly consider. In 1892, William Henry Scott had again resigned after the board had disregarded his wishes concerning a faculty appointment, and had selected the candidate to whom he had specifically objected. The board, however, did not accept the resignation. Later in that year, Scott created a sensation at the university by publicly demitting the ministry and withdrawing from membership in the Methodist church. Speaking in chapel, he stunned the students by his action

3. Hayes, *Diary*, entry for December 10, 1890; Ross, *History of Iowa State College*, pp. 113–15.
4. Mendenhall, op. cit., pp. 165–66.

which he said he took for conscience sake and in order to enjoy "a freer, broader, and higher religious life." Alexis Cope anticipated a great deal of controversy as a result of his action, and said that it seemed quite likely that his resignation would now have to be accepted. In June of 1893, Scott again submitted his resignation, and this time it was accepted to take effect when his successor was named.[5]

One of the chief obstacles to finding a successor, however, was the salary limit, set by the legislature, which prohibited the board from paying a salary of more than $3,000 a year. This was the figure first established in 1870 for the president's salary, and, although less had been paid on occasion, the salary had never exceeded that limit. It made it increasingly impossible to secure a man of the proper character and attainments.[6]

One of the men considered for the presidency was Hayes's preferred choice, Dr. Washington Gladden, but he would not accept the post at the salary which the board was authorized to pay. Hayes and Cope corresponded about Gladden as a possible choice as early as June of 1891. At that time, Cope indicated that Gladden had been approached once before but had indicated that he was not interested. A year later, L. B. Wing of the board of trustees, told Hayes that Gladden was being considered for the presidency at the Illinois Agricultural College and that if Hayes wanted him in Ohio he should "head off" the Illinois movement. Hayes immediately made contact with Gladden who confirmed the Illinois offer, and also indicated that he had already turned down one eastern institution. "There seems to be an alarming scarcity of timber out of which to make college presidents," he told Hayes, but he indicated that while he was in doubt about his course of action, it was becoming clearer to him. The presidency of a western university seemed to be his fate, he thought, and the Ohio State University position was merely a "bird in the bush." "I must not too hastily decline" the offer from Illinois, he concluded. Nevertheless, he did decline, but told Hayes that his action in no way assumed

5. Ibid., p. 151; Alexis Cope to R. B. Hayes, October 6, 1892, Hayes Papers.
6. *Record of Proceedings of the Board of Trustees*, pp. 41, 160; Mendenhall, op. cit., pp. 157–58.

any commitment from the board of trustees of the Ohio State University.[7]

In July of 1892, Hayes and Cope met with Gladden and indicated that he would be elected when the legislature was induced to raise the salary limitation. Cope, however, disagreed with the way Hayes proposed to bring the election about. "I do not see how the informal and inconclusive action of the trustees can be kept from the public," he wrote Hayes. Scott's position was certain to be further weakened, he said, and Gladden would be "hung up by a vague and uncertain promise." Cope advised that the matter be made definite by having the board elect Dr. Gladden to assume office on January 1, 1893. He urged Hayes to attend the next board meeting to see that the election took place. Hayes, however, replied that his old regiment was holding a reunion at the time of the board's session and that he had to go. It was almost as though it were the last such reunion he expected ever to attend and he wanted to be there. "Dr. Gladden will wait for our action a reasonable time—say until the next session of the legislature has time to act." Unless the meeting were "of life and death importance," said Hayes, he intended to miss it. The job now was to get action in the legislature whether the arrangement leaked out or not. Hayes closed his letter to Cope by saying, "To fight is the condition of existence. Let it come. What is worth having is worth fighting for." [8]

The possibility of Gladden's election, however, did leak out, and retention of the salary limitation appeared to be an effective way of preventing his formal election. The Columbus pastor's social, political, economic, and theological views marked him as a liberal and unacceptable to many. His volume *Who Wrote the Bible?* which popularized the new theology had not been well received by those of more conservative religious views. Two other books, *Applied Christianity*, which appeared in 1886, and *Tools and the Man: Property and Industry Under Christian Law*, which was to

7. Alexis Cope to R. B. Hayes, June 10, 1891; L. B. Wing to R. B. Hayes, June 29, 1892; Washington Gladden to R. B. Hayes, July 2 and July 11, 1892, Hayes Papers.

8. Alexis Cope to R. B. Hayes, July 13, 1892, Hayes Papers; R. B. Hayes to Alexis Cope, July 13, August 12, 1892, R. B. Hayes Correspondence, Manuscript Collection, Ohio State University Library.

appear that very year, set forth his social views in greater detail. He was opposed to socialism, but he did favor government ownership of public utilities. He maintained that the church should endorse no particular economic system but should attempt to Christianize whatever system existed. These views, together with his support of labor unions and his opposition to the popular nativist and anti-Catholic American Protective Association, which he had denounced, made it increasingly obvious to the board that he could not be chosen if they hoped for any kind of continuing legislative support. Other candidates were considered, but none was interested at the salary offered. One advised the board to get the salary raised first and then look for candidates.[9]

Then on January 17, 1893, Rutherford B. Hayes, who had served effectively as the peacemaker on the board for several years, died leaving a void that was practically impossible to fill. His work on behalf of the university had been of crucial importance; he had made peace with the farmers and had helped to secure a new departure in the state's attitude toward its university. He had also held the presidency in escrow for delivery to a man like Gladden after he reclaimed the University, but he held it too long. His hold on the functions of the presidency was not in keeping with the pattern of academic administration emerging elsewhere in the nation, and he unwittingly set a pattern for the university that was difficult to change. He felt, however, that the president should be "large enough in head and character" to preside effectively over men of many and diverse views. Neither Scott nor Chamberlain was such a man. Gladden, he was sure, was such a one, but he was not really sure that the office was sufficiently protected that such a man could serve in it.

Thomas C. Mendenhall, who from 1870 to 1878, and from 1881 until 1884 had been professor of physics at the university, was strongly supported as a candidate. He had first left the Ohio State University faculty in 1878 to become professor of physics at the

9. For a succinct outline of the life of Washington Gladden see the biographical sketch in the *Dictionary of American Biography*, pp. 325–27; see also Washington Gladden, *Recollections* (Columbus, Ohio: Houghton Mifflin Co., 1909); Mendenhall, op. cit., pp. 154, 155.

Imperial University at Tokyo. After returning to Columbus, he served three more years on the faculty before leaving to join the U. S. Signal Service in Washington. From there, he had gone to Rose Polytechnic Institute at Terre Haute, Indiana, as president. In 1889, President Benjamin Harrison appointed him as superintendent of the United States Coast and Geodetic Survey.[10]

Considering Professor Mendenhall for the post raised some of the same questions which Dr. Gladden's candidacy had raised. W. I. Chamberlain, himself a disappointed candidate, was not satisfied with the prospects which Mendenhall's election would create. Of particular concern, of course, was the matter of religious orthodoxy. Mendenhall had suggested that the school should adopt the practice instigated by President Eliot of Harvard, of having various leading clergymen serve as university chaplain, thus absolving the president of that responsibility and making his orthodoxy a less crucial matter. If the university were unable to change the salary limitation, however, there would be no problem anyhow, because Mendenhall would not leave the Coast and Geodetic Survey to take a position at a lower salary than that which he was then receiving.[11]

Members of the board of trustees asked Governor William McKinley to recommend that the limitation be raised when he addressed the general assembly, but he refused. The president of the Ohio State University was paid less than a good eastern headmaster, but the legislature refused to recognize its shortcoming in this respect and the governor was not inclined to call it to their attention. A bill was introduced in the assembly to effect the change anyway, but it was opposed by those who objected to Mendenhall for many of the same reasons that they had objected to Dr. Gladden. Others opposed it who objected to W. I. Chamberlain's conduct of affairs as a trustee. He reportedly had advised a popular professor to submit his resignation as a device enabling the board to grant him a salary increase without raising salaries generally. At Chamberlain's suggestion, however, the board accepted the

10. Ibid., pp. 159–60.
11. Ibid., p. 160.

resignation and subsequently named a friend of Chamberlain's from Iowa to the post. Representative N. R. Hysell, a good friend of the university and author of the first tax bill in its behalf, became a leader of the group demanding the former professor's reinstatement. Students and the Columbus newspapers also criticized Chamberlain and intimated that he had deliberately entrapped the professor. Matters went from bad to worse with rumors of an attempted bribe of the Senate Finance Committee by the ousted professor in an attempt to get it to report the pay raise bill unfavorably. In subsequent developments, the bill passed but left in its wake an investigation of corruption by the grand jury of Franklin County.[12]

The committee appointed to select Scott's successor then wrote again to T. C. Mendenhall offering him the post. The contents of the letter, which W. I. Chamberlain drafted, were not revealed, and no record was kept of the board meeting at which the action transpired, but evidently Chamberlain did not offer the full salary which the legislature had authorized. Mendenhall also had offers to return to Rose Polytechnic Institute, and to become president of the Worcester Polytechnic Institute in Worcester, Massachusetts; he accepted the latter offer and declined the offer of the Ohio State University. He intimated that, in spite of the legislature's action, an inadequate salary had been offered and that Chamberlain's letter had indicated that the new president would not have his own way in the election and dismissal of faculty members. The refusal was totally unexpected by the trustees, and many, including Alexis Cope, suspected that Chamberlain had aborted their efforts. A delegation of them sought to have Mendenhall reconsider his decision. In his final declination, however, Mendenhall said:

> While I am free to say that if they had put the matter in the beginning as they did at the end, with the assurance of their continued support, which they were ready to give last night, I should have been much less likely to decline, yet I must also say that several things were brought out in the discussion, relating especially to the opposition to me growing out of the unfortunate fact that I do not

12. Ibid., pp. 161–65.

sing and pray in public places, which were calculated to strengthen me in the belief that I would very quickly become a target for criticism and even abuse which would endanger the peace and success of the University.[13]

Publicity attending the negotiations with Mendenhall hurt further efforts, according to Chamberlain, and he wished for less newspaper scrutiny of the committee's search. The group then considered Merrill E. Gates, president of Amherst, and a former president of Rutgers, but he decided not to consider another change. Chamberlain then wrote to Herbert Baxter Adams of Johns Hopkins to broach the subject with him. Adams, however, raised questions about the administrative structure of the university. He was concerned, he said, about the instability of tenure and the president's lack of power in the appointment of faculty and the determination of university policy. He also questioned the president's role as chaplain, and the absence of a dean in the university structure. He was also concerned, he said, about a salary that could be fixed by the trustees but altered by the legislature. "I should be reluctant," he wrote politely, "to change my present stable position for an insecure tenure of office, with a salary subject to modification by a changing majority of the board or by the action of the legislature." [14]

At about this same time, the board contacted Dr. Ethelburt Dudley Warfield, president of Lafayette College in Pennsylvania, and, from 1888 to 1891, president of Miami University of Ohio. The board also contacted Dr. Woodrow Wilson, a professor at Princeton College and a former student of Herbert Baxter Adams. Wilson and Warfield consulted about the Ohio position and Wilson indicated to Warfield that although he had been thinking of undertaking administrative duties in a college, the conditions offered at Ohio State failed to provide the scope of action which he wanted to carry out his views about university administration. Warfield had already had one unhappy experience at Oxford in Ohio, and had no great desire to return to Ohio. Because of his eastern background and customs, he had been characterized as a dude in

13. Ibid., pp. 167–70; quoted in Mendenhall, op. cit., p. 170.
14. Ibid., p. 171.

Oxford, and his faculty was called the "dude-faculty." Neither
Warfield nor Wilson went beyond the first inquiry in negotiations
with the committee.[15]

The committee considered several other candidates and was
beginning to suffer from the insistence of Ohio newspapers that
immediate action be taken. They became torn between the pressure to act rapidly and the almost impossible task of finding an
appropriate candidate under the increasing scrutiny of the newspapers, the legislature and the general public. It was a deepening
crisis for the university in which the state's local problems pushed
the committee toward a selection, while salary limitations and
emerging customs and sectionalism in the academic world made
an appropriate selection increasingly difficult.

At this point, L. B. Wing, one of the members of the selection
committee, decided to contact James H. Canfield, chancellor of
the University of Nebraska, to see if he would be interested in
being considered. Canfield had written the committee at the request
of another aspirant. Wing wrote him about several persons who
were being considered and concluded his letter by asking Canfield
for his reaction to the possibility of his own selection for the office.
Canfield indicated a possible interest, and, after checking other
men in the field, the trustees made a formal tender of appointment
to Dr. Canfield.

Charles W. Eliot of Harvard had recommended him highly, indicating that he was a graduate of Williams College under Mark
Hopkins and an experienced teacher and administrator. He was a
ready worker, a good speaker, decidedly vigorous and breezy in
manner, said Eliot, and the board felt that it had made a wise
choice.[16] To their dismay, however, Canfield declined the offer
in a letter released to the Nebraska newspapers. A friend of Canfield's wrote to Alexis Cope, secretary of the board, implying that
the offer should be made again in about nine months and stating
that a crisis at Nebraska and unbelievable public pressures had
made Canfield's public refusal necessary. Nevertheless, it was a
stunning and unexpected surprise to the Ohio board. They con-

15. Ibid., p. 152; Walter Havighurst, *The Miami Years, 1809–1959* (New
York: G. P. Putnams' Sons, 1958), 146–54.
16. Mendenhall, op. cit., pp. 176–77, 181–82.

sidered several other candidates but eventually reconsidered Canfield and sought to discover whether he would receive their call differently if it were made again.[17]

This time, Canfield responded in a very lengthy letter asking a great many questions about the board's attitudes concerning public education and the selection of faculty and asking for a clearer specification of the duties of a president at the Ohio State University. He asked several questions about political influences in the affairs of the university, whether persons outside of the board had influence over the board, and whether there were staff members who held positions through influence and who were not really subject to the president or the board of trustees.[18] Alexis Cope responded with an equally lengthy letter attempting to answer Canfield's questions. In 1887, he said, when Rutherford B. Hayes came to the board, he threw his influence behind industrial education, strengthening it and winning the support of the people for the university. Now the time was ripe for a new man to do a great service for the people of Ohio and for popular education. Canfield accepted the position and arrived in Columbus to assume his duties in 1895.

One of James Hulme Canfield's primary interests was that the state university provide the crowning element of a superior statewide system of public instruction. This, in his view, was the full mission of the state university with a land grant foundation. It should supervise all public instruction, provide needed programs to meet the aspirations of the state and its youth in all fields from the humblest to the most advanced, and coordinate and standardize the entire system of higher education within the state. Furthermore, he saw the Ohio State University as the state's graduate and professional institution, determining standards of accreditation and certification for teachers, nurses, pharmacists, and the like.[19]

He also perceived the university president with commensurate administrative authority to supervise and direct his own campus and to influence affairs on other campuses in the state. Unfortu-

17. Ibid., pp. 179–81.
18. Ibid., pp. 193–95.
19. Veysey, op. cit., pp. 78, 111, 356; Mendenhall, op. cit., p. 252; Pollard, *History of the Ohio State University*, p. 144.

nately for his plans, neither his board of trustees, his faculty, nor the other colleges of Ohio agreed with him. The trustees resisted his efforts to control faculty appointments. The faculty resisted his efforts to construct the complete university by opposing, for instance, his efforts to add a medical college to the university complex. Both faculty and trustees resisted his efforts to assume powers that had previously resided with the board or with the faculty.[20]

Other colleges in the state resented his efforts to gain support for legislation subjecting them to state supervision. It was Canfield's belief that a central state agency should supervise the educational activities of all degree-granting institutions within the state, and he advocated legislation to bring such oversight about. The Association of Ohio Colleges, however, had considered such a coordinating and standardizing function for the state nearly twenty years before Canfield had arrived on the scene and had decided at that time that cooperative self-regulation was the better course. Ohio college leaders resented Canfield's efforts and their association was stimulated to better organized opposition. Members of the association used their influence in the legislature to circumscribe what they chose to identify as the state university's program.[21]

Canfield, in other words, advocated the state university as the keystone of the state's entire educational system, but was unable to gain sufficient support. By 1899, Canfield had resigned, and the university was again looking for a president. He could not work, Canfield said, under the "existing conditions and precedents at this university," and he saw no prospect of things becoming more like executive responsibilities under "more usual conditions." He alluded primarily to the role played by W. I. Chamberlain on the board of trustees, and the amount of authority delegated to the board's secretary.[22] After he resigned in 1899, the state and its university were still suspended between the East, where private education fulfilled the major role, and the West, where the state university did so, evidently unwilling or unable to go either direction, and as yet uncertain of any unique educational philosophy which needed

20. Mendenhall, op. cit., pp. 251–54; 258–62.
21. Pollard, *History of the Ohio State University*, pp. 140, 160–62, 164.
22. Ibid., pp. 197–200, 278–79.

institutional embodiment in Ohio and lacking an effective compromiser like Rutherford B. Hayes to arrange a reconciliation.

There was, as the students had correctly perceived, a university movement in Ohio in the 1890's, which grew out of the emerging national emphasis on higher education. There was also, by 1890, a distinctive midwestern educational spirit, and Canfield exemplified it. Utility became the creed of regionalism which reacted against the eastern model in higher education. It was a more balanced expression of that prejudice against the eastern institution which James M. Comly had identified earlier when he described Ohio institutions, with all their weaknesses, as superior to the "extravagant follies" of the eastern seaboard, or the derision exemplified when residents of Oxford, Ohio, called Miami's Princetonian faculty—a dude faculty.[23]

Canfield, as chancellor of the University of Nebraska, had attacked the eastern model fullsomely; he called the eastern colleges "institutions that seem to love scholarship and erudition for their own sake; who make these ends and not means; who hug themselves with joy because they are not as other men. . . ." Such a characterization of the eastern institution was not without widespread support in the Midwest of the 1890's.[24]

Canfield promoted utilitarian education and urged students to put vocational training first in their own educational plans. He attacked Greek-letter social fraternities and denominational colleges and criticized them as undemocratic and contrary to the spirit of American higher education. To Canfield's way of thinking, every college student would be better off in a state university. "My entire political creed, my entire political activity," he is reported to have claimed, "can be summed up in a single sentence: A thousand students in the state university in 1895; 2,000 in 1900." Presumably, he foresaw a continuing trend of that order of magnitude.[25]

23. *Makio*, XI (1891), 10–12; *Ohio State Journal* (Columbus, Ohio), May 31, 1881; Veysey, op. cit., p. 109.

24. James H. Canfield, "Ethical Culture in the College and University," National Education Association, *Proceedings*, 1892, p. 111, quoted in Veysey, op. cit., p. 78.

25. Canfield is quoted in H. W. Caldwell, "Education in Nebraska," U. S. Bureau of Education, *Circular of Information*, no. 3 (Washington, D. C.: U. S. Government Printing Office, 1902), p. 35.

If this was the spirit of the western state university, it was not entirely aceptable in Ohio with its diverse peoples, its multitude of denominational and private colleges, and a traditional sectionalism that reflected itself in the state legislature. Nor, on the other hand, was the spirit of the eastern university acceptable either. For one thing, there were the social objections which James Comly has identified. For another, there were the preachments of those men who had refused the institution's presidency about how the university should be run. The most detailed instructions had come from the eastern candidates. There was also a regional reaction to the spirit of the German university with its emphasis on research and science as too abstract and theoretical and as too far removed from the practical interests of the people as anything could be. In this Western view, the work of the people's university should be work that was related to the people.[26]

In 1897, one writer identified the Western view in an article entitled, "The Spirit of the Western University." He quoted an instructor in English at Nebraska, Canfield's former school, as saying that education was divided between those who seek fact and those who seek inspiration through fact. German education, he said, stood mainly on the side of the fact; England and France stood mainly for culture, and American institutions were suspended in the balance. The eastern model leaned too far toward the German idea while the western model sacrificed culture to practical utility.[27]

26. Hugo Munsterberg, *American Patriotism and Other Social Studies* (New York: Moffat, Yard and Co., 1913), pp. 49–51; see also R. K. Richardson, "Yale of the West—A Study of Academic Sectionalism," *Wisconsin Magazine of History*, XXXVII (1953), 258–61, 280–83.

27. Quoted in Veysey, op. cit., pp. 180–81.

A Scattered Harvest

As a successor to the excitable James H. Canfield, the board of trustees picked robust, balding, calm William Oxley Thompson, a native of Ohio and, at the time, president of Miami University at Oxford. Thompson served the university as president from 1899 to 1925 and brought a stability to the institution which it had not previously known. During that quarter of a century he eclipsed Rutherford B. Hayes as the determinant personality in the institution. William Isaac Chamberlain, with whom Canfield had clashed, ended his career as a trustee as Canfield ended his administration as president. Edward Orton, first president and for over a quarter of a century an influential member of the university faculty, died four months after Thompson became president. Four years later, Alexis Cope ended his twenty year career as secretary of the board of trustees. Thus the old generation relinquished control as William Oxley Thompson came into office, the strong president, broad in heart and character, for whom Hayes had so diligently and so vainly sought.

Thompson embodied much of the spirit of the western state university as did Canfield but without the militant fervor, and thus he was less objectionable to many in the state. During his college days at Muskingum, Thompson had taken time out to work in Illinois and Iowa. Later as a Presbyterian minister he travelled to Denver, Cheyenne, Laramie and points west. In 1885, as president of Longmont College near Denver, he became firmly identified with the West before returning to Ohio to become president of Miami University in 1890. He was a robust, hearty, confident, imposing, windburned, son of the West—as Miami's historian described him—still known as the best farm hand in Muskingum County and as a harvester who could take one side of a wagon and keep up with any two men on the other side.[1]

But Thompson was also a man of intellectual acumen and political strength, and he brought financial strength to Miami for the first time in its history. He won the support of the legislature by his capacity to discuss farming in a believable manner and because he was shrewd enough or just natural enough to let the farmer in him show. He enjoyed it and so did the members of the predominantly rural legislature. They liked and trusted William Oxley Thompson and shortly after his return to Ohio, provided Miami with an annual state appropriation of $15,000. In 1896, Thompson went to Columbus to ask for passage of the Sleeper bill and succeeded; Miami then had the support of an annual tax levy. In its first year the levy produced $22,000 for the university—an amount almost as great as Ohio State's annual income from the Morrill Land Grant itself. Finally, Miami was fully a state-supported university and Thompson had accomplished it with relative ease. He persuaded the trustees to abolish tuition in advance of the state's legitimate request in order to show his appreciation of recent legislation. A man of such achievements was quite naturally considered for the presidency of the Ohio State University and with Canfield's resignation he was unanimously elected to the post in June of 1899.

In the closing months of Canfield's administration a plan to add a medical school to the university had elicited strong opposition and probably hastened his decision to resign. Thompson, on the

1. For a lengthy treatment of the life and personality of William Oxley Thompson see James E. Pollard, *William Oxley Thompson: Evangel of Education* (Columbus: Ohio State University Press, 1955); see also Walter Havighurst, *The Miami Years: 1809–1959*, particularly chap. xii, pp. 155–68.

other hand, strongly agreed with the opposition and denied the need for a college of medicine at the University. He tended to deemphasize the university movement altogether—at least temporarily—taking a more limited view of the function of the people's college. "Let us thank our stars," he later told the Association of Land Grant Colleges and Universities, "that the Land Grant Act makes no provisions for a University. It provided for a college and only a college."[2] And yet, during Thompson's long administration the modern dimensions of the Ohio State University emerged with various colleges including law, medicine, and education.

In his first year as president, Thompson showed the strength of his diplomacy in abolishing compulsory chapel services on the campus without serious repercussions. He also changed the procedure for handling the legislature by taking personal charge of all relations with members of the legislature individually or in committees. He minimized opposition and suspicion by his personal effort to meet with and talk with all who were in any way concerned with the University or its affairs. Thompson had no inaugural, gave no inaugural address and finished his first year with a succinct five-page report. He was a man of action, not of reports, and one example was his preference for conversation with, rather than reports to, men whose opinions would make a difference for the university. This in itself commended him to legislators.

Thompson's comments on the idea of the university were equally pleasing. In characterizing the spirit of the land grant college movement, William Oxley Thompson observed that "the agricultural college professor was to be a field marshall, not ashamed to wear overalls or to have a little mud on his boots." This was, he said, "perfectly dreadful in the polite circles of classical people," but it was "the spirit of life and progress in this great central west where a journey always begins at home." He spoke disparagingly of professors in dressing gowns, pipes in mouths, meditating where

2. William Oxley Thompson, "The Spirit of the Land-Grant Institution," *Address Delivered at the Forty-fifth Annual Convention of the Association of Land-Grant Colleges and Universities at Chicago, Illinois, November 16–18, 1931* (n.p., n.d.), p. 59.

students could not bother them on subjects which had no practical meaning for the students or the state. This, he insisted, was not to be at the land grant institution.[3]

Ohio, however, had not merely established a land grant agricultural college, it had created a state university with the land grant idea in tandem. Advocates of the one attempted to ignore the other and there were periods when one seemed to dominate the other. The problem of developing both together, as Rutherford B. Hayes hoped that they would be developed, had still not been resolved though many believed that William Oxley Thompson had the educational skill, the political acumen, and the personal strength to do so.

At the turn of the century, however, Ohio was still involved in the debate about the nature and purpose of its state university, unable to agree and to instruct the legislature on the basis of that agreement. The institution itself, in many respects, was marking time. The state held back from the eastern model which emphasized liberal culture, scientific research and an independent academic community, though there was much in it that appealed to people in the state. Many of Ohio's private schools turned increasingly in that direction although most of them were marking time as well. Ohio, generally, leaned toward the western model in the sense that William Oxley Thompson represented it, with its emphasis upon utilitarianism and democracy, and not in the sense that James H. Canfield had. Fundamentally, however, the people of the state had not yet decided that they should have a state university at all, at least not like any other that had been pointed out to them. In this situation, as Thompson had said that it must, the University looked to its people for their determination of its nature and its purpose and it reflected the same indecision and vacillation.

Thompson himself was aware of indecision and vacillation and he despaired about the future of the University. He was circumspect in his comments, but recognized early in his twenty-six year administration the dilemma of growing enrollments and restricted funds. The state would never limit enrollment, he observed, yet the funds for faculty salaries and facilities never caught up with the demands.

3. Ibid., p. 60.

Twenty years ahead of its adoption he advocated a term or quarter system that would permit enlarged enrollments with limited faculties and facilities. Yet in spite of Thompson's finesse in the lobbies of the legislature and his skill in making the state university acceptable to the rank and file of Ohioans, he did not bring the kind of prosperity to the University for which he had hoped.[4]

The dimensions of indecision and vacillation were observed in other quarters as well. The Ohio State University "might become an institution like the University of Wisconsin," observed the president of the Carnegie Foundation for the Advancement of Teaching, but he spelled out some big "ifs" upon which such a development would depend. The state program for higher education in Ohio, said the Carnegie Foundation's Henry S. Pritchett, was "wasteful" and "demoralizing". In fact, he observed, the attempt to maintain three state universities in the Ohio of 1900 deprived the very term "university" of all of its meaning. The foundation had spoken out about the Ohio situation as it considered whether to include state university faculties in Andrew Carnegie's generous scheme for faculty retirement funds. In Carnegie's original grant, he had assumed that the states would not want to involve their institutions in a private scheme and, therefore, they had been excluded. At a later date he added additional funds to allow selected state university faculties to be included.[5]

In the foundation's surveys, Henry S. Pritchett noted in 1907 that while higher education in the East rested upon the private endowments derived from accumulated wealth, in the West it rested upon state support because accumulated wealth was lacking. Uniquely, however, Ohio had more state universities, as well as more private schools than other states, whether east or west. It presented something of a confusion of the two patterns. Futhermore, it was suggested that Ohio had the most active and powerful independent state college association among all the states of the union and that this derived from the multiplicity of institutions in the state. The Ohio College Association, observed Pritchett in 1908, included

4. Pollard, *William Oxley Thompson*, p. 128.
5. *Bulletin of the Carnegie Foundation for the Advancement of Teaching: Papers Relating to the Admission of State Institutions to the System of Retiring Allowances of the Carnegie Foundation*, No. 1 (March, 1907).

twenty-two of the state's fifty-two colleges and universities. It sought primarily to safeguard the standards of higher education in Ohio by excluding schools which failed to live up to minimum standards. President Guy Potter Benton of Miami explained that the Ohio College Association was powerful because the state's legitimate institutions had no legislative protection for their degrees and could survive only by rigorous collective action. The legislature seemingly issued college charters with little or no sense of responsibility, and sanctioned the weak as well as the strong while creating no agency to hold institutions accountable once charters were granted. When Canfield had suggested such a standardizing role for the Ohio State University, however, the majority of other colleges resisted with strength and resolution. Henry S. Pritchett described the Ohio College Association as a protective association in that sense but without fixing blame, alluded to state shortcomings in provision for the regulation and protection of colleges and universities.[6]

As a matter of fact, few state legislatures had chartered more colleges than the legislature of Ohio, and if practice really made perfect, the Charter Act of the Ohio State University should have been a model document. Between 1803 and 1860, for instance, the Ohio General Assembly passed legislation incorporating fifty-six colleges and universities. Some never saw the light of day; some died in infancy; others merged with other institutions. In any event, only twenty-two were in existence as college-level institutions by 1860. By 1907, however, the number had swelled again to a total of fifty-two chartered institutions. In every case the legislature had passed measures entrusting the fate of an educational institution to a board of trustees, and from that point on considered its responsibility fulfilled. Even in the original creation of Ohio and Miami Universities on federal land grants, the Ohio legislature had remained essentially uninvolved in the educational enterprise once charters for the institutions had been granted. For over sixty years after establishing Ohio and Miami, in fact, the state had shown little concern for either except in the perfunctory act of naming trustees. This was the expectation of many in 1870 when the Ohio Agricul-

6. Ibid., p. 13; *The Carnegie Foundation for the Advancement of Teaching, Third Annual Report of the President and Treasurer* (Boston, Merrymount Press, 1908), p. 99.

tural and Mechanical College was chartered, and not until the 1890's did the official state attitude begin to change, much because of the impact of the Morrill land grant act.[7]

The final ruling of the Carnegie Foundation on Ohio's application for pension participation, however, was devastating. Governor Judson Harmon received a great deal of unfavorable publicity as a result, and the state administration generally became somewhat defensive. President Thompson included the Carnegie report in his own annual report to the board of trustees, though he did so without comment or reaction. "When the Carnegie Foundation came to consider the request of the state of Ohio," said the report, "from the standpoint of educational administration, it found that the state undertakes to maintain three institutions bearing the name university." Each, the report continued, contained a college of liberal arts, each offered what it described as "more or less" postgraduate education. Two purported to offer engineering, two conducted normal departments, while the third maintained a college of education, and two taught high school courses in a preparatory academy. "Such over-lapping," said the report, "is not only wasteful, but it results in competitive bidding for students." The end result, observed the Carnegie spokesman, was to demoralize both the colleges and the high schools because sheer competition for survival reduced all to the least common standard.

Pritchett observed that the colleges were filled with students who should have been required to remain in high school, and that better admissions standards would therefore have strengthened education throughout the length and breadth of the state. The conflicting standards of the three state institutions were, in fact, at such great variance with each other, he said, that the state's system of higher education had no constructive impact upon high-school standards at all. Pritchett did acknowledge that the Ohio State University had attempted to set satisfactory standards and to establish an acceptable procedure for evaluating high schools and their preparatory programs. All was to no avail, however, according to Pritchett, because the Ohio and Miami universities were not obliged to follow

7. *Third Annual Report of the Commissioner of Statistics to the Governor of the State of Ohio,* Table XXXI, p. 132; *Ohio State Journal* (Columbus, Ohio), September 12, 1870.

a similar course. Miami, said Pritchett, follows a course of its own, but Ohio University seems merely to do what ever would bring into the college as many students as possible, regardless of grade level, in order to create maximum impact on the legislature. In conclusion, Pritchett conceded that the Ohio State University might be fairly called a university, but that Ohio and Miami were certainly not university grade institutions. If the Ohio State University could be relieved of the pressures created by the latter two, said Pritchett, then Ohio might find itself the proud possessor of a university like the one in Wisconsin. The foundation's final descision was that education would not be served either in Ohio or in the nation by admitting the state's three universities to participation in the Carnegie retirement fund for teachers. To admit one without the other two was to do violence to the state's own system, and regardless of the foundation's verdict about the system it would not enter within the state to construct its own for pension purposes. It was a serious blow to the institution and in the absence of legislative action the issue was closed.[8]

Pritchett's report was officially an indictment of the state educational system, but it was applicable equally to the public and private condition of higher education in Ohio. The twenty-two members of the Ohio College Association likewise found it difficult to uphold standards in competition with the other thirty institutions outside its ranks who enjoyed legislative charters. Many persons and groups had thought about higher education but Ohio had lacked the strong educational leadership that could coordinate and systematize the state's educational energies. The legislature on innumerable occasions sought to promote education without risk to itself, without a venturing spirit, and without commitment of itself or public resources. By the same token it acceded to petitions of practically every group that wanted to found a college, unwilling to set limits or standards and hopeful that sheer volume in numbers would absolve the state of its responsibility. One result was that, unlike Illinois where the vibrant prosperity of the University of Chicago prompted greater support for Illinois State University, Ohio

8. Henry S. Pritchett to Judson Harmon, June 9, 1909, *The Carnegie Foundation for the Advancement of Teaching, Fourth Annual Report of the President and Treasurer* (Boston: Merrymount Press, 1909), pp. 86–99.

produced no one private university capable of stimulating state higher education or of providing a friendly competitor with which to vie.[9]

Ohio, without sufficient educational statesmanship, without an acknowledged leading institution, and hopelessly divided in educational effort, was a prime example of dissipated educational energy and zeal. By 1900, the state was overbuilt in educational institutions and several generations away from the kinds of enrollment pressures that would free the institutions from a desperate kind of competition. The state's resources were spread too thin to permit any one of its fifty-two schools to become a really great university. Some, by severe self-restraint and discipline, became excellent colleges; but for many others excellence depended upon a very elusive financial prosperity and was often postponed in the search for adequate enrollments.

Even with the large numbers of institutions, however, Ohio could have provided greater support for a state university than it did. As Henry S. Pritchett had observed, state universities were carried on in most states "in spite of the people," and he implied that none would make undue sacrifices for public higher education except for one determining factor. Where a sufficient number of the influential people became sufficiently interested in the welfare of the state universitiy to make it necessary for other interests to win their support by humoring them on the state university issue—only in those states did the state university prosper. Such a power alignment had not emerged in Ohio. Where it did appear, the universities were free to develop, said Pritchett, amenable only to the public opinion of the educated and powerful classes. Where it did not emerge, the state university lacked powerful friends and failed to reach its full potential.[10]

In general, Ohioans rejected the Carnegie report. A majority reflected the mood which James M. Comly had reported somewhat earlier. The large number of struggling little colleges in Ohio, in that view, was not as bad a situation as Easterners contended. It was merely an eastern aberration that decreed that

9. Allan Nevins, *Illinois* (New York: Oxford University Press, 1917).
10. *Bulletin of the Carnegie Foundation* (March, 1907), p. 14.

Ohio's schools were too numerous, too inferior, or too inefficient. Unable to accept the verdict of the East as rendered by Henry S. Pritchett, and uncomfortable with that of the West as interpreted by James H. Canfield, Ohio continued in its own way.

According to William Oxley Thompson, Canfield's successor, the success or failure of the University hinged ultimately upon a single factor, one which could not be forced but had to evolve. "The land-grant colleges," he said, "will never find a bed of roses underneath the shadowing protection of a corporation." They were founded, supported and stimulated by the people and must eventually look not only for their support but for all their protection to that same source. "The standards of these institutions," he affirmed, "will be approved by the people." In essence, he said, the power of the university originated with the people, who delegated it to the legislature, which applied it by means of a board of trustees, who worked as much as possible through the university and its officers to give life to the desires of the people.[11]

Quite often the criticisms of the Ohio State University had an aspect of geography about them. For some, the problem with the University was that it had not become a Nebraska or an Iowa; for others it had fallen short of a Purdue in Indiana or a Cornell in New York. Particularly for those who first envisioned a great state university patterned after Cornell was the disappointment hard to bear. The Ohio State University had never received commensurate support to become a Wisconsin or a Michigan. Nevertheless, geography in itself was an oversimplification of the answer.[12]

In many western states, according to Henry S. Pritchett of the Carnegie Foundation, the combining of the land grant and the state university idea had had good results in that it prevented a struggle for existence between competing institutions, such as emerged in Ohio between Ohio State University and the two older institutions. On another occasion, however, Pritchett observed that while Wisconsin had grown strong with the land grant, Michigan grew strong without it, and he concluded his

11. *Ohio State Journal* (Columbus, Ohio), May 31, 1881.
12. *Bulletin of the Carnegie Foundation* (March, 1907), pp. 14, 31.

analysis with what he called a fundamental fact about state universities: "Those state universities have grown strong and have received generous support," he said, "which have upheld fair standards, which have made themselves the real heads of the state system of education, and which have appealed unequivocally to the state for their support as state institutions." Those three factors, plus a group of powerful friends, provided four preconditions of success, not all of which the Ohio State University enjoyed at any one time.[13]

In Ohio, the Morrill Act initiated a series of events in which several factors merged uniquely. In the Ohio of the 1860's the idea of a land grant institution was imbedded in the partisan politics typified by Benjamin Franklin Wade; it came into being, as it were, with congenital enemies. Furthermore, though agriculturists were excited about the prospect, rank and file farmers could not have been less interested. Under the circumstances, when the Morrill fund was eventually captured by those who had been denied a real state university and who despaired of ever making Miami or Ohio University into such a university, they faced partisan distrust and farmer apathy. Their success in capturing the fund, however, alienated the supporters of the two older schools, galvanizing them into action and at the same time alienated the boosters of up-and-coming towns in the state who also had need for educational opportunities. At this juncture then, the farmers themselves became more concerned about "their" university, and claimed it for themselves. They then served as the instrument which, through the legislature, could force attention to the discontents of other disappointed groups. The religious issue and questions of economic orthodoxy likewise became instruments for undermining, circumscribing, and hobbling the university movement. At this juncture, however, with the passage of the Hatch Act and the second Morrill Act, the hand of the farmer and his allies was strengthened immeasurably, and the advocates of a great state university and their early champion,

13. William Oxley Thompson, "The Influence of the Morrill Act Upon American Higher Education," *Proceedings of the Twenty-sixth Annual Convention of the Association of American Agricultural Colleges and Experiment Stations, Atlanta, Georgia, November 13–15, 1912* (n.p., n.d.), p. 24.

Rutherford B. Hayes, had to redress the balance between them and the program of the university.

Thus, years after the passage of the Morrill Land Grant College Act, Ohioans were still striving to know what to do with the opportunity bestowed upon them. A lack of educational statesmanship in the eyes of a later generation and an overabundance of educational enterprise among private groups left Ohio with a mass of small institutions and the widespread feeling that the educational needs of the people of Ohio were being effectively met. Fundamentally, it was because many in the state could not quite disassociate themselves from the private school experience of the east and that of the south, and neither set of experiences was fully adequate in the new place. Nor could the state's citizens agree to accept any very great affinity with the state school emphasis of the far west. Suspended between these emphases and oblivious to changing demands, the state's educational efforts reproduced both in miniature and with profuse monotony and regularity. The design of a unique Ohio system, or even the recognition of such a possibility, waited for newer leadership, a greater spirit of interinstitutional cooperation, and a broader vision of the role of education in society.

Bibliography

Books and Pamphlets

Adams, Herbert B., ed. *Contributions to American Educational History.* Published as U.S. Bureau of Education Circulars of Information, 1887–1903. Washington, D.C.: U.S. Government Printing Office, 1887–1903.

Atwater, Caleb. *A History of the State of Ohio, Natural and Civil.* Cincinnati, Ohio: Glezen & Shepard, 1838.

———. *An Essay on Education.* Cincinnati, Ohio: Glezen & Shepard, 1841.

Barnard, Frederick A. P. *Improvements Practicable in American Colleges.* Hartford, Conn.: F. C. Brownell, 1856.

Barnard, Henry. *Rutherford B. Hayes and His America.* Indianapolis, Ind.: Bobbs-Merrill Co., 1954.

Beach, Arthur G. *A Pioneer College: The Story of Marietta.* Chicago: John F. Cuneo Co., 1935.

Becker, Carl L. *Cornell University: Founders and the Founding.* Ithaca, N.Y.: Cornell University Press, 1943.

Beecher, Charles. *Autobiography of Lyman Beecher.* 2 vols. New York: Harper and Bros., 1864–65.

Bidwell, P. W., and Falconer, J. D. *History of Agriculture in the Northern United States, 1620–1850.* Washington, D.C.: Carnegie Institution of Washington, 1925.

Boyd, O. F. *A History of Wilmington College.* Wilmington, Ohio: Wilmington College, 1949.

Bradford, J. E., ed. *Education in the Ohio Valley Prior to 1840.* Columbus, Ohio: F. J. Heer Printing Co., 1916.

Brickman, William W., and Lehrer, Stanley, eds. *A Century of Higher Education.* New York: Society for the Advancement of Education, 1962.

Brubaker, John S., and Rudy, Willis. *Higher Education in Transition: A Popular History of American Colleges, 1636–1956.* New York: Harper and Bros., 1958.

Buck, Solon J. *The Granger Movement: A Study of Agricultural Organization and Its Political, Economic, and Social Manifestations, 1870–1880.* Cambridge, Mass.: Harvard University Press, 1913.

————. *The Agrarian Crusade: A Chronicle of the Farmer in Politics.* New Haven: Yale University Press, 1920.

Butts, Robert Freeman. *The College Charts Its Course: Historical Conceptions and Current Proposals.* New York: McGraw-Hill Book Co., 1939.

Carlton, Frank T. *Economic Influences upon Educational Progress in the United States, 1820–1850.* University of Wisconsin, Economics and Political Science Series, vol. IV, no. 1. Madison: University of Wisconsin, 1908.

Carnegie Foundation for the Advancement of Teaching. *Third Annual Report of the President and Treasurer.* Boston: Merrymount Press, 1908.

Corson, John J. *Governance of Colleges and Universities.* New York: McGraw-Hill Book Co., 1960.

Craven, A. O. *Soil Exhaustion as a Factor in the Agricultural History of Virginia and Maryland, 1606–1860.* Urbana: University of Illinois Press, 1926.

Crosbie, Laurence M. *The Phillips Exeter Academy: A History.* Norwood, Mass.: Phillips Exeter Academy, 1923.

Curti, Merle E. *The Social Ideas of American Educators.* New York: Chas. Scribner's Sons, 1935.

————, and Carstensen, Vernon R. *The University of Wisconsin: A History, 1848–1925.* 2 vols. Madison: University of Wisconsin Press, 1949.

————, and Nash, Roderick. *Philanthropy in the Shaping of American Higher Education.* New Brunswick, N.J.: Rutgers University Press, 1965.

Demaree, A. L. *The American Agricultural Press: 1819–1860*. New York: Columbia University Press, 1941.

Earnest, Ernest P. *Academic Procession: An Informal History of the American College*. Indianapolis, Ind.: Bobbs-Merrill Co., 1953.

Eckelberry, Roscoe Huhn. *History of the Municipal University in the United States*. U.S. Department of Education, Bulletin No. 2. Washington, D.C.: U.S. Government Printing Office, 1932.

Eddy, Edward Danforth, Jr. *Colleges for Our Land and Time: The Land-Grant Idea in American Education*. New York: Harper and Bros., 1956.

Ellis, David M. *Landlords and Farmers in the Hudson-Mohawk Region, 1790–1850*. Ithaca, N.Y.: Octagon Books, 1946.

Emerson, Ralph Waldo. *The Complete Works of Ralph Waldo Emerson*. Centenary Edition. Ithaca, N.Y.: Octagon Books, 1946.

Fletcher, Robert S. *A History of Oberlin College from Its Foundation through the Civil War*. 2 vols. Oberlin, Ohio: Oberlin College, 1943.

Galbreath, Charles B. *History of Ohio*. 5 vols. New York and Chicago: American Historical Society, 1925.

Gates, Paul W. *Agriculture and the Civil War*. New York: Alfred A. Knopf, 1965.

Good, Harry G. *The Rise of the College of Education of the Ohio State University*. Columbus, Ohio: College of Education, Ohio State University, 1960.

Halstead, Murat. *Caucuses of 1860: A History of the National Conventions of the Current Presidential Campaign*. Columbus, Ohio: Follett, 1860.

Havighurst, Walter. *The Miami Years 1809–1959*. New York: G. P. Putnam's Sons, 1958.

Hawes, George W. *Ohio State Gazetteer and Business Directory for 1859–1860*. Cincinnati, Ohio: G. W. Hawes, 1859.

Haworth, Paul Leland. *The Hayes-Tilden Disputed Presidential Election of 1876*. Cleveland: Burrows Bros., 1906.

Henderson, Algo D., and Hall, Dorothy. *Antioch College: Its Design for Liberal Education*. New York: Harper and Bros., 1946.

Hesseltine, William B. *Ulysses S. Grant, Politician*. New York: Dodd, Mead and Co., 1935.

————. *Lincoln and the War Governors.* New York: Alfred A. Knopf, 1955.

————. *Lincoln's Plan of Reconstruction.* Tuscaloosa, Ala.: Confederate Centennial Studies, 1960.

History of The Ohio State University (Formerly Ohio Agricultural and Mechanical College) Containing Act of Incorporation and Unrepealed Acts of the General Assembly of Ohio, December, 1878. Columbus, Ohio: Nevins and Myers, 1878.

Hodge, George B. *Association Educational Works for Men and Boys.* New York: Association Press, 1912.

Hofstadter, Richard, and Hardy, C. Dewitt. *The Development and Scope of Higher Education in the United States.* New York: Columbia University Press, 1952.

————, and Metzger, Walter. *The Development of Academic Freedom in the United States.* New York: Columbia University Press, 1955.

————, ed. *American Higher Education: A Documentary History.* 2 vols. Chicago: University of Chicago Press, 1961.

Hooper, Osman Castle. *History of the City of Columbus, Ohio, from the Founding of Franklinton in 1797 through the World War period to the Year 1920.* Columbus and Cleveland, Ohio: Memorial Publishing Company [1920].

Hoover, Thomas N. *The History of Ohio University.* Athens: Ohio University Press, 1954.

Howe, Henry. *Historical Collections of Ohio; Containing a Collection of the Most Interesting Facts, Traditions, Biographical Sketches, Anecdotes, Etc., Relating to the General and Local History.* Cincinnati, Ohio: Henry Howe, 1847.

————. *Historical Collections of Ohio.* Cincinnati, Ohio: R. Clarke and Co., 1869.

————. *Historical Collections of Ohio.* Columbus, Ohio: H. Home and Son, 1889–91.

Hubbart, Henry Clyde. *Ohio Wesleyan's First Hundred Years.* Delaware, Ohio: Ohio Wesleyan University, 1943.

In Memoriam: Edward Orton. Columbus, Ohio: Ohio State University Press, 1899.

James, Edmund Janes. *The Origin of the Land-Grant Act of 1862 (the So-called Morrill Act) and Some Account of Its Author Jonathan B. Turner.* University of Illinois Studies, vol. IV, no. 1. Urbana-Champaign: University of Illinois Press, 1910.

Jenkins, Warren. *Ohio Gazetteer and Travellers' Guide Containing a Description of the Several Towns, Townships, and Counties with Their Water-Courses, Roads, Improvements, Mineral Productions, Etc., Together with an Appendix or General Register.* Columbus, Ohio: I. N. Whiting, 1841.

Josephson, Matthew. *The Politicos, 1865–1896.* New York: Harcourt Brace, 1938.

Kay, Karl J. *History of National Normal University of Lebanon, Ohio.* Washington Court House, Ohio: Record-Republican Press, 1929.

King, Willard L. *Lincoln's Manager: David Davis.* Cambridge, Mass.: Harvard University Press, 1960.

Kinnison, William A. *Hon. Samuel Shellabarger: Lawyer, Jurist, Legislator.* Yellow Springs, Ohio: Clark County Historical Society, 1966.

Knight, George Wells. *History and Management of Land-Grants for Education in the Northwest Territory.* New York and London: G. P. Putnam's Sons, 1885.

Knight, George W., and Commons, John R. *The History of Higher Education in Ohio.* U.S. Bureau of Education, Circular of Information No. 5. Washington, D.C.: U.S. Government Printing Office, 1891.

Larson, Henrietta M. *Jay Cooke, Private Banker.* Cambridge, Mass.: Harvard University Press, 1936.

Lentz, Harold. *A History of Wittenberg College.* Columbus, Ohio: Wittenberg Press, 1946.

McGinnis, Frederick A. *A History and an Interpretation of Wilberforce University.* Wilberforce, Ohio: Wilberforce University, 1941.

Makio or Magic Mirror. Vols. I–XX, Columbus, Ohio: Fraternities of the Ohio State University, 1880–1900.

Mendenhall, Thomas C., et al., eds. *History of The Ohio State University.* 5 vols. Columbus: Ohio State University, 1920–40.

Meyer, Balthaser Henry, ed. *The History of Transportation in the United States before 1860.* Washington, D.C.: Carnegie Institution, 1917.

Miller, James M. *The Genesis of Western Culture: The Upper Ohio Valley, 1800–1825.* Vol. IX. Ohio State Archaeological and Historical Society, Ohio Historical Collections. Columbus, Ohio: Ohio State Archaeological and Historical Society, 1938.

Moore, Opha. *History of Franklin County, Ohio.* 3 vols. Indianapolis, Ind.: History Publishing Co., 1930.

Mott, Frank L. *A History of American Magazines.* Cambridge, Mass.: Harvard University Press, 1938–57.

Mumford, Frederick Blackman. *The Land-Grant College Movement.* Columbia, Mo.: Missouri Agricultural Experiment Station, 1940.

Munsterberg, Hugo. *American Patriotism and Other Social Studies.* New York: Moffat, Yard, and Co., 1913.

National Education Association. *Proceedings of the Fifteenth Annual Meeting of the National Council of Education, Buffalo, New York, 1896.* Chicago: University of Chicago Press, 1896.

———. *Proceedings of the Sixteenth Annual Meeting of the National Council of Education, Milwaukee, Wisconsin, 1897.* Chicago: University of Chicago Press, 1897.

Nevins, Allan. *Illinois.* The American College and University Series. New York: Oxford University Press, 1917.

———. *The Emergence of Modern America.* New York: Macmillan Co., 1927.

———. *The State University and Democracy.* Urbana: University of Illinois Press, 1962.

———. *The Origins of the Land-Grant Colleges and State Universities.* Washington, D.C.: Civil War Centennial Commission, 1962.

Notestein, Lucy L. *Wooster of the Middle West.* New Haven, Conn.: Yale University Press, 1937.

Ohio College Association. *College Entrance Requirements.* Wooster, Ohio: The Ohio College Association, 1913.

Orton, Edward. "Building Stones of Ohio Compiled from Notes of Professor Orton," *Ohio Geological Survey Report,* V (1884), 577–642.

———. *An Account of the Descendants of Thomas Orton, of Windsor, Connecticut, 1641.* Columbus, Ohio: Nitschke Bros., 1896.

Ohio State Centennial Educational Committee. *Historical Sketches of the Higher Educational Institutions and also of Benevolent and Reformatory Institutions of the State of Ohio.* Columbus, Ohio: n.p., 1876.

Ohio State University, The. *Alumni Register, 1878–1909.* Columbus: Ohio State University Bulletin, 1909.

"Old Woodward": A Memorial Relating to Woodward High School, 1831–1836, and Woodward College, 1836–1851, in the City of Cincinnati. Cincinnati, Ohio: "Old Woodward" Club, 1884.

Orth, Samuel P. *The Centralization of Administration in Ohio.* New York: Columbia University Press, 1903.

Owens, David B. *These Hundred Years: The Centennial History of Capital University.* Columbus, Ohio: Capital University, 1950.

Parker, William Belmont. *The Life and Public Services of Justin Smith Morrill.* Boston and New York: Houghton Mifflin Co., 1924.

Peterson, Theodore B. *Magazines in the Twentieth Century.* Urbana: University of Illinois Press, 1956.

Pfnister, Allen O. "A Century of the Church Related College," *A Century of Higher Education,* ed. by W. W. Brickman and Stanley Lehrer. New York: Society for the Advancement of Education, 1962. Pp. 80–93.

Pollard, James E. *History of the Ohio State University: The Story of Its First Seventy-Five Years, 1873–1948.* Columbus: Ohio State University Press, 1952.

———. *William Oxley Thompson: Evangel of Education.* Columbus: Ohio State University Press, 1955.

———. *Ohio State Athletics: 1879–1959.* Columbus: Ohio State University, 1959.

Pritchett, Henry S. "The Place of the College in American Education," *Annual Report.* New York: Carnegie Foundation for the Advancement of Teaching, 1907. Pp. 79–80.

Riegel, Robert Edgar. *Young America: 1830–1840.* Norman: University of Oklahoma Press, 1949.

Robson, John, ed. *Baird's Manual of American College Fraternities.* 18th ed. Menasha, Wis.: George Banta Publishing Co., 1968.

Rogers, Walter P. *Andrew D. White and the Modern University.* Ithaca, N.Y.: Cornell University Press, 1942.

Roseboom, Eugene H., and Weisenburger, Francis P. *A History of Ohio,* ed. James H. Rodabaugh. Columbus: Ohio State Archaeological and Historical Society, 1956.

Ross, Earle D. *A History of Iowa State College.* Ames: Iowa State Press, 1942.

————. *Democracy's College: The Land-Grant Movement in the Formative Stage.* Ames: Iowa State College Press, 1942.

————. *The Land-Grant Idea at Iowa State College, A Centennial Trail Balance, 1858–1958.* Ames: Iowa State College Press, 1958.

Rudolph, Frederick. "Neglect of Students as a Historical Tradition," *The College and the Student,* ed. Lawrence E. Dennis and Joseph F. Kauffman, The American Council on Education. Washington, D.C.: American Council on Education, 1966.

————. *The American College and University.* New York: Alfred A. Knopf, 1962.

————. *Hopkins and the Log.* New Haven, Conn.: Yale University Press, 1956.

Schlesinger, Arthur M., Sr. *The Rise of the City.* New York: Macmillan Co., 1933.

Schlesinger, Arthur M., Jr. *The Age of Jackson.* Boston: Brown, Little & Co., 1945.

Sears, Jesse B. *Philanthropy in the History of American Higher Education.* U.S. Bureau of Education, Bulletin No. 26. Washington, D.C.: U.S. Government Printing Office, 1922.

Shepardson, Francis W., ed. *Baird's Manual of American College Fraternities.* Twelfth and Semicentennial Edition. Menasha, Wis.: George Banta Publishing Co., 1930.

————. *Denison University, 1831–1931: A Centennial History.* Granville, Ohio: Board of Trustees, 1931.

Slater, Clarence Paul. *History of the Land-Grant Endowment Fund of the University of Illinois.* Urbana: University of Illinois, 1940.

Slosson, Edwin E. *The American Spirit in Education,* The Chronicles of America Series, ed. Allen Johnson, vol. XXXIII. New Haven, Conn., Yale University Press, 1921.

Smith, Edward C. *The Borderland and the Civil War.* New York: Macmillan Co., 1927.

Smythe, George Franklin. *Kenyon College, Its First Century.* New Haven, Conn.: Yale University Press, 1924.

Songe, Alice H. *The Land-Grant Movement in American Higher Education: An Historical Bibliography of the Land-Grant Movement and the Individual Land-Grant Institutions,* n.p.: Centennial Office, Association of State Universities and Land-Grant Colleges, 1962.

Stephenson, George M. *The Political History of the Public Lands from 1840 to 1862.* Boston: R. G. Badger, 1917.

Sullivant, Joseph. *Schedule of the Departments Proposed by J. Sullivant to Serve as a Basis in the Organization of the Ohio Agricultural and Mechanical College and School of Applied Science.* Columbus, Ohio: n.p., n.d.

————. *An Alphabetical Catalogue of Shells, Fossils, Minerals, and Zoophites in the Cabinet of Joseph Sullivant.* Columbus, Ohio: Cutler and Pilsbury, 1838.

————. *Address in Behalf of the Location of the Ohio Agricultural and Mechanical College in Franklin County.* Columbus, n.p., 1870.

————. *Hog-feeding and Pork-making.* Columbus, Ohio: n.p., 1870.

————. *A Genealogy and Family Memorial.* Columbus, Ohio: Ohio State Journal, 1874.

————. *Historical Sketch Relating to the Original Boundaries and Early Times of Franklin County.* Columbus, Ohio: Ohio State Journal, 1874.

Tarbell, Ida M. *The Nationalizing of Business.* New York: Macmillan Co., 1936.

Ten Brook, Andrew. *American State Universities, Their Origin and Progress: A History of Congressional University Land-Grants. A Particular Account of the Rise and Development of the University of Michigan and Hints toward the Future of the American University System.* Cincinnati, Ohio: n.p., 1875.

Tewksbury, Donald G. *The Founding of American Colleges and Universities before the Civil War: With Particular Reference to the Religious Influences Bearing upon the College Movement.* New York: Archon Books, 1965.

Thomas, Benjamin P., and Hyman, Harold M. *Stanton: The Life and Times of Lincoln's Secretary of War.* New York: Alfred A. Knopf, 1962.

Thwing, Charles F. *American Colleges: Their Students and Work*. New York: G. P. Putnam's, 1879.

———. *A History of Higher Education in America*. New York: D. Appleton and Co., 1906.

———. *Guides, Philosophers and Friends: Studies of College Men*. New York: Macmillan Co., 1927.

———. *The American and the German University: One Hundred Years of History*. New York: Macmillan Co., 1928.

Trefousse, H. L. *Benjamin Franklin Wade: Radical Republican from Ohio*. New York: Twayne Publishers, 1963.

Tyler, Alice Felt. *Freedom's Ferment: Phases of American Social History to 1860*. Minneapolis: University of Minnesota Press, 1944.

U.S. Bureau of Education. *Reports of the Commissioner of Education*. Washington, D.C.: U.S. Government Printing Office, 1870–82.

U.S. Department of the Interior, Office of Education Circular No. 9. *Survey of Land-Grant Colleges and Universities*. 2 vols. Washington, D.C.: U.S. Government Printing Office, 1910.

Veblen, Thorstein. *The Higher Learning in America*. New York: B. W. Huebach, 1918.

Veysey, Laurence R. *The Emergence of the American University*. Chicago: University of Chicago Press, 1965.

Waite, Frederick Clayton. *Western Reserve University: The Hudson Era*. Cleveland, Ohio: Western Reserve University Press, 1943.

Wayland, Francis. *Report to the Corporation of Brown University on Changes in the System of Collegiate Education*. Providence, R.I.: n.p., 1850.

Weisenburger, Francis P. *The Passing of the Frontier*, vol. III. *The History of the State of Ohio*, ed. Carl Wittke. Columbus, Ohio: Ohio State Archaeological and Historical Society, 1941.

———. *A Brief History of Urbana University*. Urbana, Ohio: n.p. 1950.

———. *Ordeal of Faith: The Crisis of Church-Going America, 1865–1900*. New York: Philosophical Library, 1959.

———. *Triumph of Faith: Contributions of the Church to American Life, 1865–1900*. Richmond, Va.: William Byrd Press, 1962.

Willard, G. W. *History of Heidelberg College.* Cincinnati, Ohio: Elm Street Printing Co., 1879.

Williams, Charles R., ed. *Diary and Letters of Rutherford Birchard Hayes.* 5 vols. Columbus, Ohio: Ohio State Archaeological and Historical Society, 1922–26.

Williams, E. I. F. *Heidelberg: Democratic Christian College, 1850–1950.* Menasha, Wis.: George Banta Publishing Co., 1952.

Woodward, Comer Vann. *Reunion and Reaction: The Compromise of 1877.* Garden City, N.Y.: Doubleday and Co., 1956.

Works, George Alan and Morgan, Barton. *The Land-Grant Colleges.* Washington, D.C.: U.S. Government Printing Office, 1939.

Articles in Periodicals

Adams, C. K. "Review of Ten Brook's American State Universities," *North American Review,* CXXI (October, 1875), 365–408.

Binkley, Mrs. Wilfred E. "The Evolution of Ohio Northern University," *Northwest Ohio Quarterly,* XIX (1947), 51–63.

Bossing, Nelson L. "History of Educational Legislation in Ohio from 1851 to 1925," *Ohio State Archaeological and Historical Quarterly,* XXXIX (1930), 78–397.

Brickman, William W. "College and University History," *School and Society,* LXIV (1946), 465–71.

———. "Higher Educational History," *School and Society,* LXIX (1949), 385–91.

———. "History of Colleges and Universities," *School and Society,* LXXVI (1952), 415–21.

Carnegie Foundation for the Advancement of Teaching. "Papers Relating to the Admission of State Institutions to the System of Retiring Allowances of the Carnegie Foundation," *Bulletin of the Carnegie Foundation for the Advancement of Teaching.* No. 1 (March, 1907).

Chadbourne, P. A. "Colleges and College Education," *Putnam's Magazine,* IV, No. 21 (September, 1869), 335–42.

Derby, Samuel C. "Edward Orton," *The Old Northwest Genealogical Quarterly,* III (January, 1900), 1–14.

Downes, Randolph C. "University of Toledo," *Northwest Ohio Quarterly,* XXI (1949), 149–68.

Eckelberry, R. H. "The McNeely Normal School and Hopedale Normal College," *Ohio State Archaeological and Historical Quarterly*, XL (1931), 86–119.

Fletcher, Robert S. "Bread and Doctrine at Oberlin," *Ohio State Archaeological and Historical Quarterly*, XLIX (1940), 58–67.

Gilman, D. C. "Education in America, 1776–1876," *North American Review*, CXXII (January, 1876), 191–228.

Gladden, Washington, "Professor Edward Orton, 1829–1899," *Ohio Archaeological and Historical Quarterly*, VIII (1900), 409–32.

Halstead, Murat, "The Story of the Farmer's College," *Cosmopolitan Magazine* (June, 1897), 280–88.

Harper, William Rainey. "Trend of University and College Education in the United States," *North American Review*, CLXXIV (1902), 457–65.

———. "Higher Education in the West," *North American Review*, CLXXIX (1904), 584–90.

Hewett, W. T. "University Administration," *Atlantic Monthly*, L (October, 1882), 505–30.

Hill, David J. "The Cost of Universities," *Forum*, VIII (November, 1889), 297–304.

Hyde, W. D. "The College," *Educational Review*, XXVIII (1904), 474.

Johnson, Rossiter. "College Endowments," *North American Review*, CXXXVI (May, 1883) 490–96.

Kinnison, William A. "The More Toil, the More Grace," *The Wittenberg Alumnus*, XIV (February, 1963) 8–9.

Knight, George Wells. "The State and the Private College," *Educational Review*, X (June, 1895), 57–70.

McAlpine, William. "The Origin of Public Education in Ohio," *Ohio State Archaeological and Historical Quarterly*, XXXVIII (1929), 409–77.

Miller, E. A. "History of Educational Legislation in Ohio from 1803 to 1850," *Ohio State Archaeological and Historical Quarterly*, XXVII (1918), 7–142.

Moore, Clifford H. "Ohio in National Politics, 1865-1896," *Ohio State Archaeological and Historical Quarterly*, XXXVII (April-July, 1928), 220–427.

Peterson, C. E., Jr. "Early Accrediting Society," *College and University*, XXXIX (Winter, 1964), 117–26.

Pritchett, Henry S. "The Relations of Christian Denominations to Colleges," *Educational Review*, XXXVI (October, 1908), 217–41.

Richardson, R. K. " 'Yale of the West'—A Study of Academic Sectionalism," *Wisconsin Magazine of History*, XXXVI (1953), 258–61, 280–83.

Rodabaugh, James H. "Robert Hamilton Bishop, Pioneer Educator," *Ohio State Archaeological and Historical Quarterly*, XLIV (1935), 92–102.

Ross, Earle D. "On Writing the History of Land-Grant Colleges and Universities," *Journal of Higher Education*, XXIV, no. 8 (November, 1953), 411–14, 451–52.

Rudy, S. Willis. "The 'Revolution' in American Higher Education, 1865–1900," *Harvard Educational Review*, XXI (1951), 155–74.

Shetrone, Henry Clyde. "Caleb Atwater: Versatile Pioneer, A Reappraisal," *Ohio State Archaeological and Historical Quarterly*, LIV, no. 1 (January–March, 1945), 79–88.

Weisenburger, Francis P. "Caleb Atwater: Pioneer Politician and Historian," *Ohio Historical Quarterly*, LXVIII (January, 1959), 18–37.

Unpublished Theses and Dissertations

Buis, Anne Gibson. "An Historical Study of the Role of the Federal Government in Financial Support of Education." Ph.D. diss., Ohio State University, 1953.

Chambers, Merritt Madison. "Structure and Legal Status of Governing Boards of State Universities." Ph.D. diss., Ohio State University, 1931.

Eckelberry, Roscoe Huhn. "A Study of Religious Influence in Higher Education in Ohio." Master's thesis, Ohio State University, 1923.

Hayes, Walter Sherman, Jr. "Rutherford B. Hayes and His Connection with the Ohio State University." Master's thesis, Ohio State University, 1962.

McGrath, Earl J. "The Evolution of Administrative Offices and Institutions of Higher Education in the United States." Ph.D. diss., University of Chicago, 1936.

Rodabaugh, James H. "The History of Miami University from Its Origin to 1885." Ph.D. diss., Ohio State University, 1937.

Veeck, Charles Robert. "The Senatorial Career of George E. Pugh, 1855–1861." Master's thesis, Ohio State University, 1949.

Veysey, Lawrence Ross. "The Emergence of the American University 1865–1910." Ph.D. diss., University of California, Berkeley, 1961.

Speeches and Addresses

Baker, James H. "The State University," N.E.A., *Proceedings of the Sixteenth Annual Meeting of the National Council of Education in Milwaukee, Wisconsin, 1897.* Chicago: University of Chicago Press, 1897.

Barnard, F. A. P. *Improvements Practicable in American Colleges: A Paper Read before the American Association for the Advancement of Education at Its Fifth Annual Session, in the Chapel of the University of New York, on the 30th of August, 1855.* Hartford, Conn.: F. C. Brownell, 1856.

Bourne, Henry Eldridge. *Higher Education in Ohio and Its Historical Factors.* Columbus, Ohio: n.p., 1920.

Canfield, James H. "The Opportunities of the Rural Population for Higher Education," in the *National Council of Education, Proceedings of the Ninth Annual Meeting.* Topeka, Kansas: National Council of Education, 1889. Pp. 25–51.

Ellis, John M. "Historical Sketch of the Association of the Colleges of Ohio," *Transaction of the Twenty-first Annual Meeting of the Association of Ohio Colleges in 1889.* Oberlin, Ohio: Association of Ohio Colleges, 1890. Pp. 54–66.

Emerson, Ralph Waldo. "Man the Reformer: A Lecture Read before the Mechanics Apprentices' Library Association. Boston, January 25, 1841," *The Complete Works of Ralph Waldo Emerson.* Centenary Edition. Vol. I. Boston: Houghton, Mifflin & Co., 1883–87.

———. "New England Reformers: A Lecture Read before the Society in Amory Hall on Sunday, March 3, 1844," *The Complete Works of Ralph Waldo Emerson.* Centenary Edition. Vol. I. Boston: Houghton, Mifflin & Co., 1883–87.

Hall, G. Stanley. "Student Customs," *American Antiquarian Society Proceeding, 1900–1901.* Worcester, Mass.: American Antiquarian Society, 1901. Pp. 85–88, 91.

Hopkins, Mark. *Address Delivered in Boston, May 26, 1852, before the Society for the Promotion of Collegiate and Theological Education at the West.* Boston: T. R. Marvin, 1852.

Orton, Edward. "Industrial Education, Its Character and Claims." Inaugural address of Professor Edward Orton delivered in the Senate Chamber, Columbus, Ohio, January 8, 1874. *Third Annual Report of the Trustees of the Ohio Agricultural and Mechanical College to the Governor of the State.* Columbus, Ohio: Nevins & Myers, 1874. Pp. 10–26.

———. *Address of Professor Orton, Vice President, Section E, Geology and Geography, at the Ann Arbor Meeting, August 26, 1885.* Salem, Mass.: Salem Press, 1886.

———. *The Method of Science and Its Influence upon the Branches of Knowledge Pertaining to Man: An Address Delivered before the Alumni of Hamilton College, June, 1888.* Columbus, Ohio: n.p., 1888.

Rightmire, George W. "The Land-Grant College: An Appraisement," *Presidential Address by George W. Rightmire Presented* at the *Forty-Fifth Annual Convention of the Association of Land-Grant Colleges and Universities, Chicago, Illinois, November 16 to 18, 1931.* Montpelier, Vt.: Association of Land Grant Colleges and Universities, 1931.

Scott, Walter Quincy. "Inaugural Address," in *Twelfth Annual Report of the Board of Trustees of the Ohio State University to the Governor of the State of Ohio for the Year 1882.* Columbus, Ohio: G. J. Brand, 1883. Pp. 155–75.

Scott, William Henry. *The Origin and Growth of the State University Idea in Ohio.* Columbus, Ohio: n.p., 1920.

Stanton, Robert L. "Inaugural Address," in *Addresses Delivered on the Occasion of the Inauguration of the Rev. R. L. Stanton as President of Miami University, June 27, 1867.* Oxford, Ohio: n.p., n.d.

Thompson, William Oxley. *The Colleges and Universities of Ohio: An Address Prepared for the Ohio Centennial, Chillicothe, Ohio, May 20, 1903.* Columbus, Ohio: F. J. Heer, 1903.

———. "The Influence of the Morrill Act upon American Higher Education," *The Proceedings of the Twenty-sixth Annual Convention of the Association of American Agricultural Colleges and Experiment Stations, Atlanta, Georgia, November 13–15, 1912,* n.p., n.d.

———. "The Spirit of the Land-Grant Institutions," *Addresses Delivered at the Forty-fifth Annual Convention of the Association of Land-Grant Colleges and Universities at Chicago, Illinois, November 16–18, 131,* n.p., n.d., pp. 51-60.

Documents and Manuscript Collections

Annual Reports of the Board of Trustees of the Ohio Agricultural and Mechanical College. 1870–77. Columbus, Ohio: Nevins & Myers, 1872–77.

Annual Reports of the Board of Trustees of the Ohio State University to the Governor of the State of Ohio. 1878–1900. Columbus, Ohio: Nevins & Myers, 1878–79; G. J. Brand, 1881–84; Westbote Co., 1884–1901.

Annual Reports of the Commissioner of Statistics to the Governor of the State of Ohio, 1857–68. Columbus, Ohio, 1858-69.

James H. Canfield Papers, Ohio State University Archives, Columbus, Ohio.

Alexis Cope Correspondence, Ohio State University Archives, Columbus, Ohio.

Executive Documents, Message and Annual Reports to the General Assembly, 1862–1900. Columbus, Ohio. 1863–1901.

Rutherford B. Hayes Correspondence, Manuscript Collection, Ohio State University Library. Columbus, Ohio.

Rutherford B. Hayes, Alexis Cope and William Henry Scott Correspondence, Rutherford B. Hayes Library. Fremont, Ohio.

Ohio College Association, *Transactions.* Oberlin, Ohio: Ohio College Association, 1887-1900.

Ohio General Assembly, *Journal of the House of Representatives,* 1850–1900.

Ohio General Asembly, *Journal of the Senate,* 1850–1900.

Ohio State University, Annual Circular and Catalogue, 1874–76. Ohio State University Archives, Columbus, Ohio.

Ohio Laws and Statutes: General and Local Laws and Joint Resolutions Passed by the General Assembly. Columbus, Ohio, 1803–1900.

Minutes of the Faculty of the Ohio Agricultural and Mechanical College and the Ohio State University, 1873–1900, Ohio State University Archives. Columbus, Ohio.

Edward Orton Papers, Ohio State University Archives. Columbus, Ohio.

Orton, Edward Francis Baxter. "The Place of Man in Nature." Columbus, Ohio, 1893. Manuscript, Ohio State University Memorial Library, Columbus, Ohio.

Record of Proceedings of the Board of Trustees of the Ohio Agricultural and Mechanical College and the Ohio State University. May 11, 1870 to June 25, 1890. Ohio State University Archives, Columbus, Ohio.

Walter Quincy Scott Papers, Ohio State University Archives, Columbus, Ohio.

Society for the Promotion of Collegiate and Theological Education. *Proceedings at the Quarter Century Anniversary, Marietta, Ohio, November 7–10, 1868.* New York: Trow and Smith Book Manufacturing Company, 1868.

Statistical Report of the Secretary of State to the General Assembly of the State of Ohio, 1868–1900. Columbus, Ohio, 1869–1901.

Magazines and Newspapers

American Journal of Education.

Atlantic Monthly.

Columbus Dispatch, Columbus, Ohio.

Congressional Globe.

Critic, Ohio State University, Columbus, Ohio, 1884.

Engineer and Critic, Ohio State University, Columbus, Ohio, 1888.

Farm and Fireside.

Forum.

Lantern, Ohio State University, Columbus, Ohio.

North American Review.

Putnam's Magazine.

New York Tribune.

Ohio State Journal, Columbus, Ohio.

Evening News, Springfield, Ohio.

Republic, Springfield, Ohio.

Index

Abolition movement, 12, 13, 15, 17
Academic community: customs and usages of, 102, 104; emergence of, 100, 188
Academic degrees: graduate, 118, 119; honorary, 82, 118; M.A., 119; Ph.D. 61, 74, 118, 119; standardization of, 60–61; uses of, 165
Academic freedom, 95–96, 99–102
Academic standards, 60–61, 190, 192, 194
Accreditation, 61, 181
Adams, Herbert Baxter, 179
Adelbert College, 108
Admissions standards, 76, 107, 120, 153, 191
Agricultural education, 5, 117; and chemistry, 16, 101, 139; ignored by private schools, 62; R. Leete on, 37; at Oberlin, 17–18; at Ohio State University, 85, 132–33, 142; philosophy of, 84; and state university idea, 143; J. Sullivant on, 36; and N. S. Townsend, 17–18, 71, 76
Agricultural experiment station, 101, 137, 143, 144, 149–51. See also Ohio Agricultural Experiment Station
Agricultural students. See Students
Akron, Ohio, 57
Allen, Albert, 106, 109
Alumni associations, 103, 130, 167

American Protective Association, 176
Amherst College, 77, 179
Anderson, Richard C., 39
Angel, James B., 69
Antioch College, 54–55, 59, 71, 78, 82, 132
Association of Land Grant Colleges and Universities, 187
Association of Ohio Colleges, 82, 116, 182. See also Ohio College Association
Asylum for Imbecile Youth, 17
Athens County, Ohio, 55
Attorney General of Ohio, 93
Atwater, Caleb, 13
Aultman, Cornelius, 38

"Babyism," 129
Baccalaureate degree. See Academic degrees
Bacon, Lord, 37
Band, Ohio State University, 124, 160
Baptist-Methodist conflict, 26–27
Barnard, Frederick A. P., 69
Bascom, John, 69
Baseball. See Sports
Bateham, M. B., 72
Bateham, M. B., Mrs. 15
Benton, Guy Potter, 190

Bible Teachers Training School, N. Y., 109
Biblical Authority. *See* Theology
Black laws, repeal of, 17
Bloomer costume, 15
Bonham, L. N., 133
Boston Polytechnic Institute, 77
Botany and horticulture, 49, 139, 142
Brigham, Joseph H., 148, 150–52, 155
Buchanan, James, 6, 9
Buchtel, John R., 38, 48, 57
Buchtel College, 49, 57, 146
Buckeye Mowers and Reapers, 38

Calvinism, 27, 95
Campbell, James E., 164, 166
Canfield, James H., 135, 180–83, 185–88
Cannon Act, 45: and annual election of faculty, 97; and compromise, 31–32; in conflict with developing practices, 104; debate on, in General Assembly, 31–33; R. B. Hayes's interpretation of, 158
Canton, Ohio, 19
Capital University, 41
Capital and labor, 68, 94, 96–97
Carnegie, Andrew, 189
Carnegie Foundation for the Advancement of Teaching, 189–94
Case, Leonard, 58
Case School of Applied Science, 58
Centre College, Kentucky, 38
Chamberlain, William Isaac: and board of trustees, 173–75, 185; as candidate for president, 154, 171; and J. M. Comly, 105–6; and R. B. Hayes, 154, 173; and N. R. Hysell, 177–78; at Iowa State Agricultural College, 171–72; and W. Q. Scott, 99–102, 108
Champaign County, 39, 44, 46. *See also* Urbana, Ohio
Chapel services. *See* Church-state issue
Charter Act of the Ohio State University. *See* Cannon Act
Chase, Salmon P., 17

Chemistry, 49, 58, 101, 142
Chicago, University of, 69, 109, 166
Church-state issue, 80–83, 91–93, 94; compulsory chapel, 80, 88, 92–94, 111, 113, 115, 157, 163–64, 187; Orton on, 81–83
Church, First Congregational, Columbus, 94
Churches, crisis in, 81–84. *See also* Theology
Cincinnati, Ohio: city of, 19, 29–30, 56; College, 57; Medical College, 17; University of, 31, 56, 170
Civil War: and the Morrill Act, 4–10; and nationalization of education, 89; and the Ohio College Association, 59; and postwar problems, 68, 129; and reform, 12–13
Clark County, Ohio: and Morrill Land Grant, 39, 43–47; and state fair, 40; and Wittenberg, 52–53. *See also* Springfield, Ohio, and Wittenberg College
Clark University, 165
Class conflict, 89–90. *See also* Capital and labor; Industrial classes
Classical education, 70, 117
Clay, Clement C., 8
Cleveland, Ohio: and lake trade, 19; and Morrill Land Grant, 29; and opposition to Springfield, 40–41; and Western Reserve University, 58; and YMCA College, 58
Coeducation, 113, 121
College of Physicians and Surgeons in the University of New York, 17
Colliers' Weekly, 53
Columbia University, 69, 146
Columbus, Ohio, 41, 72; alumni in, 103; and Morrill Land Grant, 29, 32, 39–46; prejudice against, 50–51; rivalry of, with Springfield, 39–40; and Sullivant, 72. *See also* Franklin County
Columbus *Dispatch*, 99
Comly, James M., 126, 130; and eastern colleges, 125–26, 183, 193; and merger of Ohio colleges, 62; and Morrill Land Grant, 45–48, 50; and Ohio State University, 33–34, 41,

74; and the *Ohio State Journal*, 43, 44; and W. Q. Scott, 98, 105, 107
Commercial education, 58, 62
Communism, 98–99, 101, 106
Comparative religion, 94. *See also* Theology
Cope, Alexis: and the board of trustees, 55, 68, 109; and J. H. Canfield, 180–81; and W. I. Chamberlain, 178; and R. B. Hayes, 145–51, 159–63, 174–75; and C. E. Thorne, 140–43; and the university movement, 167; ends career, 185
Cornell, Ezra, 42, 77
Cornell University, 42, 48, 69, 74, 100, 125, 141, 146, 194
Corwin, Thomas, 148
County Agricultural Societies, 24
Cowgill, Thomas A., 163
Cox, Jacob D., 170
Cox, Samuel S., 39
Credit Mobilier Scandal, 64, 77
Cultural education, 58
Curriculum, in agriculture, 142; basis for, at Ohio Agricultural and Mechanical College, 48–49; and board of trustees, 86, 101; at Case School of Applied Science, 58; and Ohio College Association, 60–61; Orton on, 78–79; and W. Q. Scott, 101; and J. Sullivant, 76; and N. S. Townshend, 76

Dartmouth College, 77
Darwinism, 81, 91
Dayton, Ohio, 19, 31, 44, 58. *See also* Montgomery County
Deficit financing, 161. *See also* Higher education in Ohio
Delano, Columbus, 24
Demerit system, 113, 115
Democratic party: in Ohio, 35, 84–85, 103, 166; in the U.S., 4–9, 16
Denison University, 38
Dennison, William, 36, 46, 62, 66
Denominational colleges: and Canfield, 182–83; differences of, 111; encouragement of, 58; and Ohio State University, 82–84

Department of Agriculture, 4
Depression, economic, 63–64
Doctor of Philosophy degree. *See* academic degrees
Drawing, 58
Dubois, William E. B., 147

Eastern colleges, 125
Eastern educational spirit, 183–84. *See also* Higher education, regionalism in
Eastern view of Ohio colleges, 125
Economic depression, 63–64
Education. *See* Agricultural education; Commercial education; Cultural education; Industrial education
Educational administration. *See* Higher education, administration of
Educational method, 74, 95–96, 119
Educational philosophy. *See* Philosophy of education
Elective system, 119
Eliot, Charles W., 69, 177, 180
Ellis, Seth H., 149–51
Emerson, Ralph Waldo, 12
Endowment: of Case, 58; and the Episcopal Seminary, 82; land grant as largest, in Ohio, 22; efforts to merge, of state universities, 42–43, 49; of McMicken, 56; of Springfield citizens, 52
Engineers Association, 124
Engineer and Critic, 124
Enrollments, 118, 165, 188, 193
Episcopal church, 28, 82
Essay on Education, 13
Essentialist philosophy of education, 70. *See also* Philosophy of education
Experiment stations. *See* Ohio Agricultural Experiment Station

Faculty: and Board reorganization, 86; and compulsory chapel, 80, 93; and military drill, 113; role of, in administration, 101–2, 117–21; and selection of the president, 87; and student housing, 121; tenure of, 87,

Faculty (*continued*)
  88, 97, 100, 112; and view of the
  new institution, 110. *See also* Stu-
  dent-faculty relations
Faculty psychology, 70
Fairchild, J. A., 71
Farm and Fireside, 65, 132; and agri-
  cultural graduates, 133; and the
  Hatch Act, 137, 138; and R. B.
  Hayes, 146; and opposition to Ohio
  State University, 53, 131–35, 138,
  139; and support of Ohio State
  University, 142, 152, 153
Farm journals. *See* Agricultural jour-
  nals
Farmers College, 15, 16, 59; con-
  sidered for land grant, 23, 25
Farmers institutes, 97, 134
Farm extension program, 63
Farmer: in antebellum America, 13–
  14; and distrust of reform, 16; and
  R. B. Hayes, 146; and the land
  grant college, 43–44, 62–63; life
  style of, 13–14
Foraker, Joseph B., 145, 151
Fortnightly Lantern, 122, 124
Foster, Charles, 102–3
Franklin County: interest of, in land
  grant, 29, 39, 41, 44; prejudice
  against, 50–51; selected as site for
  Ohio Agricultural and Mechanical
  College, 46–47, 50, 52–53, 66, 73,
  82; and J. Sullivant, 72; vote in,
  for bond authorization, 43–44. *See
  also* Columbus, Ohio
Franklinton, Ohio, 72
Fraternity system. *See* Greek letter
  system
Fraternity war at Ohio State Univer-
  sity, 129
Free soil movement, 5–6, 9

Galloway, Samuel, 39
Garfield, James A., 93
Gates, Merrill E., 179
General Assembly. *See* Ohio General
  Assembly
General education, 70. *See also* Phi-
  losophy of education
Geography, 142

Geology, 49, 58, 78, 88
George, Henry, 64, 96
Gilman, Daniel Coit, 69, 147
Gladden, Washington, 107; as author,
  94, 175; and R. B. Hayes, 153, 174,
  175; and W. Q. Scott, 114; social
  views of, 175–76
Grading system, 116
Graduate degrees. *See* Academic de-
  grees
Graduate enrollments, 118
Grammar school education, 58
Grange, 65, 141–42, 149. *See also*
  Patrons of Husbandry
Grant, Ulysses S., 63, 77
Greek-letter societies, 121, 126–29,
  183

Hall, G. Stanley, 129
Hamilton County, 30. *See also* Cincinnati, Ohio
Harmon, Judson, 191
Harper, William Rainey, 69, 109
Harrison, Benjamin, 177
Harvard University, 69, 71, 100, 125,
  146, 177
Harvard Law School, 38
Hatch Act, 65, 136–39, 143, 148, 195
Hayes, Rutherford B.: and board of
  trustees, Ohio State University,
  144–48, 153–61, 164, 171–75, 181,
  188, 196; and breadth of interest
  in higher education, 148; on the
  concentration of wealth, 98–99; and
  Alexis Cope, 145–51, 159–63, 174–
  75; on communism, 98–99; death
  of, 176–85; as founder of Ohio
  State University, 148; as governor,
  3, 30, 35, 40, 47, 66, 68, 72, 79,
  84; and industrial education, 147,
  151; and Negro education, 145,
  146, 147; as potential president of
  Ohio State University, 154; and
  religion, 82; and Western Reserve
  University, 108
Hayes-Ellis Settlement, 152–53
Hayes-Tilden election, 64
Hedonism, 125–26, 165
Higher criticism. *See* Theology

Higher education, American: from 1870 to 1890, 126; in the 1890's, 165

—administration of: national trends in, 102, 167–68, 171; in Ohio, 191–92

—in Ohio, financial support for: and farm view, 134, 136; growth of, hampered, 56, 63–64, 66; and R. B. Hayes, 160–62; inadequacy of, 193

—Ohio system of, 55, 83; in the Carnegie Report, 191–92; development of, delayed, 196; and proposals to merge three state universities, 42–43, 47, 49, 54–55

—philanthropy in, 165

—private, 58, 90, 192, 193

—regionalism in, 57, 125, 183–84, 185–86, 188, 189, 193–94

High schools, 59–60, 76, 120, 136, 191. See also Preparatory academies; Secondary education

Homestead Bill, 4, 6, 10

Honorary degrees. See Academic degrees

Hopkins, Mark, 180

Horticulture, 49

Horton, Valentine B., 39, 48

Howard, Solomon, 59

Howells, William Dean, 98

Hudson, Ohio, 58

Hughes Educational Fund, 57

Humanism, 74

Hysell Act, 167

Hysell, Nial R., 166–78

Illinois Agricultural College, 174

Illinois, University of, 166

Imperial University at Tokyo, 177

Industrial classes: on board of trustees, 38–39; definition of, 78–79, 84; education for, 58, 75; and R. B. Hayes, 68–69; and E. Orton, 78–79; and the Panic of 1873, 64; W. Q. Scott on, 90

Industrial education: failure of, 135, 140; R. B. Hayes's views on, 68–69, 147, 181; and the land grant college, 68–69; E. Orton on, 78–79;

and utilitarianism, 70; and YMCA schools, 58

Industrial production, 18–19

Industrialization, 18–19, 78–79, 91–92, 129

In loco parentis, 125–26

Iowa State Agricultural College, 99, 171, 194

Jones, Thomas C., 48, 141, 155

Johns Hopkins University, 69, 74, 118, 120, 147, 179

Journals, agricultural, 15–16, 62, 137, 140. See also Farm and Fireside, Ohio Cultivator, and Ohio Farmer

Kenyon College, 22, 28, 38, 59

Knights of Labor, 65

Lafayette College, 179

Land agents, 162

Land scrip, 25

Land speculation, 7–8

Lantern, 122, 124

Law schools, 55, 150, 167, 187

Lawrence Scientific School, 77

Leete, Ralph, 36–37, 47, 48, 74–75

Legislature. See Ohio General Assembly

Liberal culture and general education, 70–75, 78–79, 84, 188. See also Philosophy of education

Lincoln, Abraham, 11

London World Peace Congress, 15

Longmont College, 186

Lutheran Church, 41, 51

The Makio, 111, 112, 114–15, 122, 124, 146, 167

Manual labor system, 85–86

Manual training movement, 147

Marietta College, 38, 59

Marietta Register, 99

Massachusetts Agricultural College, 77

Masters degree. See Academic degrees

Mechanical arts, 49, 58, 79

Mechanical and scientific education, 3, 62, 117. *See also* Industrial education

Medical schools, 187; independence of, 55; opposition to, 150, 182, 186; support for, 167

Medical education, 75–76

Mendenhall, Thomas C., 71, 86, 115; as candidate for president of Ohio State University, 176–78; on Chamberlain, 173; religious views of, 82; resignation of, 85

Mental and moral discipline, 69-70, 84. *See also* Philosophy of Education

Metallurgy and mining. *See* Mining and metallurgy

Methodists, 28; influence at Ohio University, 26–27

Mexican War, 5

Miami University, 22, 25, 70, 180, 190; in Carnegie Report, 191–92; closing of, from 1873 to 1885, 53–54, 55, 61; and merger proposals, 42–43, 47, 49, 54–55; and Morrill Land Grant, 21, 23, 25; and the Presbyterians, 26–28, 51; and Sectarian influences, 26–28, 51; and state support, 22, 54, 166, 186, 190; and Thompson, 185–86

Michigan, State Agricultural College of, 133, 194

Michigan, University of, 69, 100, 146

Midwestern Educational spirit, 183–84. See also Eastern educational spirit; Higher education, regionalism in

Military drill, 113, 124

Mill, John Stuart, 101

Minimum loads, 106–7

Mining and metallurgy, 49, 58, 86

Montgomery county, 39, 44; bid of, 46; farmer vote in, 43. *See also* Dayton, Ohio

Mount Union College, 28, 59

Morrill Land Grant College Act of 1859: debate on, 4–9; Pugh's role in, 7–9; vote on, 7, 9; veto of, 9; Wade's role in, 6, 8–10

Morrill Land Grant College Act of 1862: debates on, 4, 10; Hayes on, 68; impact of, on Ohio, 3, 11–12, 21, 195; and nationalization of higher education, 35, 89–90; nature and purposes of, 79; philosophical orientation of, 71

Morrill Land Grant College Act of 1890, 195

Morrill Land Grant College System: failure of, 135; nationalized nature of, 35, 89–90; W. Q. Scott on, 92

Morrill Land Grant to Ohio: debate on, in General Assembly, 23–26, 28–33; disposition of, 23, 25–26, 30–33; legislative strategy in use of, 24–25, 29–33; opposition to, 22; proceeds of, 22, 66, 186; size of, 23

Morrill, Justin Smith, 6, 9, 10, 152

Municipal colleges, 30–31, 57, 58

Municipal education, 30–31, 58

Museum of Zoology, 77

Muskingum College, 185

McCosh, James, 69

McClung, William B., 38

McMicken, Charles: bequest of, 56

McMicken College, 56, 57

McKinley, William, 173, 177

National Association for the Advancement of Colored People, 147

Nationalization of higher education, 89–90

Native Americans, 9, 64

Nebraska, University of, 135, 180, 183, 194

Negro Education: Hayes on, 146–47; at Wilberforce, 152–53

Neil farm, 47, 48

New Hampshire, 77

New theology, 81–84. *See also* Theology

New York State Normal School, 78

Nichols, Clifton M., 40, 45, 51–52

Nihilism, 98

Nonsectarianism, 91

Oberlin College, 17, 22, 71

Ohio Agricultural Experiment Station, 63; as a focus of farm power, 148, 150; and the memorandum of understanding, 164; and Ohio State University, 144, 149–51, 164

Ohio Agricultural and Mechanical College, 16, 77, 112; and Antioch College, 54–55, 71; and the Cannon Act, 32; and farmers, 53, 63, 65; and Hayes, 35, 46, 52–53, 84; location of, 41–48, 52–53; and the Ohio College Association, 60–61; name of, changed to Ohio State University, 85, 131; organization and character of, 37–38, 39, 48, 49, 68–69, 76, 190–91; and religion, 81–83; and Sullivant's pyramid, 73; and trustees, 33, 36–39, 54, 80, 84–85. *See also* The Ohio State University

Ohio Agricultural, Military and Mechanical College, 23

Ohio College Association, 59–61, 66; in Carnegie Report, 189–92. *See also* Association of Ohio Colleges

Ohio commissioner of education, 25–26, 29, 136

Ohio Cultivator, 15, 72, 133

Ohio Editor's Association, 40

Ohio Farmer, 15

Ohio General Assembly: and college charters, 190; and disposition of Ohio's land grant, 22–25, 28–29, 31; educational leadership of, 192; Fifty-fifth Assembly of, 23–24; Fifty-ninth Assembly of, 30–32; Fifty-sixth Assembly of, 24–25; and the Hatch Act, 131, 138; and support of the Ohio State University, 83–84, 152, 162

Ohio Geological Survey, 78, 88

Ohio Land Grant. *See* Morrill Land Grant to Ohio

Ohio Municipal Education Act, 30–31, 58

Ohio State Board of Agriculture, 18, 21–23, 26, 28, 38, 40, 41, 44, 99, 102, 133, 137, 138, 148, 164, 172

Ohio State College of Arts, 23

The Ohio State Grange, 138. *See* Patrons of Husbandry and Grange

Ohio State Journal, 12, 33, 50, 97, 104, 105

Ohio State Temperence Society, 15

Ohio State University, 55, 89–90; and compulsory chapel, 80, 88, 92, 111, 113, 115, 157, 163, 187; courses offered at, 49, 60, 101, 142; criticisms of, 133–34, 138, 141, 146, 194; examination requirements of, 106, 116; and farmers, 133–34, 138, 141, 142, 144, 146; graduates of, 133; and the Hatch Act, 138; and R. B. Hayes, 146, 157, 164; and merger of Ohio University and Miami University, 42–43, 47, 49, 54–55; organization of, 117, 187; as people's college, 147; presidency at, 87, 108, 157–58, 168–69, 170–71, 174, 177–78, 179 (*see also* names of individual presidents); and rules and regulations, 116–20; and students, 115; support of, 136, 159, 161, 166, 195. *See also* Agricultural Experiment Station; Faculty; Ohio Agricultural and Mechanical College; Students

—administration of: and board of trustees, 87–89, 102–4, 138, 155–56, 158–65, and board of trustees secretary, 159–60, 182; and business management of, 85, 160; under Cannon Act, 104; Chamberlin on, 99–102; faculty view of, 86; and R. B. Hayes, 158–65, 168–69; national trends against, 71, 168, 171, 179; E. Orton on, 87; W. Q. Scott on, 88–89, 106–7; W. H. Scott on, 116–20; student view of, 112

Ohio Statesman, 26

Ohio Teachers' Association, 59

Ohio University, 23, 25, 38, 59, 146; in the Carnegie Report, 191–92; endowment of, 22; and merger with Ohio State University, 42–43, 47, 49, 54–55; and the Methodists, 26–28, 37; and Morrill Land Grant, 21, 53–54; and the Ohio College Association, 59, 61; and philosophy of education, 61, 70; and sectarianism, 26–28, 37; state's early role in, 190; and state support, 54, 166

Ohio Wesleyan University, 22, 26; and R. B. Hayes, 145, 148
Ohio Wesleyan *Collegian,* 126–27
Ohio Women's Rights Association, 15
Ohio's forest city. *See* Cleveland, Ohio
Orton, Edward, 94, 132, 185; and R. B. Hayes, 145; inaugural address of, 78–79; and merger of state universities, 54; and the presidency of Ohio State, 71, 77, 87, 170; and religious issues, 81–83
Otterbein College, 146
Oxford, Ohio, 55

Panic of 1873, 63–64
Patrons of Husbandry, 65, 141, 142, 149. *See also* Grange
Patterson, James W., 77
Peabody Education Fund, 145
Peace movement, 12, 13, 15
Pendleton, George H., 35
Perkins, Henry P., 38
Permissiveness, 126
Phillips Exeter Academy, 108
Philosophy of Education: and administrative hierarchy, 168; espoused by R. Leete, 74; in *Farm and Fireside,* 140–41; humanism, 74; industrial education, 84; lack of, in Ohio, 182; mental and moral discipline, 69–70; and the Morrill Act, 71–72; at Ohio State University, 117; Orton's support of, 78–79; in research and scientism, 71; and site selection, 46–49; J. Sullivant's support of, 73–74; N. S. Townshend's support of, 75–76; in utilitarianism, 70, 188
Political economy and civil polity, 49, 86, 101
Porter, Noah, 69
Practical farming, 13
Preparatory academies, 76, 137. *See also* High schools; Secondary education
Presbyterians: and Miami University, 26–28; and Ohio University, 26–28; and Wittenberg, 51; and Wooster College, 27, 51, 95–96

Priestly, Joseph, 37
"Prime minister" of trustees, 171
Princeton University, 69, 125, 146
Pritchett, Henry S., 189, 193–94
Psychic infantilism, 129
Public domain, 4, 5, 7
Public lands, 7–8
Public-private antagonisms, 83
Pugh, George E., 7–9
Purdue University, 194

Quarter system, 189
The Queen City. *See* Cincinnati, Ohio

Railroads, 44–45, 63–64, 101
Reform movements: general, 12–13
—agricultural: and broader reform impulses, 12–18; and educational reform, 14–15; reasserted in 1880s, 141; program for, in 1860s, 18; and Sullivant, 72
Reformers, agricultural: ineffectiveness of, 62; interest of, in Morrill Act, 12; preconceptions of, 3; and other reformers, 14–17
Registrar, 159
Religious conservatism, 83–84
The religious question, 80, 94, 98, 177. *See also* Church-state issue; Theology
Republican party, 4, 5, 6, 9, 35, 84–85, 103
Research and scientism, 70–71, 80
Rockefeller, John D., 69
Roman catholics, *See* Catholics
Rose Polytechnic Institute, 177, 178
Rural secondary education, 18, 76, 135–36, 142, 172. *See also* Secondary education; High schools; Preparatory academies

St. Mary's School for Boys. *See* Dayton, University of
Science and religion, conflict of, 91. *See also* Church-state issue; Theology
Scott, Jessup, 57
Scott, Walter Quincy, 88, 107, 111,

171; and communism, 98, 99; dismissal of, 97; economic views of, 88–91, 92, 94, 98, 99; and faculty, 88–91, 115; and farmers, 101; inaugural address of, 88–91; at Phillips Exeter, 108–9; and the public, 97; religious views of, 88–91, 115; and relations with students, 100, 103–4, 105, 107, 112; and teaching methods, 95–96; and trustees, 88–91, 100, 158; and W. H. Scott, compared with, 98; at Wooster College, 95

Scott, William Henry: compared with W. Q. Scott, 98; demission of, 173; election of, as president, 97, 170; and *Farm and Fireside*, 138, 139; and farmers, 139, 140; and the Hatch Act, 137–38; and R. B. Hayes, 146, 154, 159; and industrial education, 140; and merger of the state universities, 58; at Ohio University, 54–55; and relations with students, 113–14, 116, 121, 124; timidity of, 114

Secondary education, 18, 59–60, 120, 135–36, 191. *See also* High schools; Rural secondary education; Preparatory academies

Sectarianism, 26–28, 37, 68, 75, 90, 95–96

Secretary of the board of trustees, 39, 85, 106, 109, 158, 159

Separation of church and state. *See* Church-state issue

Shellabarger, Samuel, 39, 64

Sherman, John, 148

Slater Educational Fund, 145, 147

Slavery question, 5, 6, 89

Sleeper bill, 186

Social gospel movement, 94. *See also* Theology; The religious question; Church-state issue

Socialism, 98

Soule, Nicholas E., 108

Special nondegree program, 86

Spencer, Herbert, 101

Spiegel Grove, 144

Sports, 124, 126

Sprecher, Samuel, 59

Springfield, Ohio, 11, 29, 32, 44, 45,

59; and *Farm and Fireside*, 65; farm interests in, 19, 41; and location of the Ohio Agricultural and Mechanical College, 39–41, 45–46, 47; and opposition to Ohio State University, 131; and state fairs, 40; and Wittenberg College, 51–52. *See also* Clark County, Ohio

Springfield *Republic*, 30, 40, 44, 45, 51

Springfield Street Railway Company, 45

Standards of accreditation. *See* academic standards

Stanford University, 120, 165

Stanton, Robert Livingston, 27

Starling Medical College, 17

State Commissioner of Education. *See* Ohio Commissioner of Education

State legislature. *See* Ohio General Assembly

State supervision of higher education, 182

State system of public instruction, 181–82. *See also* Ohio system of higher education; High schools; Preparatory academies; Rural secondary education; Secondary education

State university idea in Ohio, 35–37, 39–42, 46, 62; and the Board of Trustees, 76–77; and location of the institution, 35–37, 40–42, 46–49; Hayes on, 67, 68–69; Orton on, 78, 80; W. Q. Scott on, 91–92; Townshend on, 75–76

State University, mission of, 136, 182

States rights doctrine, 7–8, 89–90

Students: activities of, 124; in agriculture, 127; and campus government, 129; and compulsory chapel, 113; culture of, 110–11, 121–24, 129–30, 165; demonstrations by, 105, 113; and faculty relations, 120–22; and faculty restrictions, 121, 122, 123–24; and Greek letter societies, 129; and Hayes, 146; housing for, 121; and Orton, 121; publications of, 111–13, 122–24, 128–29; and W. Q. Scott, 92, 112, 121; and W. H. Scott, 113–14, 116, 121, 24; and university affairs, 103–

Students (*continued*)
10, 113–14, 122; at Wooster, 96
Sullivant, Joseph: as board secretary, 85; and Franklin County's bid, 46; and Hayes, 36; pioneer family of, 41; plans of, for the university, 48, 49, 62, 72, 73, 76; as trustee, 36, 38, 39, 40, 85
Sullivant, Michael (brother), 72
Sullivant, William (brother), 72
Sullivant's pyramid, 73, 75, 76
Superintendent of public instruction. *See* Ohio commissioner of education

Tappan, Eli T., 59
Telephone, student use of, 122
Temperance movement 12, 13, 15
Tenure of faculty, 87, 88, 97, 100, 112
Theology: new directions in, 81–84; and the higher criticism, 81, 94; and orthodoxy, 81–84; and the social gospel, 94; and theological education, 109
Texas Agricultural and Mechanical College, 135
Thurman Club, 124
Thorne, Charles E., 132, 135, 136, 140, 143, 150, 151
Thompson, William Oxley, 33, 185–88, 191, 194
Tod, David, 22
Toledo, Ohio, 57
Toledo University of Arts and Trades, 57
Toledo, University of, 57
Townshend, Norton S., 6, 48, 86, 138, 139; and agricultural education, 6, 71; as reformer, 16–18; as trustee, 16–18, 38, 141; views of, 48, 75–76, 82
Tracy, Hanna M., 15
Turner, Jonathan B., 5, 71

Union Pacific Railroad, 64
Unionists, 9

Unitarianism, 75, 78, 82
United States Coast and Geodetic Survey, 177
United States Department of Agriculture, 4
United States Signal Service, 177
University movement at Ohio State University, 167, 187
Urban educational needs, 20, 39–49, 50, 76
Urban industrial America, 79–80
Urbana, Ohio, 39, 42, 44, 45. *See also* Champaign County
Urbana College, 59
Utilitarianism, 40, 70, 75, 117, 183, 188

Veterinary medicine, 49, 139, 142
Virginia Military District Cession, 103, 162–64
Vocational education, 58

Wade, Benjamin Franklin, 6, 7, 8, 10, 195
Warfield, Ethelbert Dudley, 179
Western Reserve College, 28, 58, 59, 108, 145, 148
Western spirit in higher education. *See* Regionalism in higher education
Western-Southern Alliance, 6
Western Theological Seminary, Pennsylvania, 95
Westward, migration, 15
Whig party, 9
White, Andrew D., 69
White, Wilbert Webster, 109
Wilberforce University, 152, 153
Williams College, 125
Wilson, Woodrow, 179
Wing, L. B., 174, 180
Wisconsin, University of, 69, 189, 194
Wittenberg College, 51–53, 59, 62
Woodward College, 38
Woodward Educational Fund, 57

Wooster College, 27, 51, 95–96
Worcester Polytechnic Institute, 178
World Peace Congress, 15

Yale Law School, 38
Yale University, 69, 100, 125

Yellow Springs, Ohio, 77
Youngstown, Ohio, 58
Young Men's Christian Associations,
58, 124

Zanesville, Ohio, 19